NATIONAL GEOGRAPHIC

KIDS™

ALMANAC 2013

NATIONAL GEOGRAPHIC

Gray wolves run through deep snow in Alaska, U.S.A.

NATIONAL GEOGRAPHIC KIDS™

ALMANAC 2013

NATIONAL
GEOGRAPHIC
WASHINGTON, D.C.

National Geographic Children's Books
gratefully acknowledges the following people for their help with the
National Geographic Kids Almanac 2013.

Curtis Malarkey, Julie Segal, and Cheryl Zook
of the National Geographic Explorers program;
Truly Herbert, National Geographic Communications;
and Chuck Errig of Random House

Amazing Animals

Suzanne Braden, Director, Pandas International

Dr. Rodolfo Coria, Paleontologist, Plaza Huincul, Argentina

Dr. Sylvia Earle,
National Geographic Explorer-in-Residence

Dr. Thomas R. Holtz, Jr., Senior Lecturer, Vertebrate Paleontology,
Dept. of Geology, University of Maryland

Dr. Luke Hunter, Executive Director, Panthera

"Dino" Don Lessem, President, Exhibits Rex

Kathy B. Maher, Research Editor,
NATIONAL GEOGRAPHIC magazine

Kathleen Martin, Canadian Sea Turtle Network

Barbara Nielsen, Polar Bears International

Andy Prince, Austin Zoo

Christopher Sloan

Julia Thorson, translator, Zurich, Switzerland

Dennis vanEngelsdorp, Senior Extension Associate, Pennsylvania
Department of Agriculture

Awesome Adventure

Jen Bloomer, Media Relations Manager,
The National Aquarium in Baltimore

Dereck and Beverly Joubert,
National Geographic Explorers-in-Residence

Culture Connection

Dr. Wade Davis,
National Geographic Explorer-in-Residence

Deirdre Mullervy, Managing Editor,
Gallaudet University Press

Super Science

Tim Appenzeller, Chief Magazine Editor, NATURE

Dr. José de Ondarza, Associate Professor,
Department of Biological Sciences, State University
of New York, College at Plattsburgh

Lesley B. Rogers, Managing Editor,
NATIONAL GEOGRAPHIC magazine

Dr. Enric Sala, National Geographic Visiting Fellow

Abigail A. Tipton, Director of Research (former),
NATIONAL GEOGRAPHIC magazine

Erin Vintinner, Biodiversity Specialist,
Center for Biodiversity and Conservation at the
American Museum of Natural History

Barbara L. Wyckoff, Research Editor,
NATIONAL GEOGRAPHIC magazine

Wonders of Nature

Anatta, NOAA Public Affairs Officer

Dr. Robert Ballard,
National Geographic Explorer-in-Residence

Douglas H. Chadwick, wildlife biologist and contributor to
NATIONAL GEOGRAPHIC magazine

Drew Hardesty, Forecaster, Utah Avalanche Center

Going Green

Eric J. Bohn, Math Teacher, Santa Rosa High School

Stephen David Harris, Professional Engineer,
Industry Consulting

Catherine C. Milbourn, Senior Press Officer, EPA

Brad Scriber, Senior Researcher,
NATIONAL GEOGRAPHIC magazine

Cid Simões and Paola Segura,
National Geographic Emerging Explorers

Dr. Wes Tunnell, Harte Research Institute for
Gulf of Mexico Studies, Texas A&M
University–Corpus Christi

History Happens

Sylvie Beaudreau, Associate Professor, Department of History,
State University of New York

Elspeth Deir, Assistant Professor, Faculty of Education, Queens
University, Kingston, Ontario, Canada

Dr. Gregory Geddes, Lecturer, Department of Global Studies, State
University of New York–Orange, Middletown-Newburgh, New York

Dr. Fredrik Hiebert, National Geographic Visiting Fellow

Micheline Joanisse, Media Relations Officer,
Natural Resources Canada

Dr. Robert D. Johnston,
Associate Professor and Director of the
Teaching of History Program,
University of Illinois at Chicago

Dickson Mansfield, Geography Instructor (retired),
Faculty of Education, Queens University, Kingston,
Ontario, Canada

Tina Norris, U.S. Census Bureau

Parliamentary Information and Research Service,
Library of Parliament, Ottawa, Canada

Karyn Pugliese, Acting Director, Communications, Assembly of
First Nations

Geography Rocks

Dr. Mary Kent, Demographer,
Population Reference Bureau

Dr. Walt Meier, National Snow and Ice Data Center

Dr. Richard W. Reynolds,
NOAA's National Climatic Data Center

United States Census Bureau, Public Help Desk

Dr. Spencer Wells,
National Geographic Explorer-in-Residence

Carl Haub, Senior Demographer, Conrad Taeuber Chair of Public
Information, Population Reference Bureau

Glynnis Breen, National Geographic Special Projects

AY
81
.J8
N38
2012

JUN 1 4 2012

Contents

Your World 2013

Amazing Animals

Awesome Adventure

Culture Connection

Super Science

Fun and Games

Wonders of Nature

COOL CLICK

Throughout this book, our virtual pet,
Zipper the dog, alerts you to cool clicks—
Web links that will help you find out more!

Your World
2013

Ice city!

An actual-size city of ice springs up every winter at the Harbin Ice and Snow Festival in northeast China. Artists create thousands of illuminated ice sculptures—from trains and windmills, to a replica of Rome, Italy's Colosseum. The frozen formations tower up to 16 stories tall!

Got a smart phone?
**SCAN THIS to see
more amazing things
in your world!**
(See instructions inside the front cover.)

No smart phone? Go online.
kids.nationalgeographic.com/almanac-2013

NEW 7 Wonders of Nature

Seven scenic landscapes have earned the honor of being named the new wonders of nature. To come up with the list, people from around the world emailed, texted, and phoned in their picks for the planet's most stunning spots.

Komodo National Park, Indonesia

This park—which spans several islands—was founded to protect the elusive Komodo dragon.

Puerto Princesa Underground River, The Philippines

One of the world's longest underground rivers, the Puerto Princesa winds through a cave before flowing into the South China Sea.

Iguazu Falls, Argentina and Brazil

At its highest point, Iguazu Falls stands taller than a 20-story building.

The Amazon, South America

This massive region includes more than half the world's rain forests.

Jeju Island, South Korea

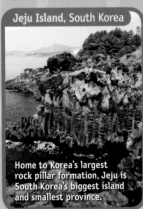

Home to Korea's largest rock pillar formation, Jeju is South Korea's biggest island and smallest province.

Halong Bay, Vietnam

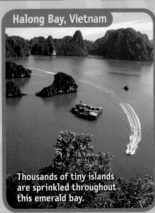

Thousands of tiny islands are sprinkled throughout this emerald bay.

Table Mountain, South Africa

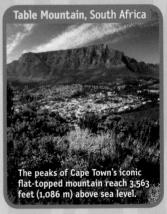

The peaks of Cape Town's iconic flat-topped mountain reach 3,563 feet (1,086 m) above sea level.

Avatar
ADVENTURER

James Cameron may best be known for directing mega-movies such as *Avatar* and *Titanic*, but he's also an inventor and a National Geographic Explorer-in-Residence. Cameron is teaming up with scientists to engineer his own state-of-the-art submarine with the hopes of one day studying some of the world's deepest places, including the Mariana Trench, 35,994 feet (10,971 m) below the Pacific Ocean's surface. But Cameron's passion for oceans doesn't end there: He has also announced that his *Avatar* sequel will explore the oceans of the alien moon Pandora. Look for that out-of-this-world adventure to hit theaters in 2014!

JAMES CAMERON FILMING FROM INSIDE A SUBMERSIBLE

ZOË SALDANA AS NEYTIRI IN *AVATAR*

Simon Says

Robots may be coming soon to a house near you! The latest models are programmed to do everything from playing games to cleaning your room. Take Simon, for example. With two arms, two eyes, and eyelids that blink every ten seconds, Simon lets you know that he's paying attention. He can learn new tasks, ask questions, and clean up. Someday you may be teaching your own version of Simon how to take out the trash! Robot designer Andrea Thomaz wanted to make a robot that could learn. That's why she built Simon to ask questions and learn from the answers. "It might be easier for a person to teach a robot if the robot responds like a person," says Thomaz.

11

FLYING RHINO RESCUE!

It's a bird. It's a plane. It's a rhino? This black rhinoceros got some serious air when it was airlifted out of its habitat on South Africa's Eastern Cape.

Why fly? These critically endangered animals are often hunted for their horns, which some cultures believe have special medicinal properties. The airlifts—which are safe for the animals—were part of the Black Rhino Range Expansion Project sponsored by the conservation organization World Wildlife Fund (WWF). Nineteen rhinos (that were tranquilized so they would be easier to transport) were flown by helicopter out of poaching-prone areas and then driven to a safer spot in the Limpopo Province, about 930 miles (1,500 km) away.

"It is just an amazing sight," project leader Jacques Flamand said of the high-flying beasts. "Each one is spectacular!"

Helicopter

HELICOPTERS CARRIED RHINOS UP TO 3,200 FEET (1,000 M) INTO THE AIR.

"It is also such a simple concept that we are all kicking ourselves that we didn't do it long ago."

Each helicopter ride lasted less than ten minutes. What's next? Flying pigs?

THE AIRLIFTED RHINOS WERE TRANSPORTED TO A SECRET LOCATION TO HELP KEEP THEM SAFE.

CALL IT A COMEBACK

Good news! Thanks to conservation efforts by humans, the numbers are increasing for several species of endangered, vulnerable, and threatened animals—including these!

Black-footed ferret

The population of black-footed ferrets, once believed to be extinct in the wild, has grown from 18 to more than 1,000 in the wild. Conservationists hope the ferrets will fall off the endangered species list for good by 2020.

Arabian oryx

The status of these antelopes improved from endangered to vulnerable after they were re-introduced into the wild. Their numbers, once as low as 200, are now up to 1,000 in the wild and up to 7,000 in captivity.

New Zealand storm petrel

For more than 150 years, biologists thought these small seabirds were extinct. But recently the birds began reappearing, and scientists have confirmed that these birds are once again flying high.

Atlantic goliath grouper

These giant swimmers were once so overfished that they were practically wiped out. But because of a fishing ban, their numbers are up along the southeastern and western coasts of the United States, though the fish remain critically endangered everywhere else in the world.

ON THE DECLINE

Sadly, some species continue to dwindle in the wild. Because of habitat destruction and hunting, these species—such as the **bog turtle**, the **San Martin titi monkey**, the **blue-eyed black lemur**—now face a greater threat of becoming extinct, according to the IUCN Red List, which tracks endangered and threatened animals.

Bog turtle

San Martin titi monkey

Blue-eyed black lemur

RAINING GOLD?

Where does gold come from? Meteors may have had something to do with it. Geologists who studied ancient rock samples found in Greenland believe that a massive meteor shower 3.9 billion years ago hit the Earth with about 20 quintillion tons of matter. These scientists think this matter may have contained precious metals, including gold and platinum. The metals were eventually stirred into the Earth's mantle, the thick layer of hot, solid rock between the crust and the core. For centuries, miners have extracted gold from the Earth to use in everything from jewelry to technology.

HOT MOVIES in 2013*

- Despicable Me 2
- The Hobbit: There and Back Again
- Iron Man 3
- Man of Steel
- Monsters University
- The Smurfs 2

*release dates and titles subject to change

IRON MAN 3

DESPICABLE ME 2

MONSTERS UNIVERSITY

Conquering Everest
The 60th Anniversary

Sir Edmund Hillary (left) and Tenzing Norgay

Mount Everest

Tenzing Norgay on the summit of Mount Everest

Fighting a freezing, whipping wind, Edmund Hillary and Tenzing Norgay scrambled to the top of a snow-covered peak. With one final step, they planted their feet on top of the world on May 29, 1953. In that instant, Hillary, a mountaineer from New Zealand, and Norgay, a Tibetan Sherpa, became the first people to summit Mount Everest, the highest point on Earth.

MICROCHIP CAT

Willow the cat came back—five years later! Willow's owners thought they would never see their pet again after she went missing from their home in Colorado, U.S.A. Then, five years after the cat disappeared, they received a surprise phone call. Authorities at a New York City shelter—some 1,600 miles (2,575 km) away—said they had Willow safe and sound! A microchip implanted when she was a kitten contained her owner's contact info, so authorities were able to to ID the cat. After seeing a picture of Willow, her shocked owners flew to New York to pick her up. No one knows how Willow wound up in New York, but now the cat is home—and hopefully staying put. Talk about a *purr*fect ending!

15

Cool Events in 2013

Happy Birthday

NATIONAL GEOGRAPHIC CELEBRATES 125 years of daring to explore.

January 13

Inauguration Day!

The U.S. President starts a new four-year term of office.

January 20

World Environment Day

Do your part to protect the planet!

June 5

Great Train Robbery

50 years ago, a gang of thieves pulled off this **$7 million** heist in Buckinghamshire, England.

August 8

World Rhino Day

Honk a horn to celebrate and to promote the protection of these at-risk animals, often hunted for their horns.

September 22

Woolly Worm Festival

How fast can a woolly worm go?

Find out in Banner Elk, North Carolina, U.S.A.

October 19-20

Santa Claus Winter Games

Santas from around the world compete in contests such as chimney climbing and reindeer racing in Gällivare, Sweden.

Late November

Sporty Celebration!

Get your kicks in today— whether you call it football or soccer, the modern version of the world's most popular sport started in England 150 years ago.

December 8

Polar Bear's Swim
Sets Record

Polar bears are strong swimmers. But did you know they have incredible endurance, too? One female polar bear recently swam for nine days straight in the Beaufort Sea north of Alaska, U.S.A., covering 426 miles (697 km). That's about the same length as 14,000 Olympic-size swimming pools! Just why did this polar bear paddle so far? With global warming causing sea ice to melt, the animals have to swim longer distances to reach land, often with their cubs. These marathon swims are dangerous to both the adults and the cubs, many of which don't make it through the trip. This particular polar bear lost 22 percent of her body weight on her record-setting swim. Unless people do something to curb climate change, experts say she and other polar bears may have to make this dangerous journey every year as the ice continues to shrink.

Want to do your part to help the polar bears? Check out tips to reduce your carbon footprint on p. 211.

sports funnies
X Games Edition

BMX races. Ski jumping. Snowboard SuperPipe. It's taking sports—to the extreme! In 2013, the action-packed X Games will add three new international sites to its lineup, expanding to six thrilling sports competitions per year. More X Games? More fun!

HEY, IS THAT SOME LOOSE CHANGE DOWN THERE?

American Gary Young competes in the BMX Freestyle Park Elimination in Los Angeles, California, U.S.A., in 2011.

NOW, WHERE DID I PUT THAT SNOWMOBILE?

U.S.A.'s Caleb Moore performs a trick in the best tricks contest at the Winter X Games 15 in Aspen, Colorado, U.S.A., in 2011.

Amazing Animals

Two young giant pandas cuddle on a tree stump at the Wolong Nature Reserve in Sichuan Province, China.

Got a smart phone?
SCAN THIS to see more
cool stuff about animals!
(See instructions inside the front cover.)
No smart phone? Go online.
kids.nationalgeographic.com/almanac-2013

WHAT IS
Taxonomy?

Since there are billions and billions of living things, called organisms, on the planet, people need a way of classifying them. Scientists created a system called **taxonomy**, which helps to classify all living things into ordered groups. By putting organisms into categories we are able to better understand how they are the same and how they are different. There are seven levels of taxonomic classification, beginning with the broadest group, called a domain, down to the most specific group, called a species.

Biologists divide life based on evolutionary history, and they place organisms in three domains depending on their genetic structure: Archaea, Bacteria, and Eukarya. (See p. 129 for "The Three Domains of Life.")

Where do animals come in?

Animals are a part of the Eukarya domain, which means they are organisms made of cells with nuclei. More than one million species of animals have been named, including humans. Like all living things, animals can be divided into smaller groups, called phyla. Most scientists believe there are more than 30 phyla into which animals can be grouped based on certain scientific criteria, such as body type or whether or not the animal has a backbone. It can be pretty complicated, so there is another, less complicated system that groups animals into two categories: vertebrates and invertebrates.

Chinese stripe-necked turtle

SAMPLE CLASSIFICATION
KOALA

Domain:	Eukarya
Phylum:	Chordata
Class:	Mammalia
Order:	Diprotodontia
Family:	Phascolarctidae
Genus:	*Phascolarctos*
Species:	*P. cinereus*

TIP
Here's a sentence to help you remember the classification order:
Dear **P**hillip **C**ame **O**ver **F**or **G**ood **S**oup.

BY THE NUMBERS

There are 10,158 vulnerable or endangered animal species in the world. The list includes:

- **1,134 mammals**, such as the snow leopard, the polar bear, and the fishing cat.
- **1,240 birds**, including the Steller's sea eagle and the Madagascar plover.
- **2,011 fish**, such as the Mekong giant catfish.
- **664 reptiles**, including the American crocodile.
- **746 insects**, including the Macedonian grayling.
- **1,910 amphibians**, such as the Round Island day gecko.
- **And more**, including 19 arachnids, 596 crustaceans, 231 corals, 135 bivalves, and 1,434 snails and slugs.

COOL CLICK

For more information about the status of threatened species around the world, check out the IUCN Red List. iucnredlist.org

Vertebrates Animals WITH Backbones

Fish are cold-blooded and live in water. They breathe with gills, lay eggs, and usually have scales.

Amphibians are cold-blooded. Their young live in water and breathe with gills. Adults live on land and breathe with lungs.

Reptiles are cold-blooded and breathe with lungs. They live on both land and water.

Birds are warm-blooded and have feathers and wings. They lay eggs, breathe with lungs, and usually are able to fly. Some birds live on land, some in water, and some on both.

Mammals are warm-blooded and feed on their mothers' milk. They also have skin that is usually covered with hair. Mammals live on both land and water.

Bird: Bald eagle

Fish: Clown anemonefish

Invertebrates Animals WITHOUT Backbones

Sponges are a very basic form of animal life. They live in water and do not move on their own.

Echinoderms have external skeletons and live in seawater.

Mollusks have soft bodies and can live either in or out of shells, on land or in water.

Arthropods are the largest group of animals. They have external skeletons, called exoskeletons, and segmented bodies with appendages. Arthropods live in water and on land.

Worms are soft-bodied animals with no true legs. Worms live in soil.

Cnidaria live in water and have mouths surrounded by tentacles.

Cnidaria: West Coast sea nettle

Worm: Earthworms

Arthropod: Red-kneed tarantula

Cold-blooded versus Warm-blooded

Cold-blooded animals, also called ectotherms, get their heat from outside their bodies.

Warm-blooded animals, also called endotherms, keep their body temperature level regardless of the temperature of their environments.

Amazing Animal Friends

Like humans, animals can take care of each other. Sometimes it doesn't matter if they're different species. These stories prove that friendship comes in all shapes and sizes.

HEY, BUDDY! HOW ABOUT YOU GRAB A LADDER AND COME UP HERE, I NEED SOME FACE TIME.

GIRAFFE hangs with GOAT

Bristol, England
Eddie the goat and Gerald the giraffe have been living together for four years. The staff at Noah's Ark Zoo Farm were worried that Gerald would be lonely. At the time, he was the only giraffe at the zoo. "Eddie is a particularly friendly goat, so we moved him into the giraffe house."

Soon, the giraffe and goat became best friends. Sometimes Gerald leans over to lick the goat on his noggin. Eddie often wraps his legs around the giraffe's long neck and rubs him with his head.

"Gerald and Eddie need connection and companionship," says animal behavior expert Marc Bekoff at the University of Colorado. "It doesn't matter if that connection is with a different species."

RACCOON adopts CAT

WHO IS THIS MASKED MAN?

Warstein, Germany

Raccoons usually hang out with their mom and siblings, but not in this case! This raccoon seems to have taken in a cat, who cuddles with the raccoon and its family as they lounge on rocks, and snoozes with them in a cave. The masked gang even lets the kitty have first dibs when feeding time rolls around.

Most cats are solitary, and raccoons can be territorial. So rangers at Wildpark Warstein tried to remove the cat several times. But the feline always returned to the welcoming paws of the raccoon family. "Raccoons often live in families," park chief Henning Dictus says. "I think the raccoons see the cat as part of theirs."

YES, I LOVE YOU. BUT KISSING ME IN PUBLIC IS NOT COOL!

DOG loves OWL

Cornwall, England

Before Bramble the owl takes to the sky for her daily flight, Sophi the English springer spaniel clears her for takeoff by licking the bird's beak. The Eurasian eagle owl and spaniel became best friends when two-week-old Bramble arrived at Ancient Art Falconry. "Sophi sniffed and licked the chick," says Sharon Bindon, the dog's owner, who also runs a sanctuary for birds of prey.

"Soon Bramble hopped down, toddled over to Sophi, and started following her everywhere." They're still practically inseparable, even though in the wild this friendship would never exist. A wild owl would prey on small mammals such as mice, rabbits, and even foxes, which are about Sophi's size.

CRITTER CREATIONS

Oklahoma City, Oklahoma

MARSHA KEEPS A STIFF UPPER LIP WHILE PAINTING.

I'M CALLING THIS ONE "SELF-PORTRAIT."

IT'S WILD HOW SCARLET'S FEATHERS MATCH THE GRAY PAINT.

Marsha the black rhino paints with her upper lip. Wiley the grizzly bear steps in paint and lumbers across a canvas. Then there's Midgie the sea lion, who paints with a brush in her mouth, then "signs" her work with a noseprint.

It's all part of an enrichment program at the Oklahoma City Zoo, in which dozens of animals express their wild side through art. Scarlet the African gray parrot makes masterpieces with delicate strokes, holding a small brush with his beak. "But if the canvas isn't set up when he's ready, watch out," says zoo spokesperson Tara Henson. "Scarlet will paint whatever's closest: a wall, a trash can ... even his keeper walking by."

PIG IN BOOTS!

A pig's funny-looking snout helps the animal dig.

MOST PIGS LOVE WALLOWING IN THE MUD—BUT NOT CINDERS! WHEN SHE REFUSED TO PLOD THROUGH PUDDLES, HER OWNERS FIT HER WITH TINY BOOTS TO PROTECT THE PIG'S HOOVES.

24

ANIMAL MYTHS BUSTED

Some people mistakenly think adult opossums hang by their tails, or that porcupines shoot their quills. What other misconceptions are out there? Here are some common animal myths.

MYTH Elephants are afraid of mice.

HOW IT MAY HAVE STARTED People used to think that mice liked to crawl into an elephant's trunk, which could cause damage and terrible sneezing. So it makes sense that elephants would be afraid of the rodents.

WHY IT'S NOT TRUE Although elephants do get anxious when they hear sounds they can't identify, their eyesight is so poor that they could barely even see a mouse. Plus, if an elephant isn't afraid to live among predators such as tigers, rhinos, and crocodiles, a mouse would be the least of its worries!

Who are you again?

MYTH Goldfish only have a three-second memory.

HOW IT MAY HAVE STARTED While an adult human's brain weighs about three pounds (1.4 kg), an average goldfish's brain weighs only a tiny fraction of that. So how could there be any room for memory in there?

WHY IT'S NOT TRUE Research has shown that goldfish are quite smart. Phil Gee of the University of Plymouth in the United Kingdom trained goldfish to push a lever that dropped food into their tank. "They remembered the time of day that the lever worked and waited until feeding time to press it," Gee says. One scientist even trained goldfish to tell the difference between classical and blues music!

MYTH Bulls charge when they see red.

HOW IT MAY HAVE STARTED Traditionally, a red cape is part of a bullfighter's colorful costume. When the bullfighter flashes the cape at the bull, the bull charges.

WHY IT'S NOT TRUE Movement actually makes a bull charge. "I've seen bulls chase everything from red to blue to plaid," says Temple Grandin of the Colorado State University. "It's the motion of the bullfighter's cape, not the color."

Mystery of the Disappearing FROGS

Frogs survived the catastrophic extinction of the dinosaurs. But strangely, the world's frogs and toads have suddenly begun to disappear. Some species that were common 25 years ago are now rare or extinct. And individual frogs are showing up with deformities such as too many legs. Scientists are not sure exactly what is going on.

But scientists do agree that because frogs drink and breathe through their thin skin, they are especially vulnerable to pesticides and pollution. A deformed frog often indicates that all is not well with the environment. And frogs live just about everywhere on Earth.

Frogs are amphibians, which means "double life." They generally hatch in water as tadpoles and end up living on land as fully formed frogs. Frogs' skin must stay moist, so they're usually found in wet places.

Because frogs are so sensitive to environmental changes, they act as an early-warning system.

Their dwindling numbers may be a sign that our planet is not as clean and healthy as it once was. By studying how frogs are affected by the environment around them, scientists may be able to predict—and sound an alarm—that a neighborhood needs to cut back on lawn fertilizers or that a chemical-dumping factory should clean up its act. The hidden message in frogs' familiar peeps and croaks? "I'm jumpy for a reason!"

SOME FROGS GLOW WHEN THEY EAT FIREFLIES.

CALLING ALL FROGS

Frogs bark, croak, cluck, click, grunt, snore, squawk, chirp, whistle, trill, and yap. Some are named for the noise they make. A chorus of barking tree frogs sounds like a pack of hounds on a hunt. The carpenter frog sounds like two carpenters hammering nails, and the pig frog grunts like—you guessed it—Porky's cousin! Here a male Australian red-eyed tree frog (top of page) inflates his throat pouch, which helps make his female-attracting calls louder.

Do Animals Have FEELINGS?

A scientist sat observing wild chimpanzees in Tanzania, in Africa. The chimp she called Flint had always been unusually attached to his mother. When his mother died, Flint withdrew from other chimps. He hardly ate. He climbed a tree to the nest he and his mother had shared. For a long time he stood there, staring into space. "It was as though he were remembering," says Jane Goodall, the world-famous chimp expert who witnessed the scene.

Stories like this suggest that animals have emotional feelings. Add up all such stories (there are many), and they suggest something more: evidence. It is evidence that researchers like Goodall hope will convince skeptics of something most people with pets already believe— that animals do have feelings.

Not everyone agrees that there is proof of animal emotions. Why the doubt? "You can't do an experiment to find out," says Joseph LeDoux, professor of neuroscience.

"An animal can't tell you, 'Yes, that's how I feel.'"

Scientists used that same argument with Goodall nearly 50 years ago. But she didn't buy it. "Look into a chimp's eyes," she says, "and you know you're looking into the mind of a thinking, feeling being."

But LeDoux says this doesn't prove feelings. Complex emotions—such as jealousy, grief, or embarrassment—may require a neocortex, the wrinkled outer part of the brain. Only primates and a few other animals have this brain structure.

Though most scientists believe that many animals do have some feelings, they also suspect that animal feelings are different from human feelings. How different? We may never know for sure.

Goodall believes that researchers will eventually gather enough data to draw some conclusions. "Until then, let's give all creatures the benefit of doubt," she suggests.

> Want to help at-risk chimps? Check out Jane Goodall's Roots & Shoots online: rootsandshoots.org. Discover how kids around the world have supported chimps, whales, the environment, and more through this organization.

Jane Goodall sits quietly observing chimpanzees, animals she has studied for more than 40 years.

27

The Fox Next Door

T he sun starts to set in northern Virginia, and a red fox wakes up, ready to search for dinner. She steps silently through the bushes, following an appetizing scent to a wooden fence. The red fox squeezes through a narrow gap in the fence, then leaps up, over the edge of . . . an open garbage can. She tears through a plastic bag and snatches some scraps of grilled chicken. As the fox climbs out, the garbage can tips over with a crash. Backyard lights turn on, but the sly fox has already disappeared with her meal.

RED FOXES COULD BE MOVIN

URBAN WILDLIFE

This dinnertime scenario is becoming more and more common across the United States. Cities and suburbs are spreading into the countryside, swallowing up red fox habitat. But instead of moving, these clever wild animals learn to thrive near people. "Red foxes can be scavengers or predators, whatever they need to get food and find den sites," says Vicky Monroe, a wildlife biologist in Fairfax County, Virginia, U.S.A., just outside Washington, D.C. To avoid people, skillful red foxes hunt at

PEOPLE MUST NEVER FEED FOXES AND SHOULD ALWAYS MAINTAIN A DISTANCE FROM THEM. WILDLIFE BIOLOGIST VICKY MONROE ADVISES COVERING GARBAGE CANS AND BRINGING PETS AND PET FOOD IN AT NIGHT.

night in backyards, gardens, and city parks. Although rabbits as well as mice and other rodents are their favorite fare, red foxes will eat birds, frogs, snakes, grasshoppers, and even berries. A hungry red fox will also jump into an open dumpster or garbage can for tasty leftovers or nibble on pet food that is left out on the porch.

MOVING IN

As winter begins near Denver, Colorado, U.S.A., two red foxes pair up to mate and raise a family. Needing a place to nestle, the foxes sneak under a porch. This is prime real estate, hidden from people, with plenty of rodents nearby. They'll stay here until their six pups, or kits, start to explore the world. By October, the members of the red fox family will leave the safety of the porch, each in search of its own den site.

The clever red foxes find creative accommodations. They have been known to squeeze through gates, scale high fences, and break into sheds and garages. One scientist says he knew of a red fox that found its way into a college football stadium and slept on the field during the off-season.

STREET SAVVY

In the woods of Illinois, U.S.A., a red fox is prowling for new territory. Other foxes have marked their range already, so this male ventures farther away where there will be less competition for food. The red fox

LOCATION, LOCATION, LOCATION
Red foxes are the most widespread meat-eating mammals in the world. Their natural range covers much of the Northern Hemisphere.

NTO YOUR NEIGHBORHOOD.

wanders to a suburban park. His search is over; here he will live closer to other foxes than he would in the countryside, but there is plenty of food and no predators in sight.

But that doesn't mean this fox is out of danger. His ears pick up a sound he recognizes. He freezes at the park's edge. He sits and waits. A car zooms past. Satisfied that the threat is gone, the fox trots across the road, slinking into the bushes on the other side.

Why did the fox cross the road? Because people put it there.

CANINE COUSINS
They are small and seem catlike, but red foxes are relatives of dogs, wolves, and coyotes.

6 Tips Every Polar

L ife in the frozen wilds of the Arctic Circle isn't exactly easy, even if you're a polar bear, the world's largest land-dwelling predator. To withstand the subzero temperatures, snow-covered landscapes, and day after day without sun, you're going to need to put all 1,500 pounds (680 kg) of your muscle, bone, and body fat to good use. If you were a polar bear, here's what you'd need to know to survive on the Arctic ice.

1

Walk, Don't Run . . . Or Better Yet, Sit Still.

When walking or running, a polar bear expends more than twice the energy used by most other mammals. Want to save energy? Don't move at all. If you decide to run, make it a short trip. After a five-mile run, even young bears in good shape can become overheated.

2

Bearfoot . . . *hmm . . . B*arefoot Is Best.

Ever wonder why your paws are so big? On an adult, they're huge—up to 12 inches (30 cm) across. Working like snowshoes, they spread weight across the snow and ice, keeping you from sinking. That way your paws don't make any crunching noises, which could warn prey that "Bigfoot" is on the way.

3

Don't Let Cubs Become Polar Bear Snacks.

It's a harsh fact of Arctic life that adult males sometimes kill and eat polar bear cubs, so mother bears are very protective. Most will chase away male polar bears much bigger than they are. Male bears are not the only threats from which moms defend their cubs. Some brave mothers will rear up on their hind legs to leap at hovering helicopters!

Bear Should Know

Fat's Where It's At.

Since you live in the cold Arctic climate, having a layer of fat is a good thing. That fat, called blubber, works like a fleece vest—it insulates your body from the frosty air and near-freezing water. When food is scarce, your four-inch (10-cm)-thick blubber gives you energy and helps keep you afloat when you swim because fat weighs less than water.

5

4

Neatness Counts. So Does Drying Off.

A clean bear is a warm bear. That's because dirty, matted fur doesn't hold body heat like clean fur does. After eating, spend up to 15 minutes cleaning yourself—licking your chest, paws, and muzzle with your long tongue. In summertime, take baths right after you eat. Then dry yourself by shaking off excess moisture or using snow like a thick, fluffy towel to rub the water away.

6

Always Wear White.

You may have noticed that the hairs in your thick fur coat aren't really white. Each is transparent with a hollow core that reflects light. This helps you blend with your surroundings—a neat trick, especially while you're hunting wary seals. Good thing wearing white is always stylish for polar bears.

Meerkat CITY

Meerkats always have something to do. These mongoose relatives live in a busy community, with no time to sit around being bored. In their family groups of up to 40 members, everyone pitches in to get all the jobs done.

A SENTINEL KEEPS WATCH.

Guards

Meerkats are very territorial. Guards, called sentinels, are always on the lookout for rival meerkats that try to move in on their territory. If a sentinel (left) spots any intruding meerkats, it sends out an alarm call. The whole group gathers together and stands tall to try to scare away the rivals. If that doesn't work, meerkats quickly decide whether to fight or retreat.

Predators such as eagles or jackals rate a different warning call. If a sentinel spots the predator first, it lets out an alarm call that sends all the meerkats scurrying into the nearest bolt hole—an underground safety den where the eagle can't follow.

Babysitters

Within a meerkat group, the alpha, or leader, female and the alpha male are usually the only ones that have babies. When their babies are too young to follow along while they search for food, meerkat parents have to go without them. So they leave their pups with babysitters—other adult meerkats in the group. The pups stay inside their family's underground burrow for the first three weeks of life, protected and cared for by the babysitters.

Diggers

Picture yourself looking for a tasty bug to eat (below) when suddenly you hear the alarm call for "eagle." You dash left, you dash right, and you finally find a bolt hole.

Bolt holes provide fast getaways for meerkats in danger. Members of the group cooperate to make sure bolt holes are properly dug out, that nothing is blocking the entry, and that there are enough bolt holes in every area.

Meerkats are built to be superdiggers. All four of their paws have long, sturdy claws that they use like rakes. They dig to find food, such as lizards and other small reptiles, insects and their larvae, and scorpions.

HOME SWEET BURROW

DIGGING FOR FOOD

WILD DOGS OF AFRICA

The puppy-dog eyes and pleading squeals of a five-month-old African wild dog named Cici can mean only one thing: dinnertime. An older sister in Cici's pack responds, dragging over a meaty impala bone. In African wild dog society, puppies have all the power. "It's up to the older siblings to take care of the puppies," says Micaela Gunther, a scientist who studies wild dogs, including Cici's family. "The doting grownups even deliver toys, such as a strip of impala skin perfect for puppy tug-of-war." Imagine your big brother or sister working hard to hand you snacks and games while you eat, play, and rest all day.

DOG DAYS

Like wolves, wild dogs live in a pack of up to 15 dogs. Pups stay in the pack for about two years. Then some may break off to start packs of their own, while others stay with their mom and dad.

When the pups are newborn, every member of the pack works together to provide for them. At first the puppies stay near the den, often under the watch of a babysitter while the pack hunts. Returning pack members throw up meat for the pups. Sound gross? Puppies love these leftovers.

PACK ATTACK

By the time the pups are six months old, they join the pack on hunting expeditions. First they learn how to stalk prey, and eventually they participate in the kill. Single 60-pound dogs rarely catch larger prey on their own, but a pack of 20 proves that there really is strength in numbers. Together they can take down a zebra or wildebeest weighing up to a thousand pounds.

Hunting wild dogs often pursue herds of gazelle for miles, fresh dogs trading places with tired ones. Eventually the weakest of the chased animals tires. The dogs surround it and attack from every direction. This teamwork is bred from the pack's intense social bonding, such as the daily greeting ceremonies and puppy play sessions. Team-building is the reason wild dogs spoil the pups, who grow up united and ready to contribute to the strength of the pack.

SuperShark AWARDS

FASTER THAN A SPEEDING BULLETFISH, LEAPING SMALL BOATS IN A SINGLE BOUND . . . it's Super Shark! Most of the 450 to 500 shark species go about their lives in secrecy, but a few stand out. Here are some of the world's super sharks.

Fantastic Fish

Whale sharks are the world's largest shark—and fish. Possibly reaching lengths up to 65 feet (20 m), it's larger than two city buses. Weighing up to 74,970 pounds (34,006 kg), it doesn't just tip the scales, it smashes them!

Best Burp (and bark)

When threatened, a swell shark doubles its size by gulping water. Once safe it makes a doglike bark and burps out all the water.

During the day, as many as 36 nurse sharks pile on top of each other as they rest in caves and crevices.

Best Dog Pile

Peewee Predators

One of the smallest sharks, the dwarf lanternshark is only 6.6 to 7.8 inches (17–20 cm)—about as long as a pencil.

Speed Chaser

Shredding the water at 31 miles per hour (50 kph), a shortfin mako shark is the world's fastest shark. Makos are faster than bottlenose dolphins (22 mph/35 kph) and killer whales (30 mph/48 kph). Their speed makes them too fast for most predators—except humans.

High Jump

A shortfin mako leaps 20 feet (6 m) above the water surface. That's higher than a giraffe's head.

DOLPHINS IN DISGUISE

If you think *you* have a few odd relatives . . . imagine having a second cousin who's six times your size or an uncle covered in scars from a lifetime of fighting. Welcome to the dolphin family, made up of more than 30 species that inhabit every ocean—and even some rivers. You probably know the common bottlenose dolphin, seen frolicking in aquariums. Now meet its surprisingly diverse relatives.

HOURGLASS DOLPHINS

Dolphin data Sailors once called these small mammals "skunk dolphins," but not because they smelled bad. The dolphin's white markings are similar to a skunk's stripe.

Spinning in air Leaping out of the water, hourglass dolphins make spectacular midair spins. "No one knows for sure why they spin," says Mark Simmonds, a dolphin biologist. "Theories include that they do it for fun, as a form of communicating to others, or to help get rid of parasites."

Where they live Frigid waters in the Antarctic

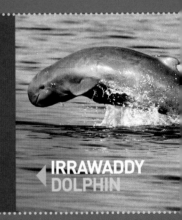

Dolphin data With its stubby dorsal fin and permanent grin on its beakless head, the Irrawaddy dolphin looks like a bottlenose dolphin reflected in a fun house mirror—recognizable but oddly misshapen. These dolphins, found in coastal waters and some freshwater rivers, are experts at catching dinner. They spit streams of water to confuse fish, making them a cinch to snatch.

Perfect catch Fishermen in Myanmar, in Asia, appreciate the Irrawaddy dolphin's fishing skills, too. In a tradition passed down for generations, the fishermen signal the dolphins to drive schools of fish into nets. These special dolphins don't do it for free—they snap up fish that get away.

Where they live Along the coasts of India and Southeast Asia, and in some Southeast Asian rivers

◀ IRRAWADDY DOLPHIN

ORCA ▶

Dolphin data Don't let its titanic size or "killer whale" nickname fool you. A male orca may grow to the length of a school bus, but it is actually a dolphin. It's also the sea's top predator, using teamwork to hunt seals, sea lions, and other large prey—hence the killer alias. Researchers have even seen orcas gobbling up great white sharks!

Mother knows best Orcas love their moms. Elder females typically lead each family, or pod. Male orcas who wander off to mate in other pods return to their mothers' sides and never see their young. "It's unusual among mammals," says Val Veirs, who studies orcas. "This top predator gets all its marching orders from Mom."

Where they live Frigid coastal waters across the globe

**BOTTLENOSE
DOLPHINS**

Dolphin data In the wild, bottlenose dolphins can swim at speeds of more than 18 miles an hour (29 kph). They surface often to breathe, doing so two or three times a minute.

Superstars They are well known as the intelligent and playful stars of many aquarium shows. Their curved mouths give the appearance of a friendly smile, and they can be trained to perform complex tricks.

Where they live In tropical oceans and other warm waters around the globe

Dolphin data Small and curious, the Commerson's dolphin is known for its playful nature and striking black-and-white coloring. These sleek swimmers look like they're wearing white capes!

Boat buds Many dolphin species enjoy playing with boats, but the dolphins seem especially excited to surf on a ship's wake and twirl in propeller turbulence. "One time two dolphins spent more than an hour playing with our research boat," says Vanesa Tossenberger, who studies Commerson's dolphins. "It certainly makes our work easier."

Where they live Off the southern tip of South America

**COMMERSON'S
DOLPHIN**

PROBLEM SOLVED!

Dolphins certainly aren't sitting around on the ocean floor figuring out jigsaw puzzles. But they do problem solve! Scientists say that dolphins have the ability to think through a problem from beginning to end—and anticipate outcomes. They're just not sure if the animals are acting on instinct or learning by trial and error.

DINNER IS SERVED

Buster the wild bottlenose dolphin is an underwater sushi chef! Her specialty? Cuttlefish. So far, she's the only animal known to prepare them.

Every May, swarms of these strange-looking, eight-armed creatures gather in Upper Spencer Gulf, South Australia, to mate and lay eggs. It looks like an all-you-can-eat buffet, but the cuttlefish are full of terrible-tasting black ink and have a big, chalky, flat bone.

Not one to waste food, Buster catches a cuttlefish. She kills it by ramming it into the sand. Then, she pounds it so hard that the ink pours out. Finally, she rubs the cuttlefish along the seafloor to remove the skin and release the bone. Only the meaty fillet is left. Sounds like this dolphin really uses her head!

NEVER TRUST A DINNER INVITATION FROM A DOLPHIN.

CUTTLEFISH

UNDER the ICE

Jellyfish (right) with 30-foot (9-m) -long tentacles are just one of the surprises beneath the surface of Antarctica's frozen seas.

Another is **sea spiders**. Found in oceans worldwide, they are usually less than an inch (2.54 cm) long. But in Antarctica they often reach the size of a human hand (below). Luckily, people aren't their chosen snack food. They prefer to chow down on coral, anemones, and sponges.

EMPEROR PENGUINS

1 Emperors are the largest of the 17 penguin species.

2 One colony can number as many as 60,000 penguins.

3 These penguins can live 20 years or more in the wild.

4 Emperors eat fish, squid, and shrimplike krill.

5 Parents feed chicks every three to four days.

Incredible Powers of the OCTOPUS!

POTIONS AND POISONS

Blue-ringed octopuses make one of the deadliest poisons in the world. They have enough poison in their saliva to kill a human, though these mollusks mostly use their venom to paralyze prey or to defend themselves from enemies.

TRICK ARMS

When faced with danger, some octopuses will break off an arm and scoot away. The arm keeps wriggling for hours, sometimes crawling all over an attacker and distracting it. The octopus grows a new arm out of the stump.

THE OCTOPUS IS THE TALLER LUMP ON THE RIGHT. THAT'S BRAIN CORAL ON THE LEFT.

ESCAPE ARTIST

To confuse attackers, an octopus will squirt a concentrated ink out of its backside that forms a smokelike cloud. This allows enough time for an octopus to escape.

MAGICAL MOVES

Octopuses can squeeze through tiny holes as if they were moving from room to room through keyholes. Some can even swim through the sand, sticking up an eye like a periscope to see if the coast is clear.

Secret Life of

U ntil recently, scientists knew almost nothing about how sea turtles spend their time underwater. But with the help of a really cool underwater camera, they've gotten a peek into the turtles' private lives—and a better idea of how to protect these endangered animals.

When strapped to a Crittercam, a specially designed camera that attaches to the turtle's shell, sea turtles show scientists life from their point of view. A suction cup holds the camera in place, then releases it after a few hours. The camera floats to the surface, where scientists can recover it and see what it recorded.

JELLYFISH

LOGGERHEAD SEA TURTLE

Must-Sea TV

And what has the Crittercam captured? Plenty! As in any great reality TV show, there are surprises around every corner with sea turtles. When the cameras started rolling, scientists saw just how surprisingly social turtles are. They even have staring contests, locking eyes on each other for a few minutes before one of the turtles swims away (scientists aren't sure about the purpose of this game but found it pretty funny!).

CRITTERCAM SHOT

GREEN SEA TURTLE

SEA SPONGE

Scrub-a-Dub

The Crittercam also helped scientists discover why sea turtles have relatively clean shells, unlike the barnacle-encrusted loggerheads. Green sea turtles were seen taking sponge baths, rubbing against living sea sponges to clean their heads, flippers, and bellies. Turtles even chase others away from the best rubbing spots!

Snack Surprise

When it came to food, scientists were surprised to find out that green sea turtles didn't munch on sea grass as suspected, but instead gobbled up nearly every bite-size jellyfish that floats into view (shown above). Before Crittercam, these turtles were thought to be vegetarians. But the jellyfish diet made sense: Why choose salad when there's jelly to snack on?

After all of these amazing observations, scientists are hoping to reveal even more secrets about this unique creature using the Crittercam. After all, the more scientists learn about the life of sea turtles, the more everyone can do to help ensure the reptiles' future.

Sea Turtles

DID YOU KNOW?
All seven species of sea turtles are endangered.

DID YOU KNOW?
One of the largest green sea turtles ever recorded has lived in California's San Diego Bay for about 40 years. Affectionately called Wrinklebutt due to a shell deformity, she weighs about 550 pounds (250 kg).

WRINKLEBUTT'S UNUSUAL SHELL SHAPE

COOL CLICK

To see Crittercam in action visit online at animals.nationalgeographic.com/animals/crittercam-wildcam/

5 HARP SEALS

COOL THINGS ABOUT

With their irresistible faces and fluffy fur, harp seals are some of the cutest animals around. But their snow-white pelts and icy habitat make harp seals especially vulnerable to hunters, global warming, and other environmental threats. Here's more about harp seals—and why it's extra-important to protect these adorable animals.

1 6,000-MILE JOURNEY

Each year, harp seals migrate more than 6,000 miles (9,600 km), spending summers feeding in northern Arctic coastal waters and heading back south in the fall to breed. They migrate in small groups of up to 20 individuals. By late February, harp seals gather in large herds. As many as one million form an enormous herd found on the floating mass of pack ice in the Gulf of St. Lawrence in Canada. Once breeding season is over, the seals travel back north for the summer.

2 SEE-THROUGH COAT

When a harp seal pup is born, its coat has a yellow tint. But it turns completely white within a couple of days. The fine, silky fur is almost transparent. This allows the pup's skin to absorb the sun's rays, which helps it stay warm. The whitecoats, as they are called, look like this only for about two weeks. Then they molt, or shed, their white fur. Their new coats are gray.

DID YOU KNOW? Harp seals are known as "earless" seals because they don't have external earflaps.

3 HEART TRICK

When a young harp seal sees a polar bear, instinct takes over. The pup can't escape the predator by running away, so it hides—in plain sight. The ball of white fur plays possum. The seal lies motionless with its head tucked into its chubby neck, looking like a heap of snow (below). The pup's heart rate slows from about 80 to 90 beats a minute to only 20 to 30 beats. If the trick works, the bear doesn't see the harp seal and moves on. Then the seal can stretch out and relax. Whew!

4 DEEP DIVERS

It's not unusual for a harp seal to hold its breath for five minutes. But when it needs to, the seal can stay underwater for as long as 20 minutes and dive more than 800 feet (244 m) down. That's six times deeper than a scuba diver can go safely. Harp seals can get places fast, too—100 feet (30 m) down in 15 seconds. As the seals zip through the water hunting for fish, they also stay alert for orcas and sharks that might eat *them*.

5 QUICK-CHANGE ARTISTS

By the time a harp seal is 14 months old, it's changed coats—and nicknames—five times. A whitecoat at first, it then becomes a graycoat, a ragged jacket, a beater, and finally a bedlamer. At four years old a harp seal has a silvery gray coat with a few spots—and it's called a spotted harp. Some females look like that the rest of their lives. But males, as well as many females, develop a distinctive black pattern that is shaped like a harp, which explains the name of the species.

PANDA SHAKE-UP

BEFORE THE EARTHQUAKE, PANDAS PLAY AT THE CENTER.

AFTER THE EARTHQUAKE, MUCH WAS DESTROYED.

Giant Panda Home Gets Extreme Makeover

An earthquake rocks China, shaking the ground around the giant pandas and their caregivers at the Wolong Giant Panda Breeding Center (WGPBC) in Sichuan. Two minutes of terror destroys schools and bamboo forests, and leaves the center in shambles. The pandas are taken to temporary quarters.

WGPBC is the world's largest giant panda breeding and research facility and home to half of the world's captive pandas. Fewer than 2,000 giant pandas are left in the wild. Rebuilding the center is crucial to the giant panda's survival as a species, so it doesn't take long for the reconstruction to begin.

MOVING UP

The new breeding center will be bigger and better than the one destroyed in the 2008 earthquake. In the nursery section, panda mothers and human caregivers will take care of newborns. When a cub is a year old and ready to leave its mother, it will move into the panda kindergarten. That's where it will learn how to find food and explore new environments before being released into the wild.

The new captive panda center will also create enormous panda enclosures by encircling bamboo-rich forests with electric fencing. Here, pandas will be able to experience a wild setting while scientists monitor their health and safety.

THIS 37-DAY-OLD GIANT PANDA CUB RESTS IN AN INCUBATOR.

ASIA
CHINA

Earthquake epicenter

SICHUAN

Giant panda breeding center

LIVING AS NEIGHBORS

As scientists plan the new breeding center, they also are working to restore habitats where human activities have left groups of wild pandas isolated. The goal is to restore wildlife corridors between habitats so that smaller panda populations do not become permanently isolated and unable to reproduce.

43

ROCK-A-BYE
MONKEY

INTAN ENJOYS ACROBATICS.

INTAN CUDDLES WITH HER MOM WHEN SHE'S READY TO REST.

Gleefully vaulting from branch to branch, Intan, a six-week-old monkey, is so daring—and so uncoordinated. She slips, then screams for help while dangling 60 feet (18 m) up a tree. Mom and other females in the troop rush to her rescue.

Ebony langurs, a kind of monkey, spend most of their lives high in the forest canopy. There they effortlessly leap from tree to tree. But today is Intan's first day in a real tree in a real forest. The troop was just released from captivity into the forest of Bromo Tengger Semeru National Park on the island of Java in Indonesia.

Monkey Business

Illegally captured from the wild and sold as pets, the monkeys in this troop are survivors. The Indonesian Conservation Department rescued them, bringing them to a center where caregivers prepare them for release back into the wild. Little Intan is born while the troop is at the center.

When the monkeys are released, biologists and photographers hide on an observation platform high in a tree to watch them settle in. But the monkeys easily find the observers.

Nice Trip. See You Next Fall!

Intan's mother becomes exasperated as she rescues her baby from climbing predicaments. After a few falls, she carries Intan to the not-so-secret blind, and puts her in photographer Djuna Ivereigh's lap.

Before Ivereigh can move the baby from her lap, Intan leaps up to play with a stick. Chasing it across the platform, Intan accidentally topples over the edge. The humans watch in horror as the baby tumbles 25 feet (8 m) to the ground!

Shrieking langurs rush toward the motionless monkey. Scooping up Intan, Mom gently rocks her baby. Very soon, Intan peeks out, unharmed. She bounds away for more monkey mischief.

The dirty looks the troop give Ivereigh suggest their opinion of her babysitting skills. The near-disastrous result may achieve one goal, though: No troop member will ever trust a human with one of its own again.

Will the RED PANDA Survive?

A mask marks one of the cutest faces in the forest. The red panda looks a little like a raccoon, a bit like a fox, and somewhat like a puppy. Soft, cuddly, reddish fur blankets its body, which is a tad larger than a big house cat's. These harmless creatures live in the high mountain forests of the Himalaya in southeastern Asia. But their numbers in the wild are dwindling.

As loggers and firewood collectors chop down trees, and ranchers allow overgrazing by domestic livestock, the fragile mountain habitat of the red panda erodes.

SPECIALIZED DIET

The diet of the red panda also makes it vulnerable, because it is one of just a few mammal species in the world that eat mainly bamboo. It's not the most nutritious stuff. This giant grass has tough stems and leaves that make it difficult to chew and digest. A bamboo diet doesn't give red pandas much energy, so they have to conserve as much as possible.

SLOW-MOVING SLEEPYHEADS

Red pandas save energy simply by keeping activity to a minimum. They spend six to eight hours a day moving around and eating. The rest of their time is spent resting and sleeping. Their bodies are built to conserve energy. When the weather is cold, the pandas curl into a tight ball on a tree branch and go into a very deep sleep. This reduces their metabolism, or the amount of energy they use. When red pandas wake up, their metabolism returns to normal. But as soon as they go back to sleep their metabolism drops again, saving energy.

Saving the BLUE IGUANA

Found only on the Caribbean island of Grand Cayman, in the Cayman Islands, the blue iguana is one of the most endangered species of lizards in the world. It can't protect itself against threats such as the construction of houses and roads, or predators such as snakes, cats, and dogs. When the number of these wild, dragonlike creatures dropped to fewer than 25 several years ago, experts took action. They began breeding them in captivity. The program has been so successful that more than 650 blue iguanas now live wild on the island. Luckily, it may be blue skies ahead for these living "dragons."

COOL CLICK

Test your knowledge of endangered animals at animals.nationalgeographic.com/animals/endangered-animals-quiz/

Animal

Bear

UP IN A TREE

The spectacled bear cub is terrified. A plane slammed into a mountainside in northern Peru, causing an explosion that either killed or scared off her mother. At just three months old, the confused and hungry cub doesn't know what to do next.

Spectacled bears are a threatened species and the only bear native to South America. A farmer takes the cub from the crash site, and she's eventually relocated to Chaparri Reserve, a bear rescue center 115 miles (185 km) away.

Six months pass, and Chaparri officials move her into a huge habitat with rocky terrain, big trees, and bushes that grow fruits that wild bears normally eat. Her interaction with humans is also limited.

Finally, nearly five years after the plane crash, the bear is released. Although she ventures away from the center, she returns each year during the dry season. High in a tree, she observes her old home—from the outside.

Wombat

NEWBORN WOMBAT IN INCUBATOR

JENSEN IS BOTTLE-FED.

Rescues

Dog

A **weary dog clings to a chunk of ice** drifting down the swift-moving Vistula River in Poland. If he tries to swim to the shore, he could be crushed by ice blocks slamming into each other or drown. No one knows how the dog got stranded on the ice floe. The river picks up speed as it rushes into the Baltic Sea. Hours pass. The dog floats 15 miles (24 km) out to sea.

Aboard the Polish sea research vessel *Baltica,* an officer sees a shape moving on the ice. They move closer, and the ship's engineer lowers an inflatable rubber boat into the icy water. From the boat, he reaches for the dog and pulls him to safety by the scruff of the neck. Back aboard *Baltica* the crew wraps the dog in blankets and gives him bits of food from the ship's kitchen. Amazingly, he is unharmed. The crew names him Baltic and unsuccessfully tries to locate his owner. So he stays with the crew, accompanying the ship's engineer on sea research missions. Now, wherever Baltic goes, he's a hero—and the ship's cook always has a special treat for him.

PUP STRANDED ON ICE

SAFE IN THE ARMS OF A RESCUER

"I **t's dead, but something is moving in the wombat's pouch."** That's the call an animal shelter in Australia's Victoria state gets after an adult wombat is struck by a car as she crosses a highway. Like kangaroos, wombats are marsupials and the females carry their young, called joeys, in their pouches for about six months. The victim's baby is only about three-and-a-half months old, hairless, and has yet to open his eyes. But he is alive. The shelter employee tucks the premature joey into a fabric pouch with a hot water bottle. Once at the shelter, she places him in an incubator to warm up.

Every four hours, the tiny patient is fed one tablespoon (14.8 ml) of formula with a plastic syringe. Week by week, the wombat joey, now named Jensen, grows. He feeds from a bottle and opens his eyes. Over the next two months, Jensen triples in weight and reaches the size of a small bowling ball. He eats grass, complete with roots and dirt like he'd find in the wild—where he's headed. After a year at the shelter, Jensen is released near an empty burrow in a grassy area of a protected forest, where he can progress with his life.

HEALTHY, HAPPY JENSEN!

47

WILD CAT
Family Reunion

There are 37 species of wild cats.

After studying their DNA, scientists have divided them into eight groups, called lineages. Here are representatives from each lineage. The domestic house cat comes from the lineage that includes the sand cat.

CHEETAH
(46 to 143 pounds: 21 to 65 kg)
- Often scans for prey from a high spot
- Can sprint up to 70 miles an hour (113 kph)
- From Puma lineage, which includes three species

CANADA LYNX
(11 to 38 pounds: 5 to 17 kg)
- Its main prey is the snowshoe hare
- Big paws act like snowshoes
- From Lynx lineage, which includes four species

OCELOT
(15 to 34 pounds: 7 to 15 kg)
- Most of an ocelot's prey is small
- Found from Texas to Argentina
- From Ocelot lineage, which includes seven species

TIGER
(165 to 716 pounds: 75 to 325 kg)
- Tigers are the only striped wild cats
- These big cats will hunt almost any mammal in their territory
- From Panthera lineage, which includes seven species, such as the lion and jaguar

ND CAT (3 to 7.5 pounds: 1 to 3 kg)

e sand cat lives in dry deserts of northern
rica and the Middle East

arely drinks; gets water from food

om Domestic Cat lineage, which includes
e species of cat

MARBLED CAT
(4 to 11 pounds:
2 to 5 kg)
- Its long, bushy tail
is sometimes longer
than its body
- Very little is known
about this rare,
nocturnal, and shy
wild cat
- From Bay Cat lineage,
which includes
three species

SERVAL
(15 to 30 pounds: 7 to 14 kg)
- Longest legs,
relative to its
body, of any
cat species
- Big ears used
to listen
for prey
- From Caracal
lineage, which
includes three
species

FISHING CAT
(11 to 35
pounds:
5 to 16 kg)
- A strong
swimmer, it
has slightly
webbed feet
- Eats mainly fish
- From Leopard
Cat lineage,
which includes
five species

How to tell a cat by its
SPOTS

JAGUAR: little dots in the middle of larger rings
(body); small black spots (head)
Home: mainly Mexico, Central and
South America
Average Size: 80 to 350 pounds
(36 to 159 kg)
Cat Fact: Third largest in the cat
family after tigers and lions, the jaguar
is the largest feline in the Western Hemisphere.

LEOPARD: rings without the jaguar's
smaller dots inside
Home: much of Asia and Africa
Average Size: 62 to 200 pounds
(28 to 91 kg)
Cat Fact: Some leopards are dark and
look spotless. They're called black panthers.

CHEETAH: evenly spaced, solid black splotches
the size of a human thumbprint
Home: parts of Africa
Average Size: 46 to 143 pounds
(21 to 65 kg)
Cat Fact: The fastest land animal,
the cheetah has dark lines on its face
from the inner corner of each eye
to the outer corners of its mouth.

SERVAL: usually a series of single
black dots that can vary from the size
of a freckle to one inch (2.54 cm) wide
Home: many parts of Africa
Average Size: 15 to 30 pounds
(7 to 14 kg)
Cat Fact: A serval uses its huge ears
to hunt by sound, surprising prey with a pounce.

OCELOT: solid or open-centered
dark spots that sometimes merge to
look like links in a chain; fur in the
center of open spots is often darker
than background coat color.
Home: South, Central, and
North America
Average Size: 15 to 34 pounds (7 to 15 kg)
Cat Fact: An ocelot's main prey is rodents.

Nature's SUPERCATS LEOPARDS

POWERFUL PROWLERS

No big cat is more at home in a tree than a leopard. It's in the trees that leopards often reveal their trademark strength. Thanks to muscular necks and stocky legs, these cats are made for pouncing and climbing. Plus, their massive heads pack powerful jaws that let leopards haul prey that's twice their weight up the trunks of trees two stories high. That would be like climbing a ladder while carrying your dad or big brother—with your teeth! The cats scramble skyward not only to hide prey from scavengers or escape from lions, but also to mount attacks from tree limbs, pouncing on unsuspecting prey below.

ADAPTABLE FELINE

Not all leopards spend their lives in trees, though. The cats are also perfectly happy hiding their dinners in the brush. This ability to adapt has helped the leopard become the most widespread member of the cat species. Leopards also adapt their diet to whatever prey is plentiful. They'll go after crocodiles, zebras, and other big animals. But they also snack on smaller prey, like rodents, lizards, and hares—no meal is too tiny for this wild cat.

A LEOPARD TAKES HER PREY UP A TREE.

Tjololo the leopard is playing tug-of-war in a tree, and he's in no mood to lose. His opponents: two hyenas that had darted out of the night to swipe Tjololo's freshly killed impala. Not about to let the hyenas steal his meal, Tjololo (pronounced cha-LO-lo) did what leopards do best: He grasped the impala in his powerful jaws and carried it straight up the tree.

NAT GEO EXPLORER

Dereck and Beverly Joubert: Award-winning Wildlife Filmmakers from Botswana

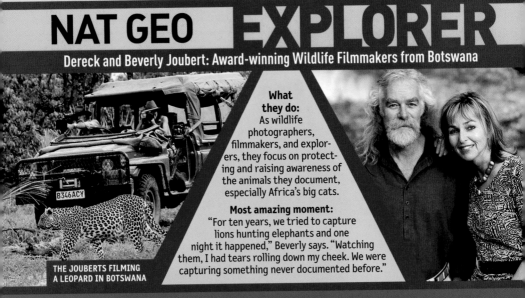

What they do: As wildlife photographers, filmmakers, and explorers, they focus on protecting and raising awareness of the animals they document, especially Africa's big cats.

Most amazing moment: "For ten years, we tried to capture lions hunting elephants and one night it happened," Beverly says. "Watching them, I had tears rolling down my cheek. We were capturing something never documented before."

THE JOUBERTS FILMING A LEOPARD IN BOTSWANA

LIONS OF THE KALAHARI DESERT

ROARRR!
On a still night the sound of lions roaring can carry for five miles (8 km). Roaring often is used to tell other lions, "This is my piece of land."

E yes half-closed against the wind-blasted sand, a sleek, black-and-gold-maned lion (above) strides along a dry riverbed in the Kalahari Desert. He is one of the lions that roam the desolate sand dunes of southern Africa's Kalahari and Namib Deserts. These lions thrive in an intensely hot landscape. They have learned to go without water for weeks.

Life for a desert lion is very different from life as a lion in the grassy plains of Africa, such as in the Serengeti of Kenya and Tanzania. There, large prides of up to 20 lions spend most of their time together. A pride is very much like a human family.

Fritz Eloff, a scientist who spent 40 years studying the desert lions of the Kalahari, found that desert lions live, on average, in smaller groups of fewer than six. Family ties are just as strong, but relationships are long-distance. Desert lions often break up into smaller groups.

BUSY NIGHTS

Life for Kalahari lions is a constant battle against thirst and high temperatures. In summer during the day, the surface temperature of the sand can be 150°F (66°C). That's hot enough to cook an egg.

Not surprisingly, Kalahari lions hunt mostly after the sun has gone down. The big cats usually rest until the middle of the night, waiting for a cool desert wind. Then they spend the rest of the night walking—looking for food.

In the Serengeti, food is very plentiful. Lions rarely have to walk more than a couple of miles before they find a meal. But life in the desert is not so easy. With only a few scattered animals such as porcupines and gemsboks—horse-size antelopes—for prey, desert lions have to walk farther and work harder to catch dinner.

DANGEROUS DINNER

When Kalahari lions do find something to eat, it is usually spiky or dangerous. One out of every three animals they catch is a porcupine. The desert lion's main prey is the gemsbok, which can provide ten times as much meat as a porcupine. But gemsboks are difficult to bring down; they've been known to kill lions by skewering them on their three-foot-long, saberlike horns.

Water is scarce in the Kalahari, so the desert lions have to be as resourceful at finding a drink as they are at finding a meal. One hot day, just as a light rain began to fall, Eloff watched two lionesses. Side by side, they licked the raindrops off each other.

These lean, strong lions have amazingly learned to survive, and by cooperating they manage to thrive in an inhospitable, almost waterless world.

THINK LIKE A *Tiger*

Getting inside a tiger's mind could help save a species

A TIGER CAN TELL IT'S IN ANOTHER'S TERRITORY BY SNIFFING TREES MARKED WITH URINE.

TIGERS LIVE IN BOTH COLD AND HOT CLIMATES.

TIGERS ARE SO RARE that only about 3,500 remain in the wild. The problem is not so much that the forests are disappearing, says Ullas Karanth, a senior conservation scientist with the New York–based Wildlife Conservation Society. "Worldwide, there is habitat enough to support 50,000 tigers."

The problem is that the forests are empty. Local human hunters have wiped out the deer, wild pigs, and wild cattle that tigers prey on. Without food—at least the equivalent of one elk-size deer a week—tigers can't survive and multiply. "They vanish," says Karanth.

Karanth believes tigers need their own space. This can be done by finding a potential tiger habitat and paying the people who live there to move to new settlements. But first scientists must know how many tigers there are and where they live.

To find that out, Karanth developed a way to count tigers. He places hundreds of motion-activated cameras in a forest in India. These cameras sense animals passing by and snap their picture. To figure out where to place the cameras to catch the elusive tigers, Karanth tries to think like a tiger.

TIGER SECRETS

Where can you find a tiger? And how do they get there? Water holes are always a good bet. Tigers go there to drink to cool off, and to ambush prey. A hungry tiger might also visit a salt lick, where soil is naturally salty. Deer often gather there.

TIGERS ARE STEALTH HUNTERS, EVEN IN WATER!

To reach their destinations, tigers usually opt for the easiest route. They follow old logging trails, dry riverbeds, and dirt roads. Footprints are easy to spot in soft soil, and a tiger marking its territory might scratch the ground and drop waste three times each mile (1.6 km). However, distinguishing tiger droppings from that of a leopard or wild dog takes some experience, as does smelling urine spray on bushes or trees. Karanth can pick up the scent of tiger urine in the air. It smells strong—musky and sweet.

SMILE, PLEASE
After lazing about all afternoon, a tiger yawns and rises to his feet. He's getting hungry. He goes on the hunt. Spying him from a grassy hillside, a herd of deer suddenly raise their tails and scream an alarm call. No matter. Even if it takes him 30 tries to make a kill, his belly will soon be full. Before long, the wild cat ambles past a motion sensor and click! A camera snaps a portrait of one well-fed tiger that gives Karanth a reason to smile.

ALMOST ANY ANIMAL A TIGER CAN CATCH IS ON ITS MENU.

CHEETAHS: Built for SPEED

This wild cat's body makes it an incredible predator.

Breathing deeply, the cheetah prepares her body for the chase. Head low, eyes focused on an impala, she slowly inches forward. In three seconds this streamlined, superfast cat is sprinting at 60 miles an hour (96 kph), eyes locked, laserlike, on the fleeing impala.

> **Long, muscular tail for balance in tight turns**

The legendary Jamaican runner Usain Bolt is the world's fastest human. Bolt ran 200 meters in 19.19 seconds, about 23 miles an hour (37 kph), but that's slow compared with the cheetah. Cheetahs can run about three times faster than Bolt. At top speed a sprinting cheetah can reach 70 miles an hour (113 kph). Next time you're in a car on the highway, imagine a cheetah racing alongside you. That will give you an idea of how fast this speedy cat can run.

Several adaptations help cheetahs run so fast. A cheetah has longer legs than

> **Small, short face with enlarged nostrils to take in lots of air**

other cats. It also has a long, extremely flexible spine. These features work together so a running cheetah can cover up to 23 feet (7 m) in one stride—about the length of five 10-year-olds lying

head to feet in a row.

Most other cats can retract their claws when they're not using them. Cheetahs' claws stick out all the time, like dogs' claws. Cheetahs use these strong, blunt claws like an athlete uses cleats on track shoes—to help push off and quickly build up speed. The large center pad on the cheetah's foot is covered with long ridges that act like the treads on a car tire. A sprinting cheetah needs to be able to stop fast, too. It is able to spread its toes wide, and its toe pads

> **Strong, blunt claws and ridged footpads to grip the ground**

are hard and pointed. This helps a cheetah turn quickly and brake suddenly. It can stop in a single stride from a speed of more than 20 miles an hour (32 kph).

All these body adaptations add up to extraordinary hunting abilities. A cheetah stalks up close to a herd of impalas, then streaks forward with lightning speed. As the herd bolts, the cat singles out one individual and follows its twists and turns precisely. As it closes in on its prey the cheetah strikes out with a forepaw, knocks the animal off its feet, and clamps its jaws over the prey's throat.

THE MYSTERY OF THE BLACK PANTHER

Are you superstitious? Do you think it's bad luck if a black cat crosses your path?

Many people once believed that black cats partnered with the devil. They show up regularly in comic books, posters, and movies. But in real life these big cats are as rare as parents who allow kids to eat dessert before dinner. What are these mysterious black cats, and where do they live?

"Black panthers are simply leopards with dark coats," says scientist John Seidensticker. "If you look closely, you can see the faint outline of spots in the dark fur," he adds.

Biologists used to think that black panthers were a separate species of leopard. The fierce black cats had a reputation for being more aggressive than spotted leopards, the way dark-maned lions are more aggressive than those with lighter manes. But zookeepers noticed that normal spotted leopards and black leopards can sometimes be born in the same litter (see below)—just as kids in the same family can have blue eyes or brown eyes.

BLENDING IN

Overall, black leopards are extremely rare in the wild. They are almost never seen in the leopard's range in Africa, and only occasionally in India. But surprisingly, these black cats are the only leopards known in the forests of Malaysia, in Southeast Asia. Black leopards are so much more common there that the local forest people don't even have a word in their vocabulary for *spotted* leopards.

Scientists don't really know why black leopards are the norm in Malaysia. One theory is that animals living in dark, humid forests like those in Malaysia tend to have darker fur for camouflage. African leopards spend most of their lives in grasslands and forests, where spots may be the best disguise.

The black cats are not evil creatures of witches and devils. They are cats at their best—evolving to blend with their habitat.

5 COOL THINGS ABOUT Butterflies

MONARCH PUPA

2

Butterflies are nature's magicians.
Butterflies begin life as caterpillars. Once grown, the caterpillar becomes a pupa. Protected by a cocoon, the pupa transforms into a butterfly, a process called metamorphosis.

1

Some butterflies start out smelly.
Not all butterflies stink, but the caterpillar of the zebra swallowtail butterfly sure does! Its nasty odor helps keep it safe from hungry animals.

ZEBRA SWALLOWTAIL

3

Butterflies taste WITH THEIR "FEET."
Butterflies have chemical receptors on their legs, similar to taste buds, that allow them to taste the sweetness of a peach just by standing on it.

4

MANY butterflies ARE poisonous.
The monarch, for example, eats only poisonous milkweed plants, making both the caterpillar and the adult butterfly a dangerous snack for predators.

5

Some are winged tricksters.
Owl butterflies startle predators with huge "eyes" on their wings. The false eyes divert an attacker's attention, giving the butterfly time for a hasty escape.

OWL BUTTERFLY

Bet you didn't know

6

facts that will BUG you!

1 **Dragonflies** appeared on **Earth** 140 million years before the **first birds.**

2 Mosquitoes prefer to **bite people** who have **smelly feet.**

3 **Raw termites** taste like **pineapple.**

4 A housefly can **turn somersaults** in the **air.**

5 **Tiny bugs** called **mites** live in your **eyebrows.**

6 Most **female fireflies can't fly.**

BIZARRE Insects

Check out some of the strangest bugs on Earth!

The bright-colored head of the puss moth caterpillar warns predators to stay away. This species, one of the most toxic caterpillars in North America, can spray acid from its head when it is attacked.

puss moth caterpillar

walking leaf

The flat, green insect is a master of disguise: It's often hard to tell between a bug and an actual leaf, thanks to its large, feathery wings. This clever camouflage provides protection from potential predators.

giraffe-necked weevil

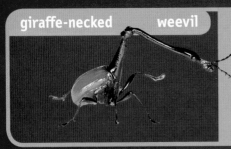

No surprise, this bug gets its name from its extra-long neck. The males have longer necks than females, which they use to fight other males for mating rights.

thorn bugs

spiny katydid

One tiny thorn bug may not be a match for a bigger predator, but when grouped together on a branch, these spiky bugs create a prickly pack no bird wants a bite of!

This katydid is covered in sharper-than-knives spikes. If a predator attacks, this species springs into action, defending itself by jabbing an enemy with its spiny legs and arms.

cockshafer beetle

The wild, feathery antennae on the male cockshafer may be cool to look at, but they're also helpful tools. They enable the bug to sniff for food and feel out its surrounding environment.

acorn weevil

The acorn weevil's hollow nose is longer than its body, perfect for drilling through the shells of acorns. A female will feast on the nut by sucking up its rich, fatty liquid, and then lay her eggs in the acorn.

crab spider

Is it a spider—or a crab? With its red-and-white coloring and pointy spines sticking out from its flat body, this arachnid looks a lot like a crustacean. But crab spiders stay on dry land, usually in the woods or in gardens.

man-faced stink bug

There are more than 4,500 species of stink bugs world-wide, including this brilliant yellow species, whose shield-shaped body displays a unique pattern resembling a tribal mask. Like all stink bugs, this species secretes a foul-smelling liquid from scent glands between its legs when it feels threatened.

rhinoceros beetle

Ounce for ounce, this insect, which gets its name from the horn-like structure on a male's head, is considered one of the world's strongest creatures. It is capable of carrying up to 850 times its own body weight.

5 SiLLY Pet Tricks

1 PIG TACKLES TEETER-TOTTER

Nelliebelle the pig's short legs make it tough for her to balance, but she still trots up and down a teeter-totter without hesitation and has never fallen. It probably helps that she's rewarded with her favorite food: vegetarian pizza. Talk about being hungry for success!

2 LIZARDS POSE FOR FANS

Larry and Lauri the Chinese water dragons bring new meaning to the term "lounge lizards." The pair poses in a reclining position on matching mini-couches for up to two hours in front of street audiences and even the family dog! The trick to having them hold their pose? "It's all about trust," says owner Henry Lizardlover (yep, that's his real name). "My lizards know they're safe with me."

HOLLYWOOD

Zachary the macaw is on a roll—literally. Although this brilliant bird has learned more than 20 tricks, cruising along on a custom-built scooter is one of Zachary's favorites. He holds the handlebars of the scooter with his beak, places one foot on the board, and then gives a big push off the ground with his other foot. It's almost as good as flying.

3 PARROT CRUISES ON SCOOTER

4 DOG PERFORMS HANDSTAND

How does Jesse the Jack Russell terrier burn off extra energy? He does handstands! Owner Heather Brook first taught Jesse this trick by encouraging Jesse to place his back paws on a wall. When Jesse held the handstand there, Brook rewarded him with his favorite squeeze toy and a chicken treat. Eventually, Jesse learned to kick off the ground directly into a handstand. But he doesn't just perform on command: "Jesse will do handstands if he has an audience," Brook says. "Especially if we have some food."

5 CAT PLAYS PIANO

Forget batting yarn and chasing mice—Nora the cat plays the piano! "One day we heard notes coming from downstairs," says owner Betsy Alexander, a piano teacher. "And there was Nora sitting at the piano like one of my students, her paws on the keys." Alexander believes that Nora associated the piano with receiving attention after observing her owner praise students, and started banging away. "To her, the piano is a giant toy," she says.

Q Why do dogs and cats NEED TAILS?

A

Dog and cat tails are multitalented. Both animals use their tails to communicate. A dog's fast-wagging tail says it wants to be friends, but a cat holds its tail high to show happiness. The tail—an extension of the backbone—also helps balance an animal's weight. That comes in handy when it jumps, lands, or even chases its tail.

NauGHty PETS

NAME **Bull**

FAVORITE ACTIVITY
Staring contests with his buddy Mac

FAVORITE TOY
Mirror

PET PEEVE
Runny noses

FIRST ONE TO BLINK HAS TO TAKE THE OWNER FOR A WALK.

PET PERKS

Why should cats and dogs get all the attention? Here's what makes some other pets so special. See if one of them is right for you.

HERMIT CRAB

Hermit crabs are easy to care for and fun—they can climb, dig, and love to crawl all over you!

GUINEA PIG

Guinea pigs love to snuggle up and have you pet their soft fur.

PARAKEET

Parakeets can be trained to talk and will perch on your finger.

The Smart Way to Find a LOST PET

Can't find Fluffy? Don't panic. Here are tips for tracking down a lost pet—plus ways you can keep your companion safe, always.

Move Fast.

Most pet owners think their pet will come home when it's ready. It usually won't—and the sooner you start looking, the more likely you are to find it. "You've got to start looking within the hour you realize it's gone," says pet detective Pat Lillis.

Put Out Bait.

Go outside and noisily open a smelly can of cat food where you think your pet went missing. "Animals return home when they're hungry," says Lillis. (And yes, even dogs go for stinky cat food!)

Look Close to Home.

Check under bushes, steps, and decks. Look up trees and in your garage or shed. Ask neighbors to search their property. When it's quiet, call your pet and listen for a meow or woof.

PROTECT YOUR PET.

Even indoor pets should wear a collar and tag. For outdoor pets, have a vet insert a microchip under its skin. That way if the pet is found, it can be scanned to read your contact information on the microchip.

Call Around—A Lot.

Check in every two or three days with local vets, shelters, and pounds. Bring a photo so they know exactly what your pet looks like.

Never Give Up.

Place rainproof "Lost" signs on doorsteps and around your neighborhood. (Signs should include a color photo of your pet showing its whole body and tear-off tabs with a parent's phone number.) Set out food where you think your pet went missing. Place its bed or uncleaned litter box outside your house for a familiar smell.

Lifestyles of the

Pssst . . . Spoiling your pet doesn't have to sap your savings. Instead, spend time—not money. Hugs, kisses, belly rubs, and baths are free for you but worth millions to your pet.

Showing love for your pet doesn't have to cost a thing. Still, pet owners spend billions of dollars a year on their pets—including hundreds on just food and treats for each cat and dog. Here's a look at some very posh pets.

DIAMONDS ARE A CODDLED KITTY'S BEST FRIEND.

◄ GETTIN' WIGGY ●━●━●━●━●━●━●

When Romeo the Yorkshire terrier wants to step out in style, he slips on a hot-pink wig. Lenny the Cavalier King Charles spaniel dons dreadlocks when he cruises the park. The price of the $40 hairpieces may cause some people to, uh, wig out. "But some owners spare no expense to keep their pets posh," says Ruth Regina, founder of the doggie-wig company Wiggles. "The dogs and the owners love how much attention they get when they wear the wigs."

RICH and FURRY

THIS PAMPERED POOCH DOESN'T MIND BEING STALKED BY THE *PAW*-PARAZZI.

▼ HOLY *"MUTT*-RIMONY" ● ● ●

JAKE AND JILL MAKE A LOVE CONNECTION.

Flowers: $1,000. Satin bridal gown: $500. *"Pup*-cakes": $100. Watching two dogs get "married" at a fancy wedding? Priceless. At least that's what some owners think when they cough up major cash for a pet wedding. "It's a way to honor the puppy love and have fun," says pet party planner Alma Rose Middleton, who has "married" dogs such as Boo Boo and Mimi after they "fell in love" at a birthday party. The cost of a to-drool-for wedding? Up to $8,000!

Try This! PAMPER YOUR PET

THESE FUN AND INEXPENSIVE COLLARS WILL GIVE YOUR PET A TASTE OF THE GOOD LIFE.

YOU WILL NEED
• FABRIC COLLAR THAT FITS YOUR PET
• NONTOXIC 3-D FASHION PAINT
• TACKY GLUE • PLASTIC GEMS AND BEADS

WHAT TO DO
Paint a design or your pet's name on the collar. Let dry. Glue on gems and beads. Lay flat and dry overnight. Make sure the gems and beads are secure before putting the collar on your pet.

28 COOL THINGS

1 PARROTS DON'T HAVE **VOCAL CORDS.**

2 IF KEPT IN THE DARK FOR A LONG TIME, **A GOLDFISH WILL TURN GRAY.**

23 Dogs often **yawn** when they are nervous or excited.

3 When doing difficult tasks, female cats tend to be **right-pawed**, while males are usually left-pawed.

4 DOGS PANT UP TO **300 TIMES** A MINUTE.

5 A hamster's teeth **NEVER STOP GROWING.**

6 Poland has **more dogs** than children.

7 A CAT'S TONGUE HAS HOOKED **TASTE BUDS** THAT WORK LIKE **VELCRO** TO HELP HOLD PREY IN ITS MOUTH.

24 A CHAMELEON'S **TONGUE** CAN STRETCH TO ONE AND A HALF TIMES ITS BODY LENGTH.

25 HORSES CAN TRAVEL UP TO **100 MILES** (160 KM) IN A DAY.

8 LAIKA THE DOG WAS THE FIRST ANIMAL TO **travel into space.**

9 Rats can't **BURP.**

10 More than half of the homes in the United States have **PETS.**

ABOUT PETS

22 A St. Bernard named Barry was said to have saved more than 40 **people** during his life.

21 CALICO CATS ARE ALMOST ALWAYS FEMALE.

20 Western hognose snakes **PLAY DEAD** when they feel threatened.

19 Hamsters can keep **food in pouches** in their cheeks for days.

18 Guinea pigs can **WALK IMMEDIATELY** after being born.

17 SNAKES USE THEIR **TONGUES** TO HELP THEM SMELL.

16 You can keep a dog from shaking water off of its coat by holding its **MUZZLE.**

15 WHEN SLEEPING STANDING UP, A HORSE **LOCKS ITS HIND LEGS** SO THAT IT DOESN'T FALL OVER.

14 DOGS CAN'T BACK DOWN A TREE LIKE CATS. THEY CAN ONLY COME DOWN FORWARD.

28 A canary CAN SING TWO DIFFERENT SONGS AT THE SAME TIME.

27 A cat's eye has **THREE EYELIDS.**

26 The oldest koi fish lived to be **226** years old.

11 A dog will **DRINK OUT OF THE TOILET** because water stays cooler there than in its bowl.

12 In Europe, **FERRETS** have been used to run television cables through pipes.

13 Ancient Egyptians **MUMMIFIED** their pet dogs, cats, and monkeys.

Prehistoric
TIME LINE

HUMANS HAVE WALKED on Earth for some 200,000 years, a mere blip in Earth's 4.5-billion-year history. A lot has happened in that time. Earth formed, and oxygen levels rose in the millions of years of the Precambrian time. The productive Paleozoic era gave rise to hard-shelled organisms, vertebrates, amphibians, and reptiles.

Dinosaurs ruled the Earth in the mighty Mesozoic. And 64 million years after dinosaurs became extinct, modern humans emerged in the Cenozoic era. From the first tiny mollusks to the dinosaur giants of the Jurassic and beyond, Earth has seen a lot of transformation.

THE PRECAMBRIAN TIME

4.5 billion to 542 million years ago

- The Earth (and other planets) formed from gas and dust left over from a giant cloud that collapsed to form the sun. The giant cloud's collapse was triggered when nearby stars exploded.
- Low levels of oxygen made Earth a suffocating place.
- Early life forms appeared.

THE PALEOZOIC ERA

542 million to 251 million years ago

- The first insects and other animals appeared on land.
- 450 million years ago (m.y.a.), the ancestors of sharks began to swim in the oceans.
- 430 m.y.a., plants began to take root on land.
- More than 360 m.y.a., amphibians emerged from the water.
- Slowly the major landmasses began to come together, creating Pangaea, a single supercontinent.
- By 300 m.y.a., reptiles had begun to dominate the land.

What Killed the Dinosaurs?

WAS IT AN ASTEROID OR A VOLCANO? These two common theories have been used by scientists to explain the disappearance of dinosaurs 65 million years ago. Researchers believe that a huge impact, such as an asteroid or comet, or a massive bout of volcanic activity might have choked the sky with debris that starved Earth of the sun's energy. The resulting greenhouse gases may have caused the temperature to soar, causing half of the world's species—including the dinosaurs—to die in a mass extinction.

DINO TIMES

THE MESOZOIC ERA

251 million to 65 million years ago

The Mesozoic era, or the age of the reptiles, consisted of three consecutive time periods (shown below). This is when the first dinosaurs began to appear. They would reign supreme for more than 150 million years.

TRIASSIC PERIOD

251 million to 199 million years ago

- Appearance of the first mammals. They were rodent-size.
- The first dinosaur appeared.
- Ferns were the dominant plants on land.
- The giant supercontinent of Pangaea began breaking up toward the end of the Triassic.

JURASSIC PERIOD

199 million to 145 million years ago

- Giant dinosaurs dominated the land.
- Pangaea continued its breakup, and oceans formed in the spaces between the drifting landmasses, allowing for sea life, including sharks and marine crocodiles, to thrive.
- Conifer trees spread across the land.

CRETACEOUS PERIOD

145 million to 65 million years ago

- The modern continents developed.
- The largest dinosaurs developed.
- Flowering plants spread across the landscape.
- Mammals flourished and giant pterosaurs ruled the skies over the small birds.
- Temperatures grew more extreme. Dinosaurs lived in deserts, swamps, and forests from the Antarctic to the Arctic.

THE CENOZOIC ERA—TERTIARY PERIOD

65 million to 2.6 million years ago

- Following the dinosaur extinction, mammals rose as the dominant species.
- Birds continued to flourish.
- Volcanic activity was widespread.
- Temperatures began to cool, eventually ending in an ice age.
- The period ended with land bridges forming, which allowed plants and animals to spread to new areas.

Who Ate What?

Herbivores
- Primarily plant-eaters
- Weighed up to 100 tons (91 t)—the largest animals ever to walk on Earth
- Up to 1,000 blunt or flat teeth to grind vegetation
- Many had cheek pouches to store food.
- Examples: *Styracosaurus, Mamenchisaurus*

Carnivores
- Meat-eaters
- Long, strong legs to run faster than plant-eaters; ran up to 30 miles an hour (48 kph)
- Most had good eyesight, strong jaws, and sharp teeth.
- Scavengers and hunters; often hunted in packs

- Grew to 45 feet (14 m) long
- Examples: *Velociraptor, Gigantoraptor, Tyrannosaurus rex*

TYRANNOSAURUS REX

Ancient dinosaur in color

What color were dinosaurs?

For decades, scientists could only take educated guesses about the color of dinosaurs. Now, we're closer to figuring out their color patterns. Thanks to pigment in dino fuzz—tiny, featherlike hairs found on some fossils—scientists have been able to determine the coloring of a 155-million-year-old prehistoric dinosaur the size of a chicken, with black-and-white spangled wings and a red feathered mohawk crown. So will dino fuzz determine the color of every species? Probably not. But these new findings do shed a bright light onto the dino's otherwise dark and mysterious past.

GIGANTORAPTOR

DID YOU KNOW?
Tyrannosaurus means "tyrant lizard." At about 40 feet (12 meters) long and about 15 to 20 feet (4.6 to 6 meters) tall, the *T. rex* was one of the largest meat-eating dinosaurs that ever lived. If it roamed the Earth today, its bite would be strong enough to dent a car.

VELOCIRAPTOR　　**SINOSAUROPTERYX**

MAMENCHISAURUS

PARASAUROLOPHUS

ERKETU

Dinosaur fossil

Fossils preserved in plaster

Paleontologists learn about dinosaurs by studying fossils—plant and animal remains that have been preserved in rock.

Bet you **didn't know**

Scientists once thought *Stegosaurus* **had a second BRAIN in its HIP!**

TUOJIANGOSAURUS

MONONYKUS

STYRACOSAURUS

71

DINO Classification

Classifying dinosaurs and all other living things can be a complicated matter, so scientists have devised a system to help with the process. Dinosaurs are put into groups based on a very large range of characteristics.

Scientists put dinosaurs into two major groups: the bird-hipped ornithischians and the reptile-hipped saurischians.

Dinosaur Superlatives

Ornithischian

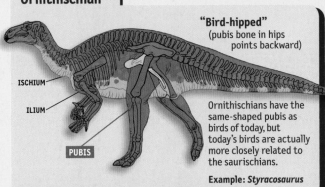

ISCHIUM

ILIUM

PUBIS

"Bird-hipped"
(pubis bone in hips points backward)

Ornithischians have the same-shaped pubis as birds of today, but today's birds are actually more closely related to the saurischians.

Example: *Styracosaurus*

Saurischian

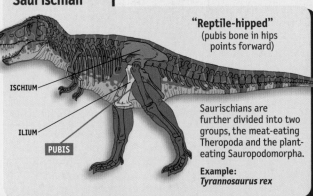

ISCHIUM

ILIUM

PUBIS

"Reptile-hipped"
(pubis bone in hips points forward)

Saurischians are further divided into two groups, the meat-eating Theropoda and the plant-eating Sauropodomorpha.

Example: *Tyrannosaurus rex*

Within these two main divisions, dinosaurs are then separated into orders and then families, such as Stegosauria. Like other members of the Stegosauria, *Stegosaurus* had spines and plates along the back, neck, and tail.

COOL CLICK

What's the largest, most complete, best preserved *T. rex*? Learn about a fossil named Sue at the Field Museum.
fieldmuseum.org/sue

Heaviest
Argentinosaurus is believed to have weighed 220,000 lbs. (99,790 kg)—more than 15 elephants!

Longest
The ***Seismosaurus*** was longer than three school buses.

Thickest skull
The ***Pachycephalosaurus's*** huge head and nine-inch-thick (23 cm) skull may have been used for head-butting.

Biggest claws
With hooklike claws almost a foot long (20-30 cm), the ***Deinocheirus*** was probably one of the most deadly dinosaurs.

Longest-lived
Sauropods are believed to have had a lifespan of about 100 years.

Longest name
Micropachycephalosaurus (23 letters)

First to be named
Megalosaurus was named in 1822 by Reverend William Buckland, an English geologist.

16 DINOS YOU SHOULD KNOW

Dinosaur (Group) *Example*
What the name means
Length: XX ft (XX m)
Time Range: When they lived
Where: Where their fossils
have been found

1 **Baryonyx** (Saurischian)
Heavy claw
Length: 28 ft (8.5 m)
Time Range: Early Cretaceous
Where: England; Niger; Spain

2 **Brachiosaurus** (Saurischian)
Arm lizard
Length: 98 ft (30 m)
Time Range: Late Jurassic
Where: U.S. (Colorado); Tanzania

5 *Lambeosaurus* (Ornithischian)
Lambe's lizard
Length: Up to 54 ft (16 m)
Time Range: Late Cretaceous
Where: U.S. (Montana); Canada (Alberta)

3 *Corythosaurus* (Ornithischian)
High-ridged tooth
Length: 8 ft (2 m)
Time Range: Early Cretaceous
Where: England; Spain; Portugal

6 *Megalosaurus* (Saurischian)
Great reptile
Length: 27 ft (8.5 m)
Time Range: Middle Jurassic
Where: England; France; Portugal

4 *Iguanodon* (Ornithischian)
Helmet lizard
Length: 30 ft (9 m)
Time Range: Late Cretaceous
Where: U.S. (Montana); Canada (Alberta)

7 *Muttaburrasaurus* (Ornithischian)
Muttaburra lizard
Length: 27 ft (7 m)
Time Range: Early Cretaceous
Where: Australia

8 *Psittacosaurus* (Ornithischian)
Parrot lizard
Length: 5.6 ft (2 m)
Time Range: Early Cretaceous
Where: Mongolia; China; Thailand

9 *Oviraptor* (Saurischian)
Egg thief
Length: 8 ft (2 m)
Time Range: Late Cretaceous
Where: Mongolia

10 *Protoceratops* (Ornithischian)
First horned face
Length: 8 ft (2 m)
Time Range: Late Cretaceous
Where: Mongolia; China

11 *Stegosaurus* (Ornithischian)
Roofed reptile
Length: 30 ft (9 m)
Time Range: Late Jurassic
Where: U.S. (Colorado, Utah, Wyoming)

12 *Spinosaurus* (Saurischian)
Spiny lizard
Length: 45 ft (13.7 m)
Time Range: Late Cretaceous
Where: Egypt; Morocco

13 *Suchomimus* (Saurischian)
Crocodile mimic
Length: 36 ft (11 m)
Time Range: Early Cretaceous
Where: Niger

TSINTAOSAURUS is sometimes called the **UNICORN DINOSAUR.**

15 *Tyrannosaurus rex* (Saurischian)
Tyrant lizard
Length: 41 ft (12 m)
Time Range: Late Cretaceous
Where: U.S. (Western); Canada (Western)

14 *Tsintaosaurus* (Ornithischian)
Lizard from Tsintao
Length: 33 ft (10 m)
Time Range: Late Cretaceous
Where: China

16 *Velociraptor* (Saurischian)
Swift robber
Length: 7 ft (2 m)
Time Range: Late Cretaceous
Where: Mongolia; China

6 NEWLY DISCOVERED DINOS

Humans have been searching for—and discovering—dinosaur remains for hundreds of years. In that time, almost 1,000 species of dinos have been found all over the world, and thousands more may still be out there waiting to be unearthed. Recent discoveries include the dog-size, 230-million-year-old Eodromaeus, found in Argentina and believed to be one of the world's earliest predators. For more exciting dino discoveries, read on.

1 *Abydosaurus* (Saurischian)
Abydos lizard
Length: 50 ft (15 m)
Time Range: Early Cretaceous
Where: U.S. (Utah)

4 *Daemonosaurus* (Saurischian)
Demon reptile
Length: Less than 5 ft (1.5 m)
Time Range: Late Triassic
Where: U.S. (New Mexico)

2 *Austroraptor* (Saurischian)
Southern thief
Length: 16 ft (5 m)
Time Range: Late Cretaceous
Where: Argentina

5 *Eodromaeus* (Saurischian)
Dawn runner
Length: 4 ft (1 m)
Time Range: Late Triassic
Where: Argentina

3 *Barrosasaurus* (Saurischian)
Lizard from Barrosa Hill
Length: 95 ft (29 m)
Time Range: Late Cretaceous
Where: Argentina

6 *Utahceratops* (Ornithiscian)
Utah horned face
Length: 20 ft (6 m)
Time Range: Late Cretaceous
Where: U.S. (Utah)

Wildly Good Animal Reports

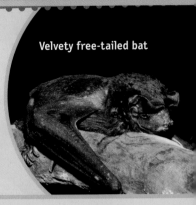
Velvety free-tailed bat

Your teacher wants a written report on the velvety free-tailed bat. By Monday! Not to worry. Use the tools of good writing to organize your thoughts and research, and writing an animal report won't drive you batty.

STEPS TO SUCCESS: Your report will follow the format of a descriptive or expository essay (see p. 98 for "How to Write a Perfect Essay") and should consist of a main idea, followed by supporting details, and a conclusion. Use this basic structure for each paragraph as well as the whole report, and you'll be on the right track.

1. Introduction
State your main idea.
The velvety free-tailed bat is a common and important species of bat.

2. Body
Provide **supporting points** for your main idea.
The velvety free-tailed bat eats insects and can have a large impact on insect populations.
It ranges from Mexico to Florida and South America.
Like other bats, its wings are built for fast, efficient flight.

Then **expand** on those points with further description, explanation, or discussion.
The velvety free-tailed bat eats insects and can have a large impact on insect populations.
 Its diet consists primarily of mosquitoes and other airborne insects.
It ranges from Mexico to Florida and South America.
 It sometimes takes refuge in people's attics.
Like other bats, its wings are built for fast, efficient flight.
 It has trouble, however, taking off from low or flat surfaces and must drop from a place high enough to gain speed to start flying.

3. Conclusion
Wrap it up with a summary of your whole paper.
Because of its large numbers, the velvety free-tailed bat holds an important position in the food chain.

KEY INFORMATION

Here are some things you should consider including in your report:

What does your animal look like?
To what other species is it related?
How does it move?
Where does it live?
What does it eat?
What are its predators?
How long does it live?
Is it endangered?
Why do you find it interesting?

FACT FROM FICTION: Your animal may have been featured in a movie or in myths and legends. Compare and contrast how the animal has been portrayed with how it behaves in reality. For example, penguins can't dance the way they do in *Happy Feet.*

PROOFREAD AND REVISE: As with any great essay, when you're finished, check for misspellings, grammatical mistakes, and punctuation errors. It often helps to have someone else proofread your work, too, as he or she may catch things you have missed. Also, look for ways to make your sentences and paragraphs even better. Add more descriptive language, choosing just the right verbs, adverbs, and adjectives to make your writing come alive.

BE CREATIVE: Use visual aids to make your report come to life. Include an animal photo file with interesting images found in magazines or printed from websites. Or draw your own! You can also build a miniature animal habitat diorama. Use creativity to help communicate your passion for the subject.

THE FINAL RESULT: Put it all together in one final, polished draft. Make it neat and clean, and remember to cite your references (see p. 257 for "Reveal Your Sources").

How to Observe ANIMALS

BOOKS, ARTICLES, and other second-hand sources are great for learning about animals, but there's another way to find out even more. Direct observation means watching, listening to, and smelling an animal yourself. To truly understand animals you need to see them in action.

VISIT

YOU CAN FIND ANIMALS in their natural habitats almost anywhere, even your own backyard. Or take a drive to a nearby mountain area, river, forest, wetland, or other ecosystem. There are animals in every natural setting you can visit. To observe more exotic varieties, plan a trip to a national park, aquarium, zoo, wildlife park, or aviary.

OBSERVE

GET NEAR ENOUGH to an animal to watch and study it, but do not disturb it. Be patient, as it may take a while to spot something interesting. And be safe. Don't take any risks; wild animals can be dangerous. Take notes, and write down every detail. Use all of your senses. How does it look? How does it act? What more can you learn?

RESEARCH

COMPARE YOUR own observations with those found in textbooks, encyclopedias, nonfiction books, Internet sources, and nature documentaries. (See p. 160 for "Research Like a Pro.") And check out exciting animal encounters in National Geographic's book series *Face to Face with Animals.*

COOL CLICK

Love to watch animals? Check out these amazing animal and pet videos.
video.kids.nationalgeographic.com/video/player/kids/index.html

TIP:
Binoculars are a good way to get up close and personal with wild animals while still keeping a safe distance.

Extreme mountain biker Aaron Chase catches air between two rock islands in the Sea of Cortez in Mexico.

Awesome Adventure

Got a smart phone?
SCAN THIS to go
on an awesome
adventure!
(See instructions inside the front cover.)
No smart phone? Go online.
kids.nationalgeographic.com/almanac-2013

DARE TO E→

Do you have what it takes to be a great explorer? Read the stories of thr

HOGAN HOLDS A TAIMEN, A GIANT MEMBER OF THE SALMON FAMILY, IN MONGOLIA.

THE AQUATIC ECOLOGIST

Zeb Hogan on traveling to Cambodia in an effort to protect megafish, such as the Mekong giant catfish, from local nets:

"The first year, we had one that weighed 595 pounds (270 kg). Bugs were swarming around my headlamp, and someone pulled on a rope and this huge fish came up out of the murk.... When we released the fish, it nearly sank us. Now we use bigger boats, but that night it was a 12-foot (3.7-m) boat dragging a 10-foot (3-m) fish. We inched along, killed the engine, and I jumped in. Giant catfish grow weak after fighting a net, and I have to grab on to them to make sure they're strong enough to swim before we release them."

Want to be an AQUATIC ECOLOGIST?

STUDY: Ecology and biology

WATCH: *Monster Fish with Zeb Hogan*

READ: *World Without Fish,* by Mark Kurlansky

DO: Volunteer at a local aquarium to discover more about fish conservation.

ADVICE: "It's okay to take risks, and it's okay to fail."

THE EXPEDITION PHOTOGRAPHER

Jimmy Chin on his adventure to the top of 20,050-foot (6,111 m) Redommaine Peak in the Himalaya which he photographed:

"After two days of following our gear-laden horses, jumping streams, and wandering through high alpine meadows, the sharp peaks of the Minya Konka range began to emerge from behind the foothills. When we finally glimpsed Redommaine, we stopped to stare. The northwest face looked incredible, steep with snow spines draped across its flanks. Cracked glaciers and icefalls surrounded the bottom of the mountain. We rounded a bend and found a gleaming lake nestled below our peak. Amazing!"

Want to be a PHOTOGRAPHER?

STUDY: Anything—then take pictures!

WATCH: *The Wildest Dream: Conquest of Everest*

READ: *National Geographic*

DO: Learn physical skills—climbing, hiking, skateboarding—to get you to great places to take photos.

ADVICE: "Create an image [you've]

XPLORE

ous adventurers, and see how you can get started on the same path.

EARLE SHOWS ALGAE TO ENGINEER MARGARET "PEGGY" LUCAS INSIDE AN UNDERWATER HABITAT.

SYLVIA EARLE

THE EXTREME OCEANOGRAPHER

Sylvia Earle on living in an enclosed underwater habitat for two weeks at 50 feet (15 m) below the surface of the Caribbean Sea to conduct marine research:

"It was a four-room underwater hotel and laboratory. There was a shower, and a complete kitchen, and even a television set, although nobody bothered much to watch it, because outside it was the greatest show on Earth, literally, with a constant changing scene of fish and other creatures that would come by. I really slept as little as I could get by with so I could be out there with the fish, constantly. The opportunity to get to know the fish was extraordinary."

Want to be an oceanographer?

STUDY: Biology and geology

WATCH: *Oceans: Sylvia Earle's Journey*

READ: *The World Is Blue*, by Sylvia Earle

DO: Head to the beach and search for creatures and shells along the shore and underwater.

ADVICE: "Never stop asking questions, and always keep looking for answers."

CHIN CLIMBING EL CAPITAN IN CALIFORNIA, U.S.A.

CHINA CONNECTION

DUDE: Marco Polo

EXPEDITION: One of the first Europeans to explore China

WHEN: Starting in 1271

Marco Polo's father and uncle ask him to travel with them from Italy to China—on horseback! The adventurous 17-year-old says yes! On his journey, Marco claims to hear "spirit voices" in the desert. The trek is worth it when he reaches the huge, glittering palace of Kublai Khan, China's ruler. There he marvels at paper money, tattoos, and rhinoceroses. Marco turns his travels into a book, which later inspires another Italian with adventurous ambitions: Christopher Columbus.

WHAT'S IN IT FOR YOU: The discovery of America

**Lion wrestling.
Ice climbing.
Rat eating.**

These are just some of the extreme experiences five awesome adventurers faced while exploring Earth's uncharted, unforgiving unknown. Want to know who wore an American flag—as underwear? Explore on ... if you dare!

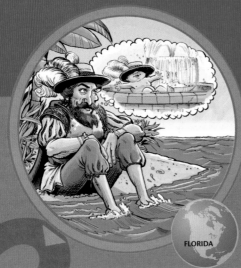

WELCOME TO THE SUNSHINE STATE

DUDE: Ponce de León

EXPEDITION: Discovered Florida, now a U.S. state

WHEN: 1513

Wealth. Fame. The chance to be young again. That, according to legend, is what awaits the first person who dips his toes into the Fountain of Youth. But the problem is no one knows where the fabled fountain is located. Spanish explorer Ponce de León sails the Caribbean to Grand Turk Island. No fountain there. San Salvador Island, too, is fountain-free. Although Ponce never finds the fountain, he scores wealth and fame by being the first European to set foot in a land he calls Pascua Florida (Flowery Easter), or Florida to you and me.

WHAT'S IN IT FOR YOU: The discovery of the future home of Disney World

AFRICA

INTO AFRICA

DUDE: David Livingstone

EXPEDITION: First European to explore Central Africa extensively

WHEN: 1841 to 1873

For Scottish doctor-missionary David Livingstone, trudging through the deserts, rain forests, and mountains of unexplored Africa (and taking lots of notes) is a dream come true. He wrestles a lion and nearly loses an arm. He sees one of the world's largest waterfalls and names it Victoria, for England's queen. He searches for the source of the Nile River and drops from sight. Five years later newspaper reporter Henry Stanley tracks down Livingstone outside a grass hut and utters the famous line, "Dr. Livingstone, I presume?"

WHAT'S IN IT FOR YOU: The knowledge that you really *should* keep distance between yourself and a lion

COOL DUDES WHO CHANGED THE WORLD

IT'S LONELY AT THE TOP. COLD, TOO.

DUDE: Robert Peary

EXPEDITION: Led the expedition that was first to reach the geographic North Pole

WHEN: 1909

Robert Peary, his trusted partner Matthew Henson, and four other men are heading north. *Way* north. They scale 50-foot (15-m) cliffs of ice and endure sub-zero temperatures and dark fog. When they finally reach the North Pole, Peary unfurls an American flag sewn by his wife—which he's worn as a warm undergarment—and rightfully feels he's on top of the world.

WHAT'S IN IT FOR YOU: The knowledge that when exploring new territory, you should always pack a flag—it could come in handy!

AROUND THE WORLD IN ... THREE YEARS

DUDE: Ferdinand Magellan

EXPEDITION: Led the first expedition to sail around the world

WHEN: Starting in 1519

Back then people thought the world was round, but no one had actually *proven* it by sailing all the way around the world—until Magellan. Terrible storms nearly sink the explorer's ships. Food runs so low that they eat rats. Three years later, just one of five ships returns to Spain. But it carries the first men to sail around the world.

WHAT'S IN IT FOR YOU: The knowledge that you won't ever fall off the edge of Earth

+ NORTH POLE

MYSTERY
IN THE DESERT

You're flying over the desert near Nasca, Peru, when you spy huge drawings in the sand below. A whale that's as long as a real blue whale, a hummingbird with the same wingspan as a 747 jumbo jet—these 2,000-year-old geoglyphs have been a mystery since they were discovered about 80 years ago.

Ancient Peruvian people, called the Nasca, created more than 1,500 of these drawings, from monkeys to spiders to a line that stretches for nine miles (14 km). But for the Nasca, these drawings weren't about art. They were about survival.

MONKEY

LINES IN THE SAND

Some archaeologists believe the Nasca created many of the geoglyphs during a drought that dried up rivers and wells. Since the Nasca likely believed that mountain and water gods controlled the rain, this would have been their way of asking the gods to send water. They drew huge creatures associated with these gods, such as hummingbirds and orcas. And they drew them so that even the gods could see them.

In the end, though, the water did not come, and the Nasca civilization ended around A.D. 650. They left no written communication, but researchers continue to read between the Nasca lines to learn more about these people. "For the Nasca, the landscape was alive," says archaeologist Johan Reinhard, a National Geographic explorer-in-residence. "It could get angry and jealous. It might send droughts to destroy the crops if someone didn't make the right offerings. They had to interact with the environment because it was a living thing."

BUILDING A NASCA LINE

How were the Nasca lines created, anyway? Scientists are pretty sure they've solved this mystery. Most of the figures are one continuous line. So working from small models, teams of 15 to 20 Nasca people would spread out from a single starting point with stakes, perhaps connected with string. They would line up the stakes, and each person would remove the dark desert rocks in his section to reveal the lighter sand underneath. They would repeat this process until a drawing was complete.

NORTH AMERICA

ATLANTIC OCEAN

PACIFIC OCEAN

SOUTH AMERICA

PERU

Nasca lines

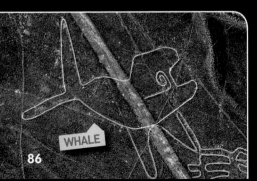

WHALE

86

Fearless Fliers

Otto Lilienthal

FAMOUS FIRST: Otto Lilienthal successfully constructed and launched an early form of airplanes, known as "gliders."

AWESOME AVIATION: He built an artificial hill in Berlin, Germany, to launch some of the 18 different models of gliders he built. That way, the gliders could take off no matter which way the wind was blowing.

SCARES IN THE AIR: While on a flight in 1896, Lilienthal lost control of his glider and fell 56 feet (17 m). He died the next day. A few years later, the **Wright brothers** picked up where he left off, adding a motor to a Lilienthal-inspired glider. In 1903, the Wright brothers' "Flyer" became known as the world's first airplane to successfully take flight.

Charles Lindbergh

FAMOUS FIRST: On May 20-21, 1927, **Charles Lindbergh** made the first-ever nonstop trip from New York to Paris, France, in a small, single-engine plane.

AWESOME AVIATION: Lindbergh's cockpit didn't have a front window, so he used a homemade periscope to look out the side for dangers. He also used charts, compasses, and the stars to guide his way.

SCARES IN THE AIR: For 2 hours during the 33½-hour flight, Lindbergh flew in total darkness and fell asleep with his eyes wide open!

Amelia Earhart

FAMOUS FIRST: In 1932, **Amelia Earhart** became the first female pilot to make a solo flight across the Atlantic Ocean.

AWESOME AVIATION: For several hours during Earhart's cross-Atlantic trip, she flew at 12,000 feet (3,658 m), watching the sun set and the moon rise.

SCARES IN THE AIR: While crossing the ocean in 1932, a severe storm battered her plane, and then ice formed on the wings, sending Earhart into a dangerous spin. Later, flames shot out of the engine, and a fuel leak dripped gas down the back of her neck, but she still managed to make land safely in Northern Ireland 15 hours after starting. In 1937, Earhart's plane disappeared mysteriously over the Pacific Ocean.

Bet you didn't know

The **WINGSPAN** OF A 747 IS LONGER than the Wright brothers' **FIRST FLIGHT.**

CRYSTAL

A ONCE HIDDEN CHAMBER REVEALS GIGANTIC, ICICLE-LIKE CRYSTALS.

It looks like a mysterious alien hideaway, with crystal structures about the height of a three-story building jutting straight into the air and crisscrossing overhead. But Mexico's Cave of Crystals isn't science fiction. It's a real cave that miners discovered only ten years ago. And scientists had never seen anything like it.

SECRET WORLD

In 2000, miners looking for lead and silver beneath Mexico's Naica Mountain began pumping water out of a flooded chamber. They were shocked when they found a hidden gallery of giant, icicle-like crystals beneath the watery depths almost a thousand feet (300 m) below the Earth's surface. Some of the crystals measured up to 37.4 feet (11.4 m) tall.

The Cave of Crystals is like no other cave in the world, but the massive glittering formations aren't the only things that make it unique. Most caves stay cool, around 60°F (15°C). But the Cave of Crystals rests atop what was once bubbling magma (hot, liquid rock). The leftover embers can make the mine hotter than the Sahara and wetter than a rain forest.

"It's like being in a sauna, only it's a thousand feet underground," says Juan Manuel García-Ruiz of the Spanish National Research Council in Granada, Spain. "As soon as I entered the cave I was dripping with sweat. My glasses fogged up from the humidity and I couldn't see."

The Cave of Crystals is made of a mineral called gypsum. Geologists call the cave's crystallized form of gypsum "selenite," after Selene, the Greek goddess of the moon. "They have the brightness and whiteness of moonlight," says crystal expert Juan Manuel García-Ruiz.

CAVE

How a Crystal Cave Grew

The superhot water that used to fill the cave contained molecules, or tiny particles, of chemicals. When those molecules bumped up against each other, they sometimes stuck together. Other molecules floating past glommed on as well, and a crystal would start to grow. Over half a million years, they grew gradually—the thickness of a human hair every 100 years—until they reached the size they are today.

DEATH-DEFYING SCIENTISTS

Harsh underground conditions are what allow the incredible crystals to grow into miniature Washington Monuments. Brave scientists put themselves in danger to study the cave, hoping to discover things such as the age of the crystals and whether tiny life-forms are living among them.

One Italian research team is developing cooling and breathing equipment to help scientists remain in the cave for long periods of time. "It's dangerous to stay too long," García-Ruiz says. "After ten minutes, I felt like I was boiling on the inside."

But to García-Ruiz and other scientists, the incredible experience inside the mysterious cave is worth the risk. "You think you're looking at icicles, but when you touch them they're hot because it's 140°F (60°C) in there," he says. "When I first saw the cave, I was so happy that I laughed out loud like a crazy man!"

PAUL NICKLEN

NICKLEN'S FRIEND GORAN TAKES HIS OWN SHOT OF THE SEAL.

The Seal Who Loved Me

WILDLIFE PHOTOGRAPHER PAUL NICKLEN DESCRIBES HIS UNDERWATER ADVENTURE IN ANTARCTICA, WHERE HE MET A LEOPARD SEAL.

Leopard seals have a reputation for being vicious beasts. As a wildlife photographer, I traveled to Antarctica, where leopard seals live and hunt penguins, to prove that they are actually misunderstood predators.

My first day out on the water, a female leopard seal swims over to our boat. She is as long as the boat and three feet (1 m) wide—massive for her species. She swims off, grabs a chinstrap penguin that was swimming out to sea, and comes back with the penguin in her jaws. She starts ramming the bird against the boat with such force that she lifts the bow out of the water.

While it is hard to watch the leopard seal kill and skin the penguin, the biologist-naturalist in me understands that she is a predator and the penguin is her prey.

It's time to get in the water, and I am momentarily paralyzed with fear. I can barely part my trembling lips to force the snorkel into my mouth. I pick up my underwater camera and slip into the cold 30°F (-1°C) Antarctic water.

Objects appear 30 percent larger underwater, so the seal seems huge in front of me. She immediately swims in my direction and, without slowing down, comes right up to me. She opens her mouth and lunges at me so that the front of my camera lens is almost at the back of her throat, her teeth virtually engulfing my camera and my head.

LEOPARD SEAL RESTING

She pulls back and observes my reaction. She repeats this threat display several times. I don't believe she will bite me. In a strange way, it is a very gentle gesture, as if she is saying, "Look how big I am."

Suddenly she stops and swims off, only to return with a live, fresh-caught penguin in her mouth. Swimming about ten feet (3 m) away from me, she holds the penguin by the feet and then releases it. The penguin swims toward me and veers off at the last second. She chases it, brings it back, and lets it go again, right in front of me.

I believe that she is trying to feed me penguins because she realizes that I am an absolutely useless predator in her ocean. She thinks I am going to starve to death if I don't receive her help.

She captures another live penguin and eats it right in front of me. She then brings me a dead penguin and withdraws a few feet, watching me. When I don't touch her offering, she blows bubbles in my face, grabs the penguin, and devours it.

Over the course of four more days, she tries to feed me penguin after penguin, and I keep shooting photos the whole time. At one point, she tenses and makes a jackhammer-like sound—a threat display that I feel through my entire body. Another leopard seal has sneaked up behind me. She is protecting me.

Knowing that I will soon leave, I feel heavy-hearted as I join the seal in the water one last time. I don't know if she ever quite figures out who or what I am, but my relationship with this seal will stay with me forever.

“ She opens her huge mouth and lunges at me so that the front of my camera lens is almost at the back of her throat... ”

WILL MY TOY CAR SURVIVE A
CROC ATTACK?

My name is Brady Barr, and part of my job as a scientist is catching crocodiles. Crocs are big, fast, good at hiding, and always alert. They're not easy to catch, but I need to get hold of them to attach tracking tags and to gather data.

I talked with some creative kids who gave me a few great ideas to help me catch crocs. So on my next trip to Africa, I set off with my scientific equipment and some toys (the kids' suggestion).

I'm helping wildlife biologists put tracking tags on a threatened population of Nile crocodiles. From our boat we spot a cluster of crocs. I set a remote-control car on the beach and steer it toward the basking crocs. I speed the car right up to one—chomp! The croc's teeth just miss the car, and it's not giving up! It chases the car and I work the joystick as if my life depends on it.

My little car is no match for a Nile crocodile—the croc's jaws close over my toy—and, temporarily, over my plans. The size and quick movements of the toy car must trigger a crocodile's predatory instinct. Conclusion: Use a faster car and improve my driving skills!

The kids' second idea: to disguise myself as a croc. I get into the water wearing a big rubber croc mask. My goal: Get close enough to wrestle a croc into our boat. When one giant male approaches, I raise the snout of my mask, which in "croc talk" lets him know I'm not looking for trouble. But he's angry—he arches his back and slaps the water with his chin. He thinks I'm a rival! At first I stand my ground, but as he comes closer, it gets too dangerous. I get out of the water ... fast! Conclusion: The disguise works.

Idea number three—I steer a remote-control boat, fitted with a small rubber croc head and a snare, toward the real crocs. Success! They act as if the boat's one of them and ignore it. Then, just as the boat's in position to snare one, the batteries die! Conclusion: The boat works, but next time I've got to remember more batteries!

A field test involves a lot of trial and error. What I learned this time will mean success the next time. Meanwhile, I reached my goal to be the first person to catch all 23 species of crocodilians!

18 EXTREME FEARS

PHOBIA	A FEAR OF
Alektorophobia	Chickens
Coulrophobia	Clowns
Bibliophobia	Books
Panophobia	Everything
Ancraophobia	Wind
Arachnophobia	Spiders
Heliophobia	Sun
Chorophobia	Dancing
Chemophobia	Chemicals
Omphalophobia	Belly buttons
Genuphobia	Knees
Peladophobia	Bald people
Zoophobia	Animals
Ablutophobia	Baths
Herpetophobia	Reptiles and snakes
Chronomentrophobia	Clocks
Pogonophobia	Beards
Phasmophobia	Ghosts

HOW TO SURVIVE...

A LION ATTACK

1 CATFIGHT
Lions usually avoid confrontations with people. But if one lunges toward you, swing a tree branch, throw rocks, or even gouge its eyes. Fighting back may make it slink away like the Cowardly Lion.

2 DON'T TAKE IT "LION DOWN"
Never crouch, kneel, or play dead. The lion might think you're ready to become a Kid McNugget.

3 ACT LIKE A PRO WRESTLER
Lions go after weaker prey, so show it that you rule. Scream, snarl, and bare your teeth (even if you have braces). Come on stronger than The Rock in a smackdown.

4 STRENGTH IN NUMBERS
Lions prefer to attack solitary prey, so make sure you safari with plenty of friends. Don't let the lion divide and conquer—keep your pals close by at all times.

5 SEE YA LATER
See an escape route? Don't wait for a permission slip, Einstein! Slowly back away—but never turn tail and run. You just might avoid a major "cat-astrophe."

QUICKSAND

1 NO MORE "SOUP-ERSTITIONS"
Quicksand isn't some bottom-less pit waiting to suck you in. It's a soupy mixture of sand and water found near riverbanks, shorelines, and marshes. It's rarely more than a few feet (one meter) deep, though it can be deeper.

2 GO WITH THE FLOAT
Not that you'd want to, but quicksand is actually easier to float on than water. So lean back, place your arms straight out from your sides, and let the sopping sand support your weight.

3 YOU FLAIL, YOU FAIL
Don't kick or struggle. That creates a vacuum, which only pulls you down. Ignore the gritty goop squishing into your underpants and remain calm.

4 LEG LIFTS
Conquer the quicksand with a slow stand. As you're lying back with your arms out, carefully inch one leg, then the other, to the surface.

5 ROLL OVER!
When both legs are afloat, pretend you're performing a dog trick. Keeping your face out of the muck, gently roll over the quicksand until you're on solid ground.

93

EXTREME
ACTION SPORTS

Forget soccer and softball: Some athletes go above and beyond when it comes to their sport of choice. These activities take a ton of skill—and plenty of guts, too. Here's a roundup of some *extreme*-ly out-there sports!

BASE JUMPING

SPECIAL GEAR
Parachute

WHY IT'S EXTREME
Instead of leaping from an airplane, BASE jumpers parachute from fixed objects, including buildings (B), antennas (A), spans (S), such as bridges, and Earth's formations (E).

EXTREME IRONING

SPECIAL GEAR
Iron, ironing board, and wrinkled clothes

WHY IT'S EXTREME
Thrill seekers iron their laundry while performing an extreme sport, like scuba diving and bungee jumping.

SNOW KITING

SPECIAL GEAR
Skis, large kite

WHY IT'S EXTREME
Skiers use large kites to propel them across the snow and ice—and off of mountains.

STILT JUMPING

SPECIAL GEAR
Jumping stilts

WHY IT'S EXTREME
Stride up to nine feet (2.7 m) with these spring-loaded stilts that you can walk, jump, and jog in.

FLARE SURFING

SPECIAL GEAR
Surfboard, flares

WHY IT'S EXTREME
Surfers create a fiery display while they ride the waves by attaching flares to the backs of their boards.

UNDERWATER HOCKEY

SPECIAL GEAR
Hockey puck, stick, swimming pool

WHY IT'S EXTREME
Players hold their breath as they dive to the bottom of the pool to go after the puck and push it to the goal.

MY SHOT

Calling all shutterbugs! Budding photographers can send their favorite pics to National Geographic Kids My Shot (ngkidsmyshot.com), where you can share, view, and rate cool images, like these taken by kids like you. So, what do you see through that lens? Break out your camera and start snapping away!

Congregate africa7

Eye loveusike

First trip in a balloon juniorasparagus

Dragonfly Matt

Funky caterpillars
the_future_batman

Seal pup yawning
alexander

TIPS FROM A PRO
How to Take Great Photos

As far as the eye can see, there are photographs waiting to be captured or created. Life swirls around us without stopping, but as a photographer, you can put a frame around moments in time. A lot more goes into taking a good photograph than just pushing a button, though.

Learn how to use a camera, but most of all, learn how to think like a photographer. Here are some valuable tips from expert photographer Neil Johnson to help you get started on your way.

COMPOSITION

- Making your subject the focus of attention does not mean that you have to put it in the middle of the frame. Placing the subject slightly off center can help lead the viewer into the picture.

SUBJECT

- When taking pictures of animals, getting down to their eye level and moving in close will improve your photographs.
- When taking pictures of people, try to get them to forget about the camera and just go about doing what they enjoy.

LIGHT

- When lighting a subject, it is important to consider not only the direction of the light (front, side, or back), but also the color of the background.
- Light does not always have to fall on the front of your subject.
- On-camera flash is most useful for subjects that are 10 to 15 feet (3 to 4 m) away.

QUICK TIPS!

- **Get close.** A lot of cameras have zoom features, but nothing beats being right there next to your subject.

- **Experiment with the different modes** on your digital camera, like portrait, sports, and macro. See what works and what doesn't.

- **Don't spend too much time** looking at the pictures on your digital camera—doing this drains the batteries! Download your photos instead.

- **Stay still,** especially if you're using a camera phone. The steadier you are, the clearer your shot will be.

How to Write a Perfect Essay

Need to write an essay? Does the assignment feel as big as climbing Mount Everest? Fear not. You're up to the challenge! The following step-by-step tips will help you with this monumental task.

1 **BRAINSTORM.** Sometimes the subject matter of your essay is assigned to you, sometimes it's not. Either way, you have to decide what you want to say. Start by brainstorming some ideas, writing down any thoughts you have about the subject. Then read over everything you've come up with and consider which idea you think is the strongest. Ask yourself what you want to write about the most. Keep in mind the goal of your essay. (The four main types of essays are described on the next page.) Can you achieve the goal of the assignment with this topic? If so, you're good to go.

2 **WRITE A TOPIC SENTENCE.** This is the main idea of your essay, a statement of your thoughts on the subject. Again, consider the goal of your essay. Think of the topic sentence as an introduction that tells your reader what the rest of your essay will be about.

3 **OUTLINE YOUR IDEAS.** Once you have a good topic sentence, then you need to support that main idea with more detailed information, facts, thoughts, and examples. These supporting points answer one question about your topic sentence—"Why?" This is where research and perhaps more brainstorming come in. Then organize these points in the way you think makes the most sense, probably in order of importance. Now you have an outline for your essay.

4 **ON YOUR MARK, GET SET, WRITE!** Follow your outline, using each of your supporting points as the topic sentence of its own paragraph. Use descriptive words to get your ideas across to the reader. Go into detail, using specific information to tell your story or make your point. Stay on track, making sure that everything you include is somehow related to the main idea of your essay. Use transitions to make your writing flow (see p. 125 for "Write With Power").

5 **WRAP IT UP.** Finish your essay with a conclusion that summarizes your entire essay and restates your main idea.

6 **PROOFREAD AND REVISE.** Check for errors in spelling, capitalization, punctuation, and grammar. Look for ways to make your writing clear, understandable, and interesting. Use descriptive verbs, adjectives, or adverbs when possible. It also helps to have someone else read your work to point out things you might have missed. Then make the necessary corrections and changes in a second draft. Repeat this revision process once more to make your final draft as good as you can.

Types of Essays

NARRATIVE ESSAY

Purpose: A narrative essay tells a story about an event.

Example: "The Seal Who Loved Me" (pp. 90-91)

Helpful Hints:
- Pick a topic that really interests you. Your excitement will come through in your writing.
- Tell your story with a clear beginning, middle, and end.
- Add fun or exciting details to highlight dramatic or unexpected moments.
- Use descriptive words to help give your reader a sense of what it was like to be there.

EXPOSITORY ESSAY

Purpose: An expository essay gives facts and information about a person, place, thing, or idea. Book reports, research papers, and biographies are types of expository writing.

Example: "Dwarf Planets" (p. 142)

Helpful Hints:
- Dig deep in your research to find interesting details.
- State your topic right away.
- Use transitional phrases to make your essay flow smoothly.

DESCRIPTIVE ESSAY

Purpose: A descriptive essay describes a person, place, or thing using sensory details to give the reader a better idea of what the subject is really like.

Example: "Discovering Tut's Treasures" (pp. 228-229)

Helpful Hints:
- Describe how the subject looks, sounds, tastes, smells, and feels.
- Use interesting comparisons.
- Be specific; find just the right adjectives and adverbs.

PERSUASIVE ESSAY

Purpose: A persuasive essay tries to convince the reader of your point of view using facts, statistics, details, and logic to make an argument.

Example: "Ocean Alert!" (p. 216)

Helpful Hints:
- State your opinion in the topic sentence.
- Use evidence to support your point of view.
- Consider the opposing views.
- Present a strong conclusion.

DON'T BE A COPYCAT

Plagiarism is presenting an idea or piece of writing as your own original work when it was actually created by someone else. It's a serious offense and will get you into trouble. Examples of plagiarism include buying or copying an essay from the Internet and handing it in as your own, or copying from a friend. Plagiarism can also occur by not citing your sources, so be careful.

In writing, you must give credit whenever you use information taken from another source. This is called citing your sources. Follow these basic guidelines to avoid plagiarism:

- **Take good notes** when researching. Keep a list of all research material you use, including details (title, author, page numbers, websites, etc.) about where you got specific pieces of information.

- **Use your own words.** Copying sentence structure but changing a few words is still plagiarism. Don't use more than three words in a row taken directly from another source.

- **Plagiarism** is not restricted to textbooks—don't copy material from the Internet, either.

- **Place quotation marks** around any phrase or sentence you take directly from another source, and cite it.

- **Double-check** your final text against your notes. Be sure that you've given credit where credit is due.

A group of dancers in Dili, East Timor, practice *capoeira*—a Brazilian dance style that features martial arts moves.

Culture
Connection

Got a smart phone?
SCAN THIS to check
out another culture.
(See instructions inside the front cover.)
No smart phone? Go online.
kids.nationalgeographic.com/almanac-2013

CELEBRATE! World Holidays 2013

1 AUSTRALIA DAY
January 26
Commemorates the creation of the first British settlement in Australia in 1788. Today, Australian families celebrate the occasion with outdoor concerts, barbecues, sports competitions, boat races, festivals, and fireworks.

2 CHINESE NEW YEAR
February 10
Also called Lunar New Year, this holiday marks the new year according to the lunar calendar. Families celebrate the occasion with parades, feasts, and fireworks. Young people may receive gifts of money in red envelopes.

3 NIRVANA DAY
February 15
Celebrated by Mahayana Buddhists, this holiday commemorates the anniversary of Buddha's death. It's not a sad day, but a day to reflect on life and celebrate.

4 NO RUZ
March 20
Also known as the Persian New Year. Millions of people of all religions gather with family and friends to celebrate this ancient festival of spring. Popular in the Middle East and Central Asia, the holiday may include storytelling and fire jumping for good luck.

5 PASSOVER
March 26–April 2
A Jewish holiday that commemorates the exodus of the Jews from Egypt and their liberation from slavery, Passover is a seven-day holiday during which observers have seders, or ritual feasts, and abstain from eating leavened bread.

6 EASTER
April 8
A Christian holiday that celebrates the resurrection of Jesus Christ, Easter is celebrated by giving baskets filled with gifts or candy to children.

7 RAMADAN AND EID AL-FITR
July 9–August 8
A Muslim religious holiday, Ramadan is a month long, ending in the Eid Al-Fitr celebration. Observers fast during this month—eating only after sunset—and do good deeds. Muslims pray for forgiveness and hope to purify themselves through observance.

8 ROSH HASHANAH AND YOM KIPPUR
September 5–6 and September 14
Rosh Hashanah is a Jewish religious holiday marking the beginning of a new year on the Hebrew calendar, and is celebrated with prayer, ritual foods, and a day of rest. Yom Kippur, known as the "Day of Atonement," is the most solemn of all Jewish holidays. It is observed with fasting and prayer, and is marked by a feast at sundown.

9 DAY OF THE DEAD
November 1–2
Known as *Día de los Muertos,* this Mexican holiday is a joyful time that honors the deceased. Festivities include parties in graveyards, where families feast, sing songs, clean tombstones, and talk to their buried ancestors.

10 HANUKKAH
November 28–December 5
This Jewish holiday is eight days long. It commemorates the rededication of the Temple in Jerusalem. It is observed with celebrations, the lighting of a menorah, and the exchange of gifts.

11 CHRISTMAS DAY
December 25
A Christian holiday marking the birth of Jesus Christ, Christmas is usually celebrated by decorating trees, exchanging presents, and having festive gatherings.

ANNIVERSARIES

Annual	1 year
Biennial	2 years
Triennial	3 years
Quadrennial	4 years
Quinquennial	5 years
Sexennial	6 years
Septennial	7 years
Octennial	8 years
Novennial	9 years
Decennial	10 years
Undecennial	11 years
Duodecennial	12 years
Tredecennial	13 years
Quattuordecennial	14 years
Quindecennial	15 years
Vigintennial or vicennial	20 years
Semicentennial or quinquagenary	50 years
Semisesquicentennial	75 years
Centennial	100 years
Quasquicentennial	125 years
Sesquicentennial	150 years
Demisemiseptcentennial or quartoseptcentennial	175 years
Bicentennial	200 years
Semiquincentennial	250 years
Tercentennial or tricentennial	300 years
Semiseptcentennial	350 years
Quadricentennial or quatercentenary	400 years
Quincentennial	500 years
Sexcentennial	600 years
Septicentennial or septuacentennial	700 years
Octocentennial	800 years
Nonacentennial	900 years
Millennial	1,000 years
Bimillennial	2,000 years

2013 CALENDAR

JANUARY

S	M	T	W	T	F	S
		1	2	3	4	5
6	7	8	9	10	11	12
13	14	15	16	17	18	19
20	21	22	23	24	25	26
27	28	29	30	31		

FEBRUARY

S	M	T	W	T	F	S
					1	2
3	4	5	6	7	8	9
10	11	12	13	14	15	16
17	18	19	20	21	22	23
24	25	26	27	28		

MARCH

S	M	T	W	T	F	S
					1	2
3	4	5	6	7	8	9
10	11	12	13	14	15	16
17	18	19	20	21	22	23
24	25	26	27	28	29	30
31						

APRIL

S	M	T	W	T	F	S
	1	2	3	4	5	6
7	8	9	10	11	12	13
14	15	16	17	18	19	20
21	22	23	24	25	26	27
28	29	30				

MAY

S	M	T	W	T	F	S
			1	2	3	4
5	6	7	8	9	10	11
12	13	14	15	16	17	18
19	20	21	22	23	24	25
26	27	28	29	30	31	

JUNE

S	M	T	W	T	F	S
						1
2	3	4	5	6	7	8
9	10	11	12	13	14	15
16	17	18	19	20	21	22
23	24	25	26	27	28	29
30						

JULY

S	M	T	W	T	F	S
	1	2	3	4	5	6
7	8	9	10	11	12	13
14	15	16	17	18	19	20
21	22	23	24	25	26	27
28	29	30	31			

AUGUST

S	M	T	W	T	F	S
				1	2	3
4	5	6	7	8	9	10
11	12	13	14	15	16	17
18	19	20	21	22	23	24
25	26	27	28	29	30	31

SEPTEMBER

S	M	T	W	T	F	S
1	2	3	4	5	6	7
8	9	10	11	12	13	14
15	16	17	18	19	20	21
22	23	24	25	26	27	28
29	30					

OCTOBER

S	M	T	W	T	F	S
		1	2	3	4	5
6	7	8	9	10	11	12
13	14	15	16	17	18	19
20	21	22	23	24	25	26
27	28	29	30	31		

NOVEMBER

S	M	T	W	T	F	S
					1	2
3	4	5	6	7	8	9
10	11	12	13	14	15	16
17	18	19	20	21	22	23
24	25	26	27	28	29	30

DECEMBER

S	M	T	W	T	F	S
1	2	3	4	5	6	7
8	9	10	11	12	13	14
15	16	17	18	19	20	21
22	23	24	25	26	27	28
29	30	31				

Kwanzaa

The soft light of black, red, and green candles casts a colorful glow in homes around the United States during Kwanzaa, a holiday commemorating African heritage. For one week each December, a candle is lit each night to represent the seven basic values of African-American family life: unity, self-determination, collective work and responsibility, coop-erative economics, purpose, creativity, and faith. Family and friends also exchange small gifts, play music, dance, and feast on foods from the harvest as they celebrate their culture and community.

CHINESE Dragon Boat FESTIVAL

Legend has it that in 278 B.C., Qu Yuan—who had been banished at the urging of jealous rivals—drowned himself in the Miluo River in despair. His friends rowed out to the river, warding off evil spirits with drums and throwing lumps of rice into the water to distract the fish from eating Qu Yuan's body. Today, people in China—and around the world—recreate that scene each year by racing colorful rowboats while beating drums, munching on rice balls, and lighting firecrackers for good luck.

What's Your Chinese Horoscope?
Locate your birth year to find out.

In Chinese astrology the zodiac runs on a 12-year cycle, based on the lunar calendar. Each year corresponds to one of twelve animals, each representing one of twelve personality types. Read on to find out which animal year you were born in and what that might say about you.

RAT
1972, '84, '96, 2008
Say cheese! You're attractive, charming, and creative. When you get mad, you can really have sharp teeth!

HORSE
1966, '78, '90, 2002
Being happy is your "mane" goal. And while you're smart and hardworking, your teacher may ride you for talking too much.

OX
1973, '85, '97, 2009
You're smart, patient, and as strong as an ... well, you know what. Though you're a leader, you never brag.

SHEEP
1967, '79, '91, 2003
Gentle as a lamb, you're also artistic, compassionate, and wise. You're often shy.

TIGER
1974, '86, '98, 2010
You may be a nice person, but no one should ever enter your room without asking—you might attack!

MONKEY
1968, '80, '92, 2004
No "monkey see, monkey do" for you. You're a clever problem-solver with an excellent memory.

RABBIT
1975, '87, '99, 2011
Your ambition and talent make you jump at opportunity. You also keep your ears open for gossip.

ROOSTER
1969, '81, '93, 2005
You crow about your adventures, but inside you're really shy. You're thoughtful, capable, brave, and talented.

DRAGON
1976, '88, 2000, '12
You're on fire! Health, energy, honesty, and bravery make you a living legend.

DOG
1970, '82, '94, 2006
Often the leader of the pack, you're loyal and honest. You can also keep a secret.

SNAKE
1977, '89, 2001, '13
You may not speak often, but you're very smart. You always seem to have a stash of cash.

PIG
1971, '83, '95, 2007
Even though you're courageous, honest, and kind, you never hog all the attention.

MYTHS BUSTED!

A wise man says, "Welcome to America!"

WAA-HOO!

WHOA!

SWEET!

THE MYTH

Chewing gum takes seven years to digest.

WHY IT'S NOT TRUE

Gum is made from a substance similar to rubber, so it's impossible for the acid in your stomach to break it down. But that doesn't mean the gum sticks around. It can't adhere to the slippery lining in your gut, so as long as you don't make meals out of it, gum will come out of your body with the rest of your waste. "In a couple days, it comes out looking pretty much the same as when it went in," says David E. Milov, a doctor at Nemours Children's Hospital in Orlando, Florida, U.S.A.

THE MYTH

Fortune cookies come from China.

WHY IT'S NOT TRUE

Fortune cookies aren't even found in China! "They most likely came from Japan," says Jennifer 8. Lee, author of *The Fortune Cookie Chronicles.* The proof: an 1878 Japanese book that shows a man baking fortune cookies. Chinese people weren't associated with the treats until at least 1907. "The cookies were brought to California by Japanese immigrants," Lee says. It's still a mystery why fortune cookies are now served mostly in Chinese restaurants.

Pop History

BUBBLE GUM IS MADE FROM SWEETENERS like sugar, a variety of different flavorings, and a chewy gum base. The gum base originally was made from a product called "chicle," which comes from *Manilkara chicle* trees.

Today, the gum base is sometimes made from a latex product or a type of rubber. But these products also come from trees. Think it's weird to chew gum from a tree? People have been doing it for centuries, ever since the ancient Maya of present-day Mexico and Central America chewed chicle thousands of years ago.

Interested in learning about other food history and fun facts?

COOL CLICK

foodfunandfacts.com/foodfun.htm

7 sweet facts about desserts

1 The **largest** **s'more** ever made used 40,000 marshmallows, **8,000** chocolate bars, and 55,000 graham crackers.

2 The oldest **chocolate** ever found was in a **2,600-year-old pot.**

3 A man once ate **49 glazed** doughnuts in 8 minutes.

4 The word **"cookie"** comes from the Dutch word **koekje,** which means **small cake.**

5 Some **astronauts** living on the *Mir* space station ate **Jell-O** every Sunday to help keep track of the days.

6 **Olive oil** ice cream is a popular **flavor** in several fancy restaurants.

7 **STRAWBERRIES** contain more **VITAMIN C** than **ORANGES.**

Piece of Cake

Some artists are making treats that look just too real to eat! Designer cakes are popping up everywhere, and this cake artist has some sneaky tricks for baking realistic creations. Want to learn more? Read on!

The word "cake" comes from the Viking word *kaka*.

NECK IN NECK

To create this 18-inch-tall, 25-pound (46-cm, 11-kg) giraffe cake, artist Debbie Goard used a plastic pipe in its neck to hold up the head—and the head is the only part not made of cake. A cake head would have been too heavy and fallen over. Her solution? Make it out of rice cereal treats. "People usually feel funny about eating the head, anyway," says Goard, of Debbie Does Cakes in Oakland, California, U.S.A.

CHI-WOW-WA

To create this doggone delicious cake, Goard molded cake around smooth wooden sticks called dowels, and a board was tucked into the belly to support the body. "I've been known to use a saw and drill," she says.

I'M A CAKE!

Ancient Egyptians baked cakes, but they were more like honey-sweetened bread.

EAT THE BEAT

You'd need to lick off your drumsticks if you played this drum. Goard used an airbrush to spray-paint on food coloring to create the blue body and silver rims. Then she brushed on edible glitter to give the drum its realistic sparkle. For the drum's logo, she hooked up her computer to a special printer that uses food coloring for ink and sheets of icing for paper.

PASTA-*LICIOUS*

The spaghetti noodles are fondant—thick icing that's easy to mold. The meatballs are walnut chocolate truffles, and it's all covered in raspberry jam for red sauce. (In case you're wondering, the actual cake is under the noodles.) The hardest part? Goard hand-rolled some 600 strings of spaghetti, one strand at a time.

109

CRAFTS Around the WORLD

TRY THESE FUN ACTIVITIES INSPIRED BY DIFFERENT CULTURES.

Ask for a parent's help and permission before you start these projects.

FUN FACT
Trolls are part of Norway's folklore. Legend has it that these creatures of the dark turn to stone if they're caught in the sun.

TROLL DOLLS

YOU WILL NEED

- GLUE
- FELT AND/OR FABRIC
- SMALL PLASTIC BOTTLE SUCH AS A SPICE JAR
- FAKE FUR
- GOOGLY EYES
- DECORATIONS SUCH AS YARN, STICKERS, AND PAPER CUTOUTS

WHAT TO DO

Decide what characters you want to make and pick out the materials you need at a craft store. Glue felt around the bottle where the face will go. Glue the fake fur along the top edge of the felt so it stands up straight. Then glue on the fabric "clothing," googly eyes, and your choice of decorations and accessories. Be sure to let each layer dry before adding the next layer of material.

FUN FACT
Navajo Indians create sandpaintings as part of healing ceremonies and other rituals.

SANDPAINTING

YOU WILL NEED

- CANVAS BOARD OR FOAM BOARD
- GLUE
- COLORED SAND (AVAILABLE IN CRAFT STORES)
- PENCIL AND BLACK MARKER

WHAT TO DO

Sketch your design on the board in pencil. When you are happy with the sketch, outline it with the marker. Starting at the top, cover a small area with glue and then one color of sand. Make sure you don't get glue and sand on the marker lines. Shake excess sand back into the container and let the glue dry. Repeat using different colors for different areas. Dry overnight.

FUN FACT
Japanese tie-dye, or *shibori*, is more than 1,000 years old. Peasants used the technique to brighten up old clothes. Tie-dye was also fashionable among royalty.

TIE-DYED T-SHIRT

YOU WILL NEED

- WHITE, 100% COTTON T-SHIRT (PREWASHED)
- RUBBER BANDS
- LARGE POT
- HOT WATER
- FABRIC DYE (ANY COLOR)
- LARGE BUCKET
- TONGS
- WATER- AND HEAT-SAFE RUBBER GLOVES

CAUTION! Dye can stain anything, even the sink. Cover your work area with plastic and read the cleaning instructions on the dye package. Always wear rubber gloves.

WHAT TO DO

1. Dampen the T-shirt. For a random pattern, twist and scrunch the fabric, using rubber bands to hold the T-shirt in that position. For a circular pattern like the one at right, grab part of the T-shirt and squeeze it into a long, skinny shape. Tie several equally spaced rubber bands around the fabric. Each rubber band will form a circle.

2. Ask a parent to boil water in the large pot. Using the measurements on the dye package, ask your parent to pour the hot water into a bucket and stir in the dye.

3. Dunk the shirt into the water with the tongs and stir constantly for about 10 to 15 minutes. (The T-shirt appears slightly darker when it's wet.)

4. Rinse the shirt under cold water. Then remove the rubber bands and rinse until the water runs clear. Dry in a clothes dryer to help set the color.

BUILD A SNOW

This snow carving of King Kong could eat Frosty the Snowman for dinner!
Create a smaller version in your backyard by following these tips from
Don Berg, head of the United States National Snow Sculpting Competition.

YOU WILL NEED

Ask for permission to use these supplies and be sure to return them clean and dry:

- SNOW SHOVEL
- GARBAGE CAN
- PLASTIC PAIL
- SQUARE AND V-SHAPED CHISELS
- GARDEN TROWEL
- SMALL PUTTY KNIFE
- IF YOU DON'T HAVE THESE ITEMS, TRY METAL KITCHEN UTENSILS OR OTHER HOUSEHOLD TOOLS.

TIPS FOR GETTING STARTED

BEGIN WITH A PICTURE of the subject you want to snow-sculpt for reference.

CARVE FROM THE TOP DOWN to make sure the bottom will support the top.

PATCH UP MISTAKES by adding slightly melted snow to your sculpture.

BUNDLE UP! The ideal temperature for carving is about 20°F to 32°F (-7°C to 0°C).

Ask for a parent's help and permission before you start this project. Be sure to wear waterproof gloves and boots.

MAKE A SNOW PILE

Shovel snow into a garbage can or pail. Stomp on the snow frequently or press hard to pack it down. Turn the can or pail upside down and lift up to release the block of snow.

START SCULPTING

1. Using a chisel, carve shallow lines to show where you want to remove snow. Slowly carve away a little snow at a time.

2. With a garden trowel, carve the gorilla's basic shape. Do not carve detailed features yet.

3. Make shallow lines where the gorilla's eyes, nose, and mouth will go. Then use the trowel to hollow them out.

4. Using a chisel, carve the lips, eyeballs, ears, and any other facial features. Use the V-shaped chisel to carve waves and layers in hair. Be careful not to dig too deep.

5. Use the putty knife to smooth out grooves or gouges.

6. Shovel away any excess snow from your work. Then watch the neighbors go ape over your creative sculpture!

SCULPTURE!

CHECK OUT OTHER COOL ANIMAL CARVINGS!

THE BIGGEST SNOW SCULPTURES IN THE WORLD, LIKE THIS ONE FROM THE SAPPORO FESTIVAL IN JAPAN, CAN WEIGH UP TO 100 TONS (90 T)— THAT'S MORE THAN 50 HIPPOS.

AT SNOW SCULPTURE COMPETITIONS, PEOPLE KNOWN AS "STOMPERS" HELP COMPRESS SNOW BY STOMPING ON IT.

TO ADD COLOR, SPRAY WATER ON THE SCULPTURE, WHICH CREATES AN ICY LAYER. THEN APPLY NONTOXIC SPRAY BODY PAINT.

THIS ELEPHANT WAS SCULPTED FROM AN EIGHT-FOOT (2.4-M)-TALL CUBE OF SNOW.

1 THE LARGEST U.S. BILL PRODUCED TODAY IS THE **$100 BILL.** BUT LESS THAN 45 YEARS AGO, YOU COULD PAY FOR STUFF WITH A **$10,000 BILL!**

2 Nearly two dozen countries—from Australia to Nigeria to Mexico—print money on SHEETS OF PLASTIC instead of paper. These brightly colored bills are so tough they can be WASHED WITH SOAP AND WATER.

MONEY AND LUCK

COOL FACTS THAT WILL MAKE YOU SAY, "KA-CHING!"

3 COINS IN ANCIENT CHINA WERE MINTED WITH HOLES IN THE CENTER SO THEY COULD BE STRUNG AND CARRIED MORE EASILY. A FEW COUNTRIES STILL USE COINS WITH HOLES, INCLUDING DENMARK, JAPAN, PAPUA NEW GUINEA, AND THE PHILIPPINES.

4 WHALE TEETH WERE ONCE HIGHLY TREASURED CURRENCY IN FIJI. IN THE 19TH CENTURY, A SINGLE WHALE TOOTH WAS WORTH ONE CANOE.

5 Until the early 1900s, **A WHOLE COCONUT** was the accepted form of currency in the **NICOBAR ISLANDS,** west of Thailand in the **INDIAN OCEAN.**

6 **LOONIE** is the nickname for the Canadian one-dollar coin, which features the image of a bird called a loon, commonly found in Canada.

7 IN 2007, MONGOLIA ISSUED A COMMEMORATIVE COIN WITH A PORTRAIT OF **U.S. PRESIDENT JOHN F. KENNEDY.** IF YOU PUSH A TINY BUTTON, THE COIN PLAYS A SOUND BITE FROM A SPEECH.

JOHN F. KENNEDY (1917-1963)

HOW TO FENG SHUI YOUR ROOM

IF FENG SHUI DOESN'T WORK FOR YOU, THAT'S OK. THIS STORY IS JUST FOR FUN!

Want to make more friends? Get better grades? Feng shui may help! Feng shui (FUNG SHWAY) is the ancient art of placement. Though it's not a science, people have been swearing by feng shui "cures" for thousands of years to bring them good luck. How? By placing or rearranging items in your home, positive chi—or energy—can flow freely and change your luck for the better. Try a few of these feng shui cures in your bedroom, then see what happens!

1
A mobile keeps positive chi moving.

2
Hang a soft-ringing bell on each side of your door to give you positive thoughts, which inspire good luck and happiness.

3
Hang three pictures of family and friends in a triangle pattern to get along better with your loved ones. In feng shui, the number three stimulates good chi.

4
Draw a picture of what you want and put it under your mattress. Your dreams just may come true.

5
Move your desk or a bookcase to the left of the door to get better grades.

6
Put a quartz crystal on your desk to improve your concentration. Girls should place theirs on the left; boys on the right.

7
Hang a bulletin board of your achievements on the wall opposite your door for inspiration and motivation.

8
Put a stuffed version of your birth-year animal (see p. 105) on your bed for extra luck.

9
Three pillows on your bed may help you have fun with your friends—or make new ones.

10
Keep a plant in your room if you crave more time with family and friends.

11
Place a light-green or purple bowl in your room, and add a coin when you enter or leave to help save money.

12
Place your bed along a wall so you have a clear view of your door. This will help you sleep better.

12 Ways to Say Happy Birthday

1 **ARABIC** Eid milaad sa'eed
2 **FRENCH (CANADA)** Bonne Fête
3 **GERMAN** Alles Gute zum Geburtstag
4 **GREEK** Hronia polla
5 **HAWAIIAN** Hau'oli La Hanau
6 **HEBREW** Yom Huledet Sameakh
7 **HINDI** Janmadin mubarak ho
8 **MANDARIN** Shengrì kuàilè
9 **RUSSIAN** S dniom rojdeniya
10 **SPANISH** ¡Feliz cumpleaños!
11 **SWAHILI** Nakutakia mema kwa siku yako ya kuzaliwa!
12 **TURKISH** Dogum günün kutlu olsun

LANGUAGES IN PERIL

TODAY, there are more than 7,000 languages spoken on Earth. But by 2100, more than half of those may disappear. In fact, experts say one language dies every two weeks, due to the increasing dominance of larger languages, such as English, Spanish, and Mandarin. So what can be done to keep dialects from disappearing? Efforts like National Geographic's Enduring Voices Project are now tracking down and documenting the world's most threatened indigenous languages, such as Tofa, spoken by only 30 people in Siberia, and Magati Ke, from Aboriginal Australia. The hope is to preserve these languages— and the cultures they belong to.

10 LEADING LANGUAGES

Approximate population of first-language speakers (in millions)

Rank	Language	Speakers
1.	Chinese (Mandarin)	845
2.	Spanish	329
3.	English	328
4.	Arabic	221
5.	Hindi	182
6.	Bengali	181
7.	Portuguese	178
8.	Russian	144
9.	Japanese	122
10.	German	90

Some languages have only a few hundred speakers, while Earth's population giant, China, has more than 845 million speakers of Mandarin. That's more than double the next-largest group of language speakers. Colonial expansion, trade, and migration account for the spread of the other most widely spoken languages. With growing use of the Internet, English is becoming the language of the technology age.

Bet you didn't know

6 FUN language facts

1 The **most commonly** used letters in the English language are **E, T, A,** and **O.**

2 The Hawaiian alphabet has **13** letters.

3 The **longest** word in English is pneumonoultramicroscopicsilicovolcanoconiosis, a lung disease.

4 **More people** speak English in **China** than they do in the **United States.**

5 People in **Papua New Guinea** speak a total of **820** languages.

6 The word **taxi** means the same thing in English, German, French, Swedish, Spanish, and Portuguese.

World Religions

A round the world, religion takes many forms. Some belief systems, such as Christianity, Islam, and Judaism, are monotheistic, meaning that followers believe in just one supreme being. Others, like Hinduism, Shintoism, and most native belief systems, are polytheistic, meaning that many of their followers believe in multiple gods.

All of the major religions have their origins in Asia, but they have spread around the world. Christianity, with the largest number of followers, has three divisions—Roman Catholic, Eastern Orthodox, and Protestant. Islam, with about one-fifth of all believers, has two main divisions—Sunni and Shiite. Hinduism and Buddhism account for almost another one-fifth of believers. Judaism, dating back some 4,000 years, has more than 13 million followers, less than one percent of all believers.

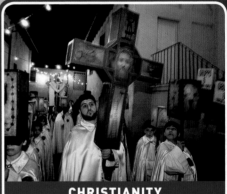

CHRISTIANITY

Based on the teachings of Jesus Christ, a Jew born some 2,000 years ago in the area of modern-day Israel, Christianity has spread worldwide and actively seeks converts. Followers in Switzerland (above) participate in an Easter season procession with lanterns and crosses.

BUDDHISM

Founded about 2,400 years ago in northern India by the Hindu prince Gautama Buddha, Buddhism spread throughout East and Southeast Asia. Buddhist temples have statues, such as the Mihintale Buddha (above) in Sri Lanka.

HINDUISM

Dating back more than 4,000 years, Hinduism is practiced mainly in India. Hindus follow sacred texts known as the Vedas and believe in reincarnation. During the festival of Navratri, which honors the goddess Durga, the Garba dance is performed (above).

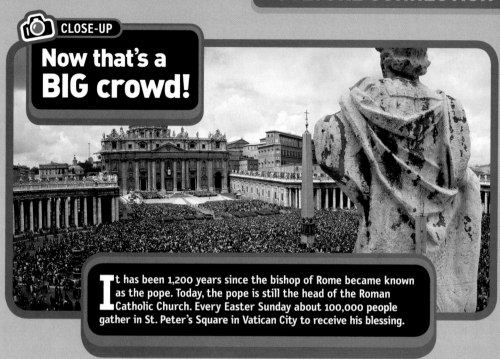

CLOSE-UP

Now that's a BIG crowd!

I t has been 1,200 years since the bishop of Rome became known as the pope. Today, the pope is still the head of the Roman Catholic Church. Every Easter Sunday about 100,000 people gather in St. Peter's Square in Vatican City to receive his blessing.

To learn more about ancient and medieval religions, go online.
historyforkids.org/learn/religion

COOL CLICK

ISLAM

Muslims believe that the Koran, Islam's sacred book, records the words of Allah (God) as revealed to the Prophet Muhammad around A.D. 610. Believers (above) circle the Kabah in the Haram Mosque in Mecca, Saudi Arabia, the spiritual center of the faith.

JUDAISM

The traditions, laws, and beliefs of Judaism date back to Abraham (the Patriarch) and the Torah (the first five books of the Old Testament). Followers pray before the Western Wall (above), which stands below Islam's Dome of the Rock in Jerusalem.

MYTHOLOGY

GREEK

EGYPTIAN

The ancient Greeks believed that many gods and goddesses ruled the universe. According to this mythology, the Olympians lived high atop Greece's Mount Olympus. Each of these 12 principal gods and goddesses had a unique personality that corresponded to particular aspects of life, such as love or death.

Egyptian mythology is based on a creation myth that tells of an egg that appeared on the ocean. When the egg hatched, out came Ra, the sun god. As a result, ancient Egyptians became worshippers of the sun and of the nine original deities, most of whom were the children and grandchildren of Ra.

THE OLYMPIANS

Aphrodite was the goddess of love and beauty.

Apollo, Zeus's son, was the god of the sun, music, and healing. Artemis was his twin.

Ares, Zeus's son, was the god of war.

Artemis, Zeus's daughter and Apollo's twin, was the goddess of the hunt and childbirth.

Athena, born from the forehead of Zeus, was the goddess of wisdom and crafts.

Demeter was the goddess of fertility and nature.

Hades, Zeus's brother, was the god of the under-world and the dead.

Hephaestus, the son of Hera, was the god of fire.

Hera, the wife and older sister of Zeus, was the goddess of women and marriage.

Hermes, Zeus's son, was the messenger of the gods.

Poseidon, the brother of Zeus, was the god of the sea and earthquakes.

Zeus was the most powerful of the gods and the top Olympian. He wielded a thunderbolt and was the god of the sky and thunder.

THE NINE DEITIES

Geb, son of Shu and Tefnut, was the god of the Earth.

Isis (Ast), daughter of Geb and Nut, was the goddess of fertility and motherhood.

Nephthys (Nebet-Hut), daughter of Geb and Nut, was protector of the dead.

Nut, daughter of Shu and Tefnut, was the goddess of the sky.

Osiris (Usir), son of Geb and Nut, was the god of the afterlife.

Ra (Re), the sun god, is generally viewed as the creator. He represents life and health.

Seth (Set), son of Geb and Nut, was the god of the desert and chaos.

Shu, son of Ra, was the god of air.

Tefnut, daughter of Ra, was the goddess of rain.

All cultures around the world have unique legends and traditions that have been passed down over generations. Many myths refer to gods or supernatural heroes who are responsible for occurrences in the world. For example, Norse mythology tells of the red-bearded Thor, the god of thunder, who is responsible for creating lightning and thunderstorms. And many creation myths, especially from some of North America's native cultures, tell of an earth-diver represented as an animal that brings a piece of sand or mud up from the deep sea. From this tiny piece of earth, the entire world takes shape.

NORSE

ROMAN

Norse mythology originated in Scandinavia, in northern Europe. It was complete with gods and goddesses who lived in a heavenly place called Asgard that could be reached only by crossing a rainbow bridge.

While Norse mythology is lesser known, we use it every day. Most days of the week are named after Norse gods, including some of these major deities.

NORSE GODS

Balder was the god of light and beauty.

Freya was the goddess of love, beauty, and fertility.

Frigg, for whom Friday was named, was the queen of Asgard. She was the goddess of marriage, motherhood, and the home.

Heimdall was the watchman of the rainbow bridge and the guardian of the gods.

Hel, the daughter of Loki, was the goddess of death.

Loki, a shape-shifter, was a trickster who helped the gods—and caused them problems.

Skadi was the goddess of winter and of the hunt. She is often represented as "The Snow Queen."

Thor, for whom Thursday was named, was the god of thunder and lightning.

Tyr, for whom Tuesday was named, was the god of the sky and war.

Wodan, for whom Wednesday was named, was the god of war, wisdom, death, and magic.

Much of Roman mythology was adopted from Greek mythology, but the Romans also developed a lot of original myths as well. The gods of Roman mythology lived everywhere and each had a role to play. There were thousands of Roman gods, but here are a few of the stars of Roman myths.

ANCIENT ROMAN GODS

Ceres was the goddess of the harvest and motherly love.

Diana, daughter of Jupiter, was the goddess of hunting and the moon.

Juno, Jupiter's wife, was the goddess of women and fertility.

Jupiter, the patron of Rome and master of the gods, was the god of the sky.

Mars, the son of Jupiter and Juno, was the god of war.

Mercury, the son of Jupiter, was the messenger of the gods and the god of travelers.

Minerva was the goddess of wisdom, learning, and the arts and crafts.

Neptune, the brother of Jupiter, was the god of the sea.

Venus was the goddess of love and beauty.

Vesta was the goddess of fire and the hearth. She was one of the most important of the Roman deities.

THE OLYMPICS

LEGEND HAS IT THAT the Olympic Games were founded in ancient times by Heracles, a son of the Greek god Zeus. Unfortunately, that can't really be proven. The first Olympic Games for which there are still written records took place in 776 B.C. There was only one event: a running race called the stade. From then on, the Olympics were held every four years until they were abolished in A.D. 393.

It wasn't until more than 1,500 years later that the Olympics were resurrected. The modern Olympic Games were held for the first time in 1896 and have continued around the world ever since.

Summer Olympic Games Sites

1896	Athens, Greece
1900	Paris, France
1904	St. Louis, Missouri, U.S.A.
1908	London, England, U.K.
1912	Stockholm, Sweden
1920	Antwerp, Belgium
1924	Paris, France
1928	Amsterdam, Netherlands
1932	Los Angeles, California, U.S.A.
1936	Berlin, Germany
1948	London, England, U.K.
1952	Helsinki, Finland
1956	Melbourne, Australia
1960	Rome, Italy
1964	Tokyo, Japan
1968	Mexico City, Mexico
1972	Munich, West Germany (now Germany)
1976	Montreal, Canada
1980	Moscow, U.S.S.R. (now Russia)
1984	Los Angeles, California, U.S.A.
1988	Seoul, South Korea
1992	Barcelona, Spain
1996	Atlanta, Georgia, U.S.A.
2000	Sydney, Australia
2004	Athens, Greece
2008	Beijing, China
2012	London, England, U.K.
2016	Rio de Janeiro, Brazil

Winter Olympic Games Sites

1924	Chamonix, France
1928	St. Moritz, Switzerland
1932	Lake Placid, New York, U.S.A.
1936	Garmisch-Partenkirchen, Germany
1948	St. Moritz, Switzerland
1952	Oslo, Norway
1956	Cortina d'Ampezzo, Italy
1960	Squaw Valley, California, U.S.A.
1964	Innsbruck, Austria
1968	Grenoble, France
1972	Sapporo, Japan
1976	Innsbruck, Austria
1980	Lake Placid, New York, U.S.A.
1984	Sarajevo, Yugoslavia
1988	Calgary, Alberta, Canada
1992	Albertville, France
1994	Lillehammer, Norway
1998	Nagano, Japan
2002	Salt Lake City, Utah, U.S.A.
2006	Torino (Turin), Italy
2010	Vancouver, British Columbia, Canada
2014	Sochi, Russia
2018	Pyeongchang, South Korea

Note: Due to World Wars I and II, the 1916 Summer Olympics and both the summer and winter games of 1940 and 1944 were not held.

Bet you didn't know

LONDON is the only city to host the **OLYMPICS THREE TIMES** (1908, 1948, 2012).

The **FLAG** of every **COUNTRY IN THE WORLD** has at least one of the five colors in the Olympic rings: **blue, yellow, black, green, and red.**

Make a Difference

There are so many ways to make a difference in the lives of others. Whether it's volunteering, donating some of your allowance to charity, or reaching out to someone in need, a small but meaningful gesture may ignite a charitable spirit that can spread around the world. Ready to get going? Here are some ways you can give back today!

1 Pet Party

HOW YOU CAN HELP

Throw a party that brings your community together for a good cause. Invite your friends and neighbors with their dogs. Ask guests to bring pet toys and supplies as donations for an animal shelter. Serve treats for dogs as well as humans, and make up dog-friendly party games like Frisbee. Each shelter's needs will differ, so call first to find out what kind of donations they prefer.

THESE PETS LIKE WEARING HATS, BUT YOUR PET MAY NOT. NEVER FORCE YOUR PET TO WEAR A COSTUME IT DOESN'T LIKE WEARING.

3 Basket of Cheer

HOW YOU CAN HELP

Brighten a sick child's day with new art supplies. Fill a big gift basket with crayons, markers, coloring books, paint sets, construction paper, beads, or other supplies. Then deliver the basket to a children's hospital.

2 Make a Change

HOW YOU CAN HELP

Ask your family to start collecting loose change in a big jar. When the jar is full, pour it into a change-counting machine at a bank or grocery store, then donate the money to the charity of your choice.

BE SURE TO CALL AHEAD TO MAKE SURE YOUR CHARITY WILL ACCEPT YOUR DONATION.

Explore a New Culture

INDIAN STAMP

5·00 MADHUBANI - MITHILA PAINTING मधुबनी - मिथिला चित्रकला भारत INDIA

MADHUBANI - MITHILA PAINTING मधुबनी - मिथिला चित्रकला 10·00 भारत NDIA

5 RUPEE COIN

INDIAN FLAG

You're a student, but you're also a citizen of the world. Writing a report on a foreign nation or your own country is a great way to better understand and appreciate how people in other parts of the world live. Pick the country of your ancestors, one that's been in the news, or one that you'd like to visit someday.

Passport to Success

A country report follows the format of an expository essay (see p. 99 for "Types of Essays") because you're "exposing" information about the country you choose.

Simple Steps

1. RESEARCH Gathering information is the most important step in writing a good country report. Look to Internet sources, encyclopedias, books, magazine and newspaper articles, and other sources to find important and interesting details about your subject.

2. ORGANIZE YOUR NOTES Put the information you gathered into a rough outline. For example, sort everything you found about the country's system of government, climate, etc.

3. WRITE IT UP Follow the basic structure of good writing: introduction, body, and conclusion. Remember that each paragraph should have a topic sentence that is then supported by facts and details. Incorporate the information from your notes, but make sure it's in your own words. And make your writing flow with good transitions and descriptive language.

4. ADD VISUALS Include maps, diagrams, photos, and other visual aids.

5. PROOFREAD AND REVISE Correct any mistakes, and polish your language. Do your best!

6. CITE YOUR SOURCES Be sure to keep a record of your sources (see p. 257 for "Reveal Your Sources").

TIP: Think about countries experiencing war or unrest, such as Afghanistan and Libya. These places would make ideal topics for your next country report.

Key Information

You may be assigned to write a report on a specific aspect of a country, such as its political system, or your report may be more general. In writing a broad survey, be sure to touch on the following areas:

GEOGRAPHY—the country's location, size, capital, major cities, topography, and other physical details

NATURE—the country's various climates, ecosystems (rain forest, desert, etc.), and unique wildlife

HISTORY—major events, wars, and other moments that affected the country and its people

GOVERNMENT—the country's political system (democracy, dictatorship, etc.) and the role of the individual citizen in the country's governance

ECONOMY / INDUSTRY—the country's economic system (capitalism, socialism, etc.), major industries and exports, and the country's place in the world economy

PEOPLE AND CULTURE—the country's major religions, spoken languages, unique foods, holidays, rituals, and traditions

GO BEYOND THE BASICS

✔ Explain the history of the country's flag and the meaning of its colors and symbols. crwflags.com/fotw/flags

✔ Play the country's national anthem. Download the anthem, words, and sheet music. nationalanthems.info

✔ Convert the country's currency into currencies from around the world. xe.com/ucc

✔ Check the local weather. Go to this website and enter the city or country's name in the bar marked "Find Weather." weather.com

✔ Figure out the time difference between the country you're studying and where you live. worldtimeserver.com

✔ Still want more information? Go to National Geographic's One-Stop Research site for maps, photos, art, games, and other information to make your report stand out. nationalgeographic.com/onestop

COOL CLICKS

Write With Power

Using good transitions makes any kind of writing read more smoothly. It provides organization, improves connections between thoughts, and helps the reader to understand. Here are a few examples of good transitions you might want to use:

Addition
also, again, as well as, besides, coupled with, furthermore, in addition, likewise, moreover, similarly

Generalizing
as a rule, as usual, for the most part, generally, generally speaking, ordinarily, usually

Emphasis
above all, chiefly, with attention to, especially, particularly, singularly

Similarity
comparatively, coupled with, correspondingly, identically, likewise, similarly, moreover, together with

Restatement
in essence, in other words, namely, that is, that is to say, in short, in brief, to put it differently

Contrast and Comparison
by the same token, conversely, instead, likewise, on one hand, on the other hand, on the contrary, rather, yet, but, however, still, nevertheless, in contrast

An artist's concept shows the new Mars rover, named Curiosity, examining a rock on the red planet. The mobile robot, launched in November 2011, is designed to find out whether Mars has ever been able to sustain microscopic life-forms called microbes.

Super
Science

Got a smart phone?
SCAN THIS to try a fun
science experiment!
(See instructions inside the front cover.)
No smart phone? Go online.
kids.nationalgeographic.com/almanac-2013

WHAT IS LIFE?

This seems like such an easy question to answer. Everybody knows that singing birds are alive and rocks are not. But when we start studying bacteria and other microscopic creatures, things get more complicated.

SO WHAT EXACTLY IS LIFE?
Most scientists agree that something is alive if it has the following characteristics: It can reproduce; grow in size to become more complex in structure; take in nutrients to survive; give off waste products; and respond to external stimuli, such as increased sunlight or changes in temperature.

KINDS OF LIFE
Biologists classify living organisms by how they get their energy. Organisms such as algae, green plants, and some bacteria use sunlight as an energy source. Animals (like humans), fungi, and some Archaea use chemicals to provide energy. When we eat food, chemical reactions within our digestive system turn our food into fuel.

Living things inhabit land, sea, and air. In fact, life also thrives deep beneath the oceans, embedded in rocks miles below the Earth's crust, in ice, and in other extreme environments. The life-forms that thrive in these challenging environments are called extremophiles. Some of these draw directly upon the chemicals surrounding them for energy. Since these are very different forms of life than what we're used to, we may not think of them as alive, but they are.

HOW IT ALL WORKS
To try and understand how a living organism works, it helps to look at one example of its simplest form—the single-celled bacterium called *Streptococcus*. There are many kinds of these tiny organisms, and some are responsible for human illnesses. What makes us sick or uncomfortable are the toxins the bacteria give off in our bodies.

A single *Streptococcus* bacterium is so small that at least 500 of them could fit on the dot above the letter *i*. These bacteria are some of the simplest forms of life we know. They have no moving parts, no lungs, no brain, no heart, no liver, and no leaves or fruit. Yet this life-form reproduces. It grows in size by producing long chain structures, takes in nutrients, and gives off waste products. This tiny life-form is alive, just as you are alive.

What makes something alive is a question scientists grapple with when they study viruses, such as the ones that cause the common cold and smallpox. They can grow and reproduce within host cells, such as those that make up your body. Because viruses lack cells and cannot metabolize nutrients for energy or reproduce without a host, scientists ask if they are indeed alive. And don't go looking for them without a strong microscope—viruses are a hundred times smaller than bacteria.

Scientists think life began on Earth some 3.9 to 4.1 billion years ago, but no fossils exist from that time. The earliest fossils ever found are from the primitive life that existed 3.6 billion years ago. Other life-forms, some of which are shown below, soon followed. Scientists continue to study how life evolved on Earth and whether or not it is possible that life exists on other planets.

MICROSCOPIC ORGANISMS

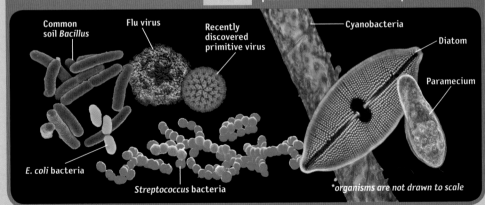

Common soil *Bacillus*

Flu virus

Recently discovered primitive virus

Cyanobacteria

Diatom

Paramecium

E. coli bacteria

Streptococcus bacteria

*organisms are not drawn to scale

The Three Domains of Life

Biologists divide all living organisms into three domains: Bacteria, Archaea, and Eukarya. Archaean and Bacterial cells do not have nuclei; they are so different from each other that they belong to different domains. Since human cells have a nucleus, humans belong to the Eukarya domain.

1

BACTERIA

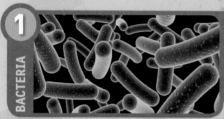

Domain Bacteria: These single-celled microorganisms are found almost everywhere in the world. Bacteria are small and do not have nuclei. They can be shaped like rods, spirals, or spheres. Some of them are helpful to humans, and some are harmful.

2

ARCHAEA

Domain Archaea: These single-celled microorganisms are often found in extremely hostile environments. Like Bacteria, Archaea do not have nuclei. but they have some genes in common with Eukarya. For this reason, scientists think the Archaea living today most closely resemble the earliest forms of life on Earth.

3

EUKARYA

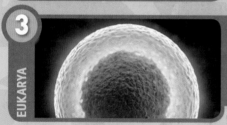

Domain Eukarya: This diverse group of life-forms is more complicated than Bacteria and Archaea, as Eukarya have one or more cells with nuclei. These are the tiny cells that make up your whole body. Eukarya are divided into four groups: fungi, protists, plants, and animals.

FYI

What is a domain? Scientifically speaking, a domain is a major taxonomic division into which natural objects are classified (see p. 20 for "What Is Taxonomy?").

FUNGI

Kingdom Fungi (about 100,000 species): Mainly multicellular organisms, fungi cannot make their own food. Mushrooms and yeast are fungi.

PLANTS

Kingdom Plantae (about 300,000 species): Plants are multicellular, and many can make their own food using photosynthesis (see p. 196 for "Photosynthesis").

PROTISTS

Protists (about 250,000 species): Once considered a kingdom, this group is a "grab bag" that includes unicellular and multicellular organisms of great variety.

ANIMALS

Kingdom Animalia (about a million species): Most animals, which are multicellular, have their own organ systems. Animals do not make their own food.

YOUR AMAZING
BODY!

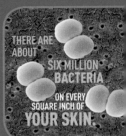

THERE ARE ABOUT **SIX MILLION BACTERIA** ON EVERY SQUARE INCH OF **YOUR SKIN.**

The human body is a complicated mass of systems— nine systems, to be exact. Each system has a unique and critical purpose in the body, and we wouldn't be able to survive without all of them.

The **NERVOUS** system controls the body.

The **MUSCULAR** system makes movement possible.

The **SKELETAL** system supports the body.

The **CIRCULATORY** system moves blood throughout the body.

The **RESPIRATORY** system provides the body with oxygen.

The **DIGESTIVE** system breaks down food into nutrients and gets rid of waste.

The **IMMUNE** system protects the body against disease and infection.

The **ENDOCRINE** system regulates the body's functions.

The **REPRODUCTIVE** system enables people to produce offspring.

Weird but true

MEN GET THE HICCUPS MORE OFTEN THAN WOMEN DO.

YOUR "FUNNY BONE" IS ACTUALLY A NERVE, NOT A BONE.

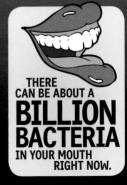

THERE CAN BE ABOUT A **BILLION BACTERIA** IN YOUR MOUTH RIGHT NOW.

BODY MYTHS BUSTED!

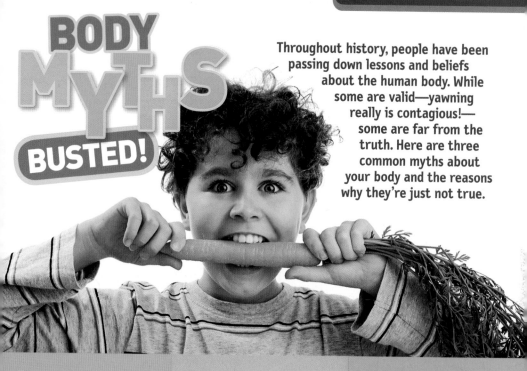

Throughout history, people have been passing down lessons and beliefs about the human body. While some are valid—yawning really is contagious!—some are far from the truth. Here are three common myths about your body and the reasons why they're just not true.

MYTH 1
Eating carrots improves your eyesight.

HOW IT STARTED
Legend has it that during World War II, British soldiers claimed to have excellent night vision because they consumed carrots. It was actually because of radar—the carrot bit was just used to confuse the Germans.

WHY IT'S NOT TRUE
Carrots do offer a high dose of vitamin A, which helps you maintain healthy eyesight. But eating extra of the orange veggies won't make you see better—only glasses can do that.

MYTH 2
Humans use only 10 percent of their brain.

HOW IT STARTED
In 1907, psychologist William James suggested that we only use a small part of our "mental and physical resources," which may have led to the 10 percent figure.

WHY IT'S NOT TRUE
Whether you're aware of it or not, your brain is firing on four cylinders almost all of the time—otherwise, you would stop breathing. Your brain activity slows when you're in a deep sleep or under anesthesia.

MYTH 3
If your ears are burning, someone is talking about you.

HOW IT STARTED
Ancient Romans believed that certain physical signs—including ringing or burning ears—were signs that someone outside of earshot was chatting about you.

WHY IT'S NOT TRUE
Outside of having a sixth sense or bionic hearing, it's impossible to know when your name is coming up in someone else's conversation when you can't actually hear or see them talking. Besides, burning ears are usually a sign of sickness, sunburn, or overheating.

Your Amazing
eyes

Discover the magic of your body's built-in cameras.

You carry around a pair of cameras in your head so incredible they can work in bright sunshine or at night. Only about an inch (2.5 cm) in diameter, they can bring you the image of a tiny ant or a twinkling star trillions of miles away. They can change focus almost instantly and stay focused even when you're shaking your head or jumping up and down. These cameras are your eyes.

A CRUCIAL PART OF YOUR EYE IS AS FLIMSY AS A WET TISSUE.

A dragonfly darts toward your head! Light bounces off the insect, enters your eye, passes through your pupil (the black circle in the middle of your iris), and goes to the lens. The lens focuses the light onto your retina—a thin lining on the back of your eye that is vital but is as flimsy as a wet tissue. Your retina acts like film in a camera, capturing the picture of this dragonfly. The picture is sent to your brain, which instantly sends you a single command—*duck!*

YOU BLINK MORE THAN 10,000 TIMES A DAY.

Your body has many ways to protect and care for your eyes. Each eye sits on a cushion of fat, almost completely surrounded by protective bone. Your eyebrows help prevent sweat from dripping into your eyes. Your eyelashes help keep dust and other small particles out. Your eyelids act as built-in windshield wipers, spreading tear fluid with every blink to keep your eyes moist

and wash away bacteria and other particles. And if anything ever gets too close to your eyes, your eyelids slam shut with incredible speed—in two-fifths of a second—to protect them!

YOUR EYES SEE EVERYTHING UPSIDE DOWN AND BACKWARD!

As amazing as your eyes are, the images they send your brain are a little quirky: They're upside down, backward, and two-dimensional! Your brain automatically flips the images from your retinas right side up and combines the images from each eye into a three-dimensional picture. There is a small area of each retina, called a blind spot, that can't record what you're seeing. Luckily your brain makes adjustments for this, too.

YOUR PUPILS CHANGE SIZE WHENEVER THE LIGHT CHANGES.

Your black pupils may be small, but they have an important job—they grow or shrink to let just the right amount of light enter your eyes to let you see.

THE EYEBALL'S TOUGH OUTER LAYERS, THE **CORNEA (1)** AND **SCLERA (2)**, GIVE IT STRENGTH.

THE COLORED **IRIS** ABSORBS BRIGHT LIGHT.

THE **PUPIL** EXPANDS AND CONTRACTS TO LET IN THE AMOUNT OF LIGHT NEEDED TO SEE.

THE **LENS**, WITH THE CORNEA, FOCUSES LIGHT.

COLORLESS, JELLYLIKE **VITREOUS HUMOR** FILLS THE EYEBALL, HELPING TO HOLD ITS SHAPE.

A MILLION FIBERS IN THE **OPTIC NERVE** CONNECT THE EYE TO THE BRAIN.

THE **RETINA** CHANGES LIGHT RAYS INTO ELECTRICAL SIGNALS SENT TO THE BRAIN.

What Your FAVORITE COLOR Says About YOU

Your favorite color can say a lot about you. Researchers say that we have two basic responses to color: physical (red can make you hot) and emotional (yellow can make you happy). These responses, as well as what some colors represent historically, mean fave colors may reflect your personality. Just for fun, see how colors may affect your mood. Feeling blue? Maybe grab some yellow! *If these personality profiles don't match you, that's okay. These are just for fun!*

ORANGE
can represent energy and warmth. It can also make you hungry and boost your health.

IF YOU LIKE ORANGE, YOU . . . are a nice person who's rarely sick. When you're not cooking or eating, you're outside enjoying the sun.

PINK
can represent health and love.

IF YOU LIKE PINK, YOU . . . are cheerful and always look out for your friends. You have no problem speaking your mind, and you express your feelings well.

RED
can represent danger. It can also excite the senses and activate blood circulation.

IF YOU LIKE RED, YOU . . . are energetic and like taking risks. Very aware of what's going on around you, you are a leader who's not afraid to speak up.

YELLOW
can represent victory. It can also help you be more organized and optimistic.

IF YOU LIKE YELLOW, YOU . . . are a positive person who likes cheering people up. Your competitiveness and organizational skills help you succeed.

PURPLE
can represent wealth or royalty. It's also associated with art and music.

IF YOU LIKE PURPLE, YOU . . . have great taste in anything from clothes to music to food, which you always share with your friends. You are also very creative.

BLUE
can represent peace and loyalty. It's also a universally popular color.

IF YOU LIKE BLUE, YOU . . . are well liked by everyone. People come to you with their problems, and you do what you can to make sure everyone gets along.

GREEN
can represent nature and growth. It may also calm people down.

IF YOU LIKE GREEN, YOU . . . spend a lot of time outside and like doing new things. You're very mellow and easygoing, never taking things too seriously.

Bet you didn't know

Some people **CAN HEAR** their eyeballs moving.

You can get a **SUNBURN** on your **eyes.**

The more you **CONCENTRATE**, the less you **BLINK.**

Your Amazing
brain

Inside your body's supercomputer

Y ou carry around a three-pound (1.4-kg) mass of wrinkly material in your head that controls every single thing you will ever do. From enabling you to think, learn, create, and feel emotions to controlling every blink, breath, and heartbeat—this fantastic control center is your brain. It is a structure so amazing that a famous scientist once called it the "most complex thing we have yet discovered in our universe."

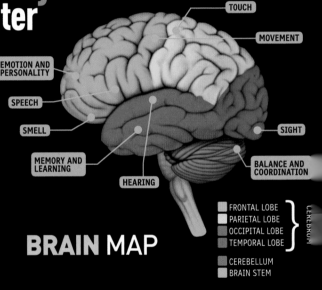

TOUCH

MOVEMENT

EMOTION AND PERSONALITY

SPEECH

SMELL

SIGHT

MEMORY AND LEARNING

BALANCE AND COORDINATION

HEARING

BRAIN MAP

■ FRONTAL LOBE
■ PARIETAL LOBE
■ OCCIPITAL LOBE
■ TEMPORAL LOBE

CEREBRUM

■ CEREBELLUM
■ BRAIN STEM

THE BIG QUESTION

WHAT TAKES UP TWO-THIRDS OF YOUR BRAIN'S WEIGHT AND ALLOWS YOU TO SWIM, EAT, AND SPEAK?

Answer: The huge hunk of your brain called the cerebrum. It's definitely the biggest part of the brain. It houses the centers for memory, the senses, movement, and emotion, among other things.

The cerebrum is made up of two hemispheres—the right and the left. Each side controls the muscles of the opposite side of the body.

All About YOU

AN AVERAGE KID'S BRAIN WEIGHS AS MUCH AS...

66 PERCENT OF ONE OF THE CROWNS WORN BY THE QUEEN OF ENGLAND

26 iPOD NANOS

ABOUT 700 GUMMY BEARS

3,823 BLUE MORPHO BUTTERFLIES

.0000008956 PERCENT OF A CRUISE SHIP

A VERY YOUNG SIBERIAN TIGER CUB

AN INDIAN FLYING FOX

.000008309 PERCENT OF THE ST. LOUIS GATEWAY ARCH IN MISSOURI

A PAIR OF GLOVES WORN BY ASTRONAUTS ON A SPACE WALK

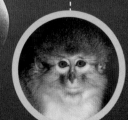

ONE TALAPOIN MONKEY

It would take **31,400** **10-year-olds' brains** TO EQUAL THE WEIGHT OF A **sperm whale.**

* Based on an average 10-year-old kid's 3-pound (1.4 kg) brain. All other numbers also based on averages.

Get Fit!

Try to work an hour of physical activity into each day. Whether you choose to play sports, go for a hike, or ride your bike, make your exercise exciting by switching things up and trying new ways to stay fit.

Exercise is awesome! Here's why:
• It makes you stronger and fitter.
• It makes you healthier.
• It makes you happier.

Ways to work out without even knowing it!

HOOF IT. Walk or bike short distances instead of riding in a car.

DO YARD WORK. Activities like gardening, mowing the lawn, and even shoveling snow are all great ways to burn calories—plus the fresh air is good for you!

STEP IT UP. Take the stairs instead of the elevators or escalators.

STICK TOGETHER. Get your friends and family together for a run, walk, or bike ride.

10 Tips for a Germ-Free School Year

Follow these tips and you might score a perfect attendance record this year!

1 **Wash your hands** with soap and water after you sneeze, cough, or use the bathroom. Count to 20 or sing a couple of rounds of "Row, Row, Row Your Boat" while you scrub!

2 **Use an alcohol-based hand sanitizer** if soap and water aren't available.

3 **Use a tissue** when you need to sneeze or cough. Throw your tissues in the trash.

4 **Take a multivitamin** every day.

5 **Don't share water bottles,** drinks, or even earbuds. That's a quick way to pick up bacteria from your friends.

6 **Stay home** from school, sports practice, and parties if you feel sick or have a fever.

7 **Eat lots of fruits and vegetables.** A healthy diet can help boost your immune system and help you fight off illnesses before they make you sick!

8 **Sleep eight or more hours** every night. A strong body will help you fend off infections.

9 **Blow kisses to your sick family** and friends instead of giving kisses and hugs.

10 **Get a flu shot** if your doctor or school recommends it.

Let's Jump!

NATIONAL GEOGRAPHIC KIDS BREAKS
GUINNESS WORLD RECORD!

So you may not live in the White House. But that doesn't mean you can't have as much fun as the First Lady of the United States. If you participated in NATIONAL GEOGRAPHIC KIDS' latest Guinness World Records attempt, that's exactly what you did!

NG KIDS readers have set the Guinness World Record for the most people doing jumping jacks in a 24-hour time period. Between October 11, 2011, and October 12, 2011, 300,265 people in 1,050 locations did one minute of jumping jacks to be counted for the record. How much do you rock? The previous record was only 20,425!

First Lady Michelle Obama kicked off the 24-hour time period, leading 464 kids in one minute of jumping jacks at the White House. "The whole world is going to see how much fun we can have not just breaking a world record but also doing some exercise," she said. The record attempt was in support of Mrs. Obama's Let's Move initiative, which is all about moving, staying active, and eating healthy.

Even though the record's over, there's still lots you can do to stay healthy and active. Who knows—you might set a record of your own!

JUMPING JACKS
AROUND THE WORLD!

People jumped in the United Kingdom, Kazakhstan, Republic of Congo, Singapore, Australia, Argentina, and more!

FRANCE

SOUTH AFRICA

CALIFORNIA

THE UNIVERSE BEGAN WITH A BIG BANG

Clear your mind for a minute and try to imagine this: All the things you see in the universe today—all the stars, galaxies, and planets—are not yet out there. Everything that now exists is concentrated in a single, incredibly hot, dense state that scientists call a singularity. Then, suddenly, the basic elements that make up the universe flash into existence. Scientists say that actually happened about 13.7 billion years ago, in the moment we call the big bang.

For centuries scientists, religious scholars, poets, and philosophers have wondered how the universe came to be. Was it always there? Will it always be the same, or will it change? If it had a beginning, will it someday end, or will it go on forever?

These are huge questions. But today, because of recent observations of space and what it's made of, we think we may have some of the answers. Everything we can see or detect around us in the universe began with the big bang. We know the big bang created not only matter but also space itself. And scientists think that in the very distant future, stars will run out of fuel and burn out. Once again the universe will become dark.

COOL CLICK

Go online for more information on the origins of the universe.
science.nationalgeographic.com/science/space/
universe/origins-universe-article.html

EARLY LIFE ON EARTH

About 3.5 billion years ago Earth was covered by one gigantic reddish ocean. The color came from hydrocarbons.

The first life-forms on Earth were Archaea that were able to live without oxygen. They released large amounts of methane gas into an atmosphere that would have been poisonous to us.

About 3 billion years ago erupting volcanoes linked together to form larger landmasses. And a new form of life appeared—cyanobacteria, the first living things that used energy from the sun.

Some 2 billion years ago the cyanobacteria algae filled the air with oxygen, killing off the methane-producing Archaea. Colored pools of greenish-brown plant life floated on the oceans. The oxygen revolution that would someday make human life possible was now under way.

About 530 million years ago the Cambrian explosion occurred. It's called an explosion because it's the time when most major animal groups first appeared in our fossil records. Back then, Earth was made up of swamps, seas, a few active volcanoes, and oceans teeming with strange life.

More than 450 million years ago life began moving from the oceans onto dry land. About 200 million years later dinosaurs began to appear. They would dominate life on Earth for more than 150 million years.

PLANETS

CERES

MARS

EARTH

VENUS

MERCURY

JUPITER

SUN

MERCURY
Average distance from the sun:
35,980,000 miles (57,900,000 km)
Position from the sun in orbit: first
Equatorial diameter: 3,030 miles (4,878 km)
Mass (Earth = 1): 0.055
Density (Water = 1): 5.43
Length of day: 58 Earth days
Length of year: 88 Earth days
Surface temperatures: -300°F (-184°C)
to 800°F (427°C)
Known moons: 0

VENUS
Average distance from the sun:
67,230,000 miles (108,200,000 km)
Position from the sun in orbit: second
Equatorial diameter: 7,520 miles (12,100 km)
Mass (Earth = 1): 0.815
Density (Water = 1): 5.25
Length of day: 243 Earth days
Length of year: 225 Earth days
Average surface temperature: 864°F (462°C)
Known moons: 0

EARTH
Average distance from the sun:
93,000,000 miles (149,600,000 km)
Position from the sun in orbit: third
Equatorial diameter: 7,900 miles (12,750 km)
Mass (Earth = 1): 1
Density (Water = 1): 5.52
Length of day: 24 hours
Length of year: 365 days
Surface temperatures: -126°F (-88°C)
to 136°F (58°C)
Known moons: 1

MARS
Average distance from the sun:
141,633,000 miles (227,936,000 km)
Position from the sun in orbit: fourth
Equatorial diameter: 4,333 miles (6,794 km)
Mass (Earth = 1): 0.107
Density (Water = 1): 3.93
Length of day: 25 Earth hours
Length of year: 1.88 Earth years
Surface temperatures: -270°F (-168°C)
to 80°F (27°C)
Known moons: 2

The **planet Mercury** is made mostly of **iron.**

This artwork shows the 13 planets and dwarf planets that astronomers now recognize in our solar system. The relative sizes and positions of the planets are shown but not the relative distances between them. Many of the planets closest to Earth can be seen without a telescope in the night sky.

FOR INFORMATION ABOUT DWARF PLANETS, SEE P. 142.

SATURN

URANUS

NEPTUNE

PLUTO

HAUMEA

MAKEMAKE

ERIS

JUPITER
Average distance from the sun:
483,682,000 miles (778,412,000 km)
Position from the sun in orbit: sixth
Equatorial diameter: 88,840 miles (142,980 km)
Mass (Earth = 1): 318
Density (Water = 1): 1.3
Length of day: 9.9 Earth hours
Length of year: 11.9 Earth years
Average surface temperature: -235°F (-148°C)
Known moons: 64*

SATURN
Average distance from the sun:
890,800,000 miles (1,433,500,000 km)
Position from the sun in orbit: seventh
Equatorial diameter: 74,900 miles (120,540 km)
Mass (Earth = 1): 95
Density (Water = 1): 0.71
Length of day: 10 Earth hours
Length of year: 29.46 Earth years
Average surface temperature: -218°F (-139°C)
Known moons: at least 62*

URANUS
Average distance from the sun:
1,784,000,000 miles (2,870,970,000 km)
Position from the sun in orbit: eighth
Equatorial diameter: 31,760 miles (51,120 km)
Mass (Earth = 1): 15
Density (Water = 1): 1.24
Length of day: 17.9 Earth hours
Length of year: 84 Earth years
Average surface temperature: -323°F (-197°C)
Known moons: 27

NEPTUNE
Average distance from the sun:
2,795,000,000 miles (4,498,250,000 km)
Position from the sun in orbit: ninth
Equatorial diameter: 30,775 miles (49,528 km)
Mass (Earth = 1): 17
Density (Water = 1): 1.67
Length of day: 16 Earth hours
Length of year: 164.8 Earth years
Average surface temperature: -353°F (-214°C)
Known moons: 13

*INCLUDES PROVISIONAL MOONS

DWARF PLANETS

Haumea

Eris

Thanks to advanced technology, scientists have been spotting many never-before-seen celestial bodies at the other end of their telescopes. One new discovery? Three bright space rocks found near Pluto, which may soon be classified as new dwarf planets. Usually smaller than Mercury and round in shape, dwarf planets lack the gravitational strength to sweep all debris out of their solar orbits. So, while regular planets orbit in a clear path around the sun, a dwarf planet also orbits other objects near it, such as asteroids.

Officially, scientists recognize five dwarf planets: Pluto, Ceres, Haumea, Makemake, and Eris. And in addition to the trio of space rocks near Pluto, there are hundreds—perhaps even thousands—of objects in the outer reaches of the solar system out there that may be added to that list. So as time and technology advance, the dwarf planet family could continue to grow.

CERES
Position from the sun in orbit: fifth
Length of day: 9.1 Earth hours
Length of year: 4.6 Earth years
Known moons: 0

PLUTO
Position from the sun in orbit: tenth
Length of day: 6.4 Earth days
Length of year: 248 Earth years
Known moons: 4

HAUMEA
Position from the sun in orbit: eleventh
Length of day: 4 Earth hours
Length of year: 284 Earth years
Known moons: 2

MAKEMAKE
Position from the sun in orbit: twelfth
Length of day: unknown
Length of year: 307 Earth years
Known moons: 0

ERIS
Position from the sun in orbit: thirteenth
Length of day: less than 8 Earth hours
Length of year: 557 Earth years
Known moons: 1

THE SUN

The sun is a star that is about 4.6 billion years old. As the anchor that holds our solar system together, it provides the energy necessary for life to flourish on Earth. It accounts for 99 percent of the matter in the solar system. The rest of the planets, moons, asteroids, and comets added together amount to the remaining one percent.

Even though a million Earths could fit inside the sun, it is still considered an average-size star. Betelgeuse (BET-el-jooz), the star on the shoulder of the constellation known as Orion, is almost 400 times larger.

A BIG BALL OF GAS

Like other stars, the sun is a giant ball of hydrogen gas radiating heat and light through nuclear fusion—a process by which the sun converts about four million tons (3,628,739 t) of matter to energy every second.

Also like other stars, the sun revolves around its galaxy. Located halfway out in one of the arms of the Milky Way galaxy, the sun takes 225 to 250 million years to complete one revolution around the galaxy.

The sun is composed of about 74 percent hydrogen, 25 percent helium, and one percent trace elements like iron, carbon, lead, and uranium. These trace elements provide us with amazing insight into the history of our star. They're the heavier elements that are produced when stars explode. Since these elements are relatively abundant in the sun, scientists know our sun was forged from materials that came together in two previous star explosions. All of the elements found in the sun, on Earth, and in our bodies were recycled from those two exploding stars.

OUR AMAZING SUN

When viewed from space by astronauts, the sun burns white in color. But when we see it from Earth, through our atmosphere, it looks yellow.

Solar flares—explosions of charged particles—sometimes erupt from the sun's surface. They create beautiful aurora displays on Earth, Jupiter, Saturn, and even distant Uranus and Neptune.

We know that the sun makes life possible here on Earth. We couldn't survive without it.

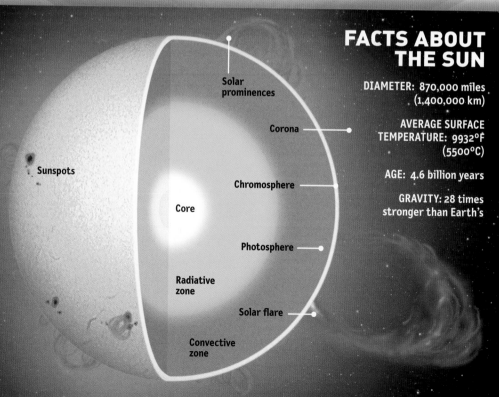

FACTS ABOUT THE SUN

Solar prominences

Corona

Chromosphere

Photosphere

Solar flare

Convective zone

Radiative zone

Core

Sunspots

DIAMETER: 870,000 miles (1,400,000 km)

AVERAGE SURFACE TEMPERATURE: 9932°F (5500°C)

AGE: 4.6 billion years

GRAVITY: 28 times stronger than Earth's

143

Sky Calendar
2013

Horsehead Nebula

Leonid meteor shower

Milky Way

January 1–5 Quadrantids Meteor Shower Peak. View up to 40 meteors per hour.

April 25 Partial Lunar Eclipse. Visible in most of Africa, Asia, Europe, and Australia.

April 28 Saturn at Opposition. Saturn is at its closest approach to Earth.

May 10 Annular Solar Eclipse. A partial eclipse can be seen in Western Australia and the Central Pacific.

May 28 Conjunction of Venus and Jupiter. Look west near sunset to view these two planets come within one degree of each other.

July 28–29 Southern Delta Aquarids Meteor Shower Peak. View up to 20 meteors per hour.

August 12–13 Perseids Meteor Shower Peak. One of the best! Up to 60 meteors per hour.

August 27 Neptune at Opposition. The blue planet will be at its closest approach to Earth. Because Neptune is so far away, binoculars or a telescope are recommended for viewing. Unless you have a very powerful telescope, Neptune will appear as a small blue dot.

October 3 Uranus at Opposition. Uranus will be at its closest approach to Earth. Because the planet is so far away, binoculars or a tele-scope are recommended for viewing. Unless you

have a very powerful telescope, Uranus will appear as a small blue-green dot.

October 21–22 Orionids Meteor Shower Peak. View up to 20 meteors per hour.

November 3 Hybrid Solar Eclipse. This eclipse will begin off the East Coast of the United States and travel east across the Atlantic and Central Africa. It will begin as a partial eclipse and change to a total eclipse as it travels.

November 17–18 Leonid Meteor Shower Peak. View up to 15 meteors per hour.

December 13–15 Geminids Meteor Shower Peak. A spectacular show! Up to 60 multicolored meteors an hour.

Dates may vary slightly depending on your location. Check with a local planetarium for the best viewing time in your area.

SOLAR AND LUNAR ECLIPSES

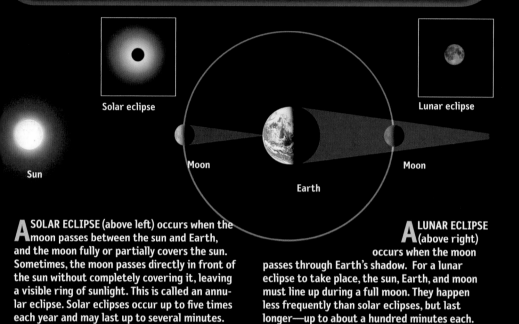

Solar eclipse

Sun

Moon

Earth

Lunar eclipse

Moon

A SOLAR ECLIPSE (above left) occurs when the moon passes between the sun and Earth, and the moon fully or partially covers the sun. Sometimes, the moon passes directly in front of the sun without completely covering it, leaving a visible ring of sunlight. This is called an annular eclipse. Solar eclipses occur up to five times each year and may last up to several minutes.

A LUNAR ECLIPSE (above right) occurs when the moon passes through Earth's shadow. For a lunar eclipse to take place, the sun, Earth, and moon must line up during a full moon. They happen less frequently than solar eclipses, but last longer—up to about a hundred minutes each.

The Big Dipper is part of the constellation commonly known as the Great Bear.

SKY DREAMS

L ONG AGO, people looking at the sky noticed that some stars made shapes and patterns. By playing connect-the-dots, they imagined people and animals in the sky. Their legendary heroes and monsters were pictured in the stars.

Today, we call the star patterns identified by the ancient Greeks and Romans "constellations." There are 88 constellations in all. Some are only visible when you're north of the Equator, and some only when you're south of it.

In the 16th-century age of exploration, European ocean voyagers began visiting southern lands. and they named the constellations

that are visible in the Southern Hemisphere, such as the Southern Cross. Astronomers used the star observations of these navigators to fill in the blank spots on their celestial maps.

Constellations aren't fixed in the sky. The star arrangement that makes up each one would look different from another location in the universe. Constellations also change over time because every star we see is moving through space. Over thousands of years, the stars in the Big Dipper, which is part of the larger constellation Ursa Major (the Great Bear), will move so far apart that the dipper pattern will disappear.

CONSTELLATIONS

Nothing to do on a clear night? Look up! There's so much to see in that starry sky. The constellations you can see among the stars vary with the season. As the following maps show, some are more visible in the winter and spring, while others can be spotted in the summer and fall.

Looking for constellations in the Southern Hemisphere? Go online. sydneyobservatory .com.au/blog/?cat=10

COOL CLICK

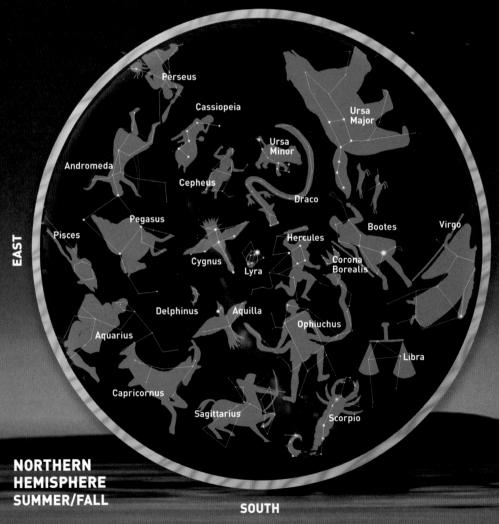

NORTH

NORTHERN HEMISPHERE SUMMER/FALL

SOUTH

EAST

Perseus
Cassiopeia
Ursa Major
Ursa Minor
Andromeda
Cepheus
Draco
Pegasus
Bootes
Virgo
Pisces
Hercules
Cygnus
Corona Borealis
Lyra
Delphinus
Aquilla
Ophiuchus
Aquarius
Libra
Capricornus
Sagittarius
Scorpio

Planet or Star?

On a clear night, you'll see a sky filled with glittering lights. But not every bright spot is a star—you may be peeking at a planet, too. How to tell a star from a planet? While stars twinkle, planets shine more steadily and tend to be the brightest objects in the sky, other than the moon. Planets also move across the sky from night to night. If you think you've spotted one, keep checking on it as the week goes by. Has it moved closer or farther away from the moon? Then it's probably a planet.

WANT TO SPOT A SATELLITE? Look for an **OBJECT** that travels quickly and steadily among **THE STARS.**

NORTH

Cepheus

Draco

Cassiopea

Ursa Minor

Andromeda

Bootes

Perseus

Ursa Major

Auriga

Aries

Virgo

Gemini

Taurus

Leo

Cancer

Canis Minor

Orion

Crater

Canis Major

Hydra

EAST

WEST

SOUTH

NORTHERN HEMISPHERE WINTER/SPRING

147

Continents on the Move

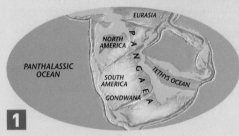

1

PANGAEA About 240 million years ago, Earth's landmasses were joined together in one supercontinent that extended from pole to pole.

2

BREAKUP By 94 million years ago, Pangaea had broken apart into landmasses that would become today's continents. Dinosaurs roamed Earth during a period of warmer climates.

3

EXTINCTION About 65 million years ago, an asteroid smashed into Earth, creating the Gulf of Mexico. This impact may have resulted in the extinction of half the world's species, including the dinosaurs. This was one of several major mass extinctions.

4

ICE AGE By 18,000 years ago, the continents had drifted close to their present positions, but most far northern and far southern lands were buried beneath huge glaciers.

A LOOK INSIDE

The distance from Earth's surface to its center is 3,963 miles (6,378 km). There are four layers: a thin, rigid crust; the rocky mantle; the outer core, which is a layer of molten iron; and finally the inner core, which is believed to be solid iron.

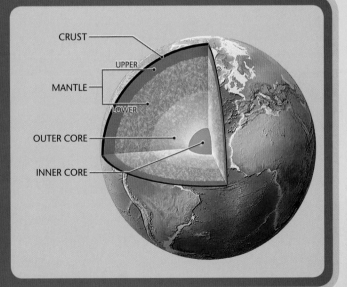

CRUST

UPPER

MANTLE

LOWER

OUTER CORE

INNER CORE

ROCK STARS

The world is full of rocks. Some big, some small, some formed deep beneath the Earth, and some starting at the surface. While they may look similar, not all rocks are created equally. Look closely, and you'll see differences between every boulder, stone, and pebble. Here's more about the three top varieties of rocks.

Igneous

Named for the Greek word meaning "from fire," igneous rocks form when hot, molten liquid called magma cools. Pools of magma form deep underground and slowly work their way to the Earth's surface. If they make it all the way, the liquid rock erupts and is called lava. As the layers of lava build up they form a mountain called a volcano. Some typical igneous rocks include obsidian, basalt, and pumice, which is so chock full of gas bubbles that it actually floats in water.

OBSIDIAN   PUMICE

Metamorphic

Like their name suggests, metamorphic rocks are the masters of change! These rocks were once igneous or sedimentary, but thanks to intense heat and pressure deep within the Earth, they have undergone a total transformation from their original form. These rocks never truly melt; instead, the heat twists and bends them until their shapes substantially change. Metamorphic rocks include slate and marble, which is used for buildings, monuments, and sculptures.

MARBLE   SLATE

Sedimentary

When wind, water, and ice constantly wear away and weather rocks, smaller pieces called sediment are left behind. These are sedimentary rocks, also known as gravel, sand, silt, and clay. As water flows downhill it carries the sedimentary grains into lakes and oceans, where they get deposited. As the loose sediment piles up, the grains eventually get compacted or cemented back together again. The result is new sedimentary rock. Sandstone, gypsum, and shale are sedimentary rocks that have formed this way.

SANDSTONE   GYPSUM

It's a Rocky World!

ROCKS AND MINERALS CAN BE FOUND **IN A WIDE RANGE** of different environments. In addition to being useful materials, they also give scientists clues to how our world has changed over time.

GRANITE Plutonic igneous rock rich in quartz and feldspar. It is a hard rock used as a building stone and for monuments.

GYPSUM Sedimentary rock that forms from the evaporation of mineral-rich water.

FOSSILS IN SHALE (ferns) Shale is a fine-grained sedimentary rock made from compacted mud. It often contains fossils of extinct organisms.

SANDSTONE Sedimentary rock that forms when sand grains get cemented back together again.

BASALT The most common type of igneous rock, basalts form most of the Earth's crust under the ocean.

OLIVINE This group of greenish minerals is found mainly in dark-colored igneous rocks such as basalt, peridotite, and gabbro.

BERYL Commonly found in pegmatite and schist. Well-formed green beryl crystals are also known as emeralds.

TOURMALINE Commonly found in both igneous and metamorphic rocks.

SULFUR AND SALT CRYSTALS They give the crater of Dallol volcano in Ethiopia its unique color.

FELDSPAR Like quartz, feldspar can be found in all three major rock types.

FLUORITE Most often found in igneous and meta-morphic rocks.

NATIVE COPPER This soft metal forms with basalt in hydrothermal vents near volcanoes.

151

Birthstones

In the past, people believed that certain gems brought good luck to those people born in different months and that these gems stood for special qualities in a person. The chart on the left lists the primary birthstone for each month as well as the unique character trait that it represents in a person.

MONTH		STONE	CHARACTER TRAIT
1 January		Garnet	Constancy
2 February		Amethyst	Sincerity
3 March		Aquamarine	Courage
4 April		Diamond	Innocence
5 May		Emerald	Love and Success
6 June		Moonstone	Health and Longevity
7 July		Ruby	Contentment
8 August		Peridot	Married Happiness
9 September		Sapphire	Clear Thinking
10 October		Pink Tourmaline	Hope
11 November		Citrine	Fidelity
12 December		Blue Topaz	Prosperity

Match Game

How's your eye at spotting a gemstone? Can you tell what your birthstone looks like before it is cut and polished? In the column to the left are the twelve birthstones the way they would look in a jewelry store. Below are the same 12 gems as they appear in nature. See if you can match the finished stone with its natural counterpart.

A B

G H

A lapidary uses a polishing wheel to finish a gemstone.

Cutting and Polishing

Gemstones in the field hardly ever look like a gem. Instead they usually look dull, with rough edges, and often resemble plain, ordinary rocks. Before a gemstone can be considered a gem, it usually has to be worked. A lapidary is the person who cuts, polishes, and engraves stones in order to make them look more attractive.

C D E F

I J K L

ANSWERS: 1E, 2K, 3C, 4I, 5A, 6G, 7F, 8L, 9D, 10J, 11B, 12H

COOL inventions

ROBOT DELIVERY

In 20 years, you might be able to walk back from the mall without carrying a bunch of bags, or go to the airport without lugging suitcases. The Cargonaut—just a concept for now—is a human-size robot that flies around picking up and delivering personal items. Containers called skyboxes would be available at Cargonaut locations in malls, airports, and hotels. To ship something ahead, you find a station, place your stuff inside a skybox, and punch in the Cargonaut location closest to your destination. That's where you pick up your package. The Cargonaut flies above the tops of buildings carrying your cargo. Meanwhile, your hands are free for more important tasks—like texting your friends about where you're off to next.

SPY PHONE

Even if you're not quite ready to join the CIA or Secret Service, you can still feel as stealthy as a spy. The MW2 is a watch that doubles as a cell phone. When you need to make a call—whether to phone in an important clue, or just to complain about your little brother's latest antics—simply dial the number on the MW2's keypad (or use the onscreen buttons), slyly lift your hand toward your mouth, and start talking. Your subjects will never know you're on the phone at all. They'll just think you're checking the time.

CLEVER
DOG WALKER

You just got home after a long day at school, and your restless four-legged friend is barking and running laps around your room. But it's cold and rainy, and the last thing you feel like doing is taking him for a walk. Relax. Lead your canine pal onto this JOG A DOG doggie treadmill, slowly turn the speed dial on the remote control to get things moving, and wait for him to work up to a trot. Fido gets a workout, and you stay dry.

SPACESHIP
FOR
TOURISTS

Prepare for liftoff! In the near future, you could be rocketing out of this world on Virgin Galactic's SpaceShip Two shuttle, the first to offer tourist trips to outer space. Leaving from a spaceport in New Mexico, an aircraft called the WhiteKnight Two will carry SpaceShip Two on its belly, taking off like a plane and climbing to 50,000 feet (15 km). At this height, the spaceship will drop off, turn upward, and zoom into space at a blazing 3,000 miles (4,828 km) an hour. Once you reach the starry blackness, you'll be able to see the curvature of the Earth below while you float weightless through the cabin. After hurtling in orbit for a while, the spaceship will turn and head back to Earth, touching down like a regular plane. It'll be a two-hour adventure of a lifetime.

SPACE Robots

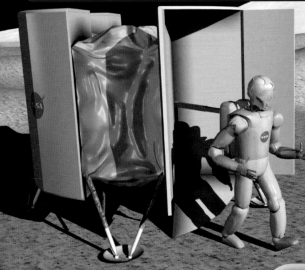

SOMEDAY YOU MIGHT CONTROL AN AVATAR ON THE MOON.

Robot avatars may one day be handy companions to space travelers, whether they're as far away as Mars or as close as a space station or moon base. Though still a concept, robonauts, controlled remotely by humans, are expected to be a huge help to astronauts. "Our goal is for robots to work side by side with humans," says NASA's Matt Ondler. "Robonauts will help our astronauts with the three D's: jobs that are dirty, dull, and dangerous."

TO THE MOON

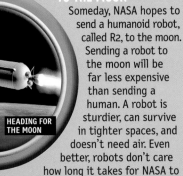

HEADING FOR THE MOON

Someday, NASA hopes to send a humanoid robot, called R2, to the moon. Sending a robot to the moon will be far less expensive than sending a human. A robot is sturdier, can survive in tighter spaces, and doesn't need air. Even better, robots don't care how long it takes for NASA to return them to Earth.

Once on the moon, the robonaut could perform experiments, send live video back to Earth, and explore the lunar surface. R2 will be able to

COLLECTING ROCK SAMPLES

move using legs, or by attaching its torso to a four-wheeled rover and becoming part of the vehicle like a Transformer. And when R2's battery is low, it can plug into a solar-powered recharging station and get some much-needed juice.

AVATARS IN SPACE

The future R2 would be designed to operate by itself. But for delicate and difficult tasks, a human operator would control it like an avatar in a video game. NASA will need people skilled at operating robonauts to ensure the success of future missions. So the next time your mom complains that you're spending too much time on video games, just tell her you're training for a job with NASA!

EXPLORING THE SURFACE

5 WAYS
You Use Satellites

Psst! Want in on a secret? Spaceships control our world! Well, not exactly. But much of the technology you use—TVs, telephones, email—relies on tons of satellites whizzing around Earth. Here's a look at five ways you use satellites.

1 TELEVISION If you've watched TV, then you've used a satellite. Broadcast stations send images from Earth up to satellites as radio waves. The satellite bounces those signals, which can only travel straight, back down to a satellite dish at a point on Earth closer to your house. Satellite transmission works sort of like a shot in a game of pool when you ricochet your ball off the side of the pool table at an angle that sinks it into the right pocket.

2 WEATHER News flash! A severe thunderstorm with dangerous lightning is approaching your town. How do weather forecasters know what's coming so they can warn the public? They use satellites equipped with cameras and infrared sensors to watch clouds. Computers use constantly changing satellite images to track the storm.

3 TELEPHONE As you talk back and forth with a relative overseas on a landline, you might experience a delay of a quarter second—the time it takes for your voices to be relayed by a satellite bounce.

4 EMAIL Satellites also bridge long distances over the Internet by transmitting emails. Communications satellites for phones and the Internet use a geostationary orbit. That means that a satellite's speed matches Earth's rotation exactly, keeping the satellite in the same spot above Earth.

5 GPS Driving you to a party at a friend's house, your dad turns down the wrong street. You're lost. No problem if the car has a global positioning system (GPS) receiver. GPS is a network of satellites. The receiver collects information from the satellites and plots its distance from at least three of them. Using this information, it can show where you are on a digital map. Thanks to satellites, you will make it to the party on time.

HOW A BASIC MOBILE CALL REACHES A FRIEND

You punch in a phone number and press SEND.

Your mobile (cell) phone sends a coded message—a radio signal—to a cellular tower, which transfers the radio signal to a landline wire. From there, the signal travels underground.

The underground signal reaches a switching center; there a computer figures out where the call needs to go next.

Through landlines the message reaches the cell tower nearest the call's destination.

Switched back to a radio signal, the call reaches the person you dialed. Let the talking begin!

WHAT IS THE "CELL" IN CELL PHONE?

A typical cellular, or mobile, tower serves a small area—about ten square miles (26 sq km). That area is called a cell. Whichever cell you are in when you make your call is the cell that picks up your data and sends it on.

SPACE VACATION

3 destinations that are out of this world

How far would you travel to play zero-gravity tag or go on safari to another planet? Here are three out-of-this-world vacations that scientists believe will someday be possible.

DESTINATION 1

The Space Elevator

Press the button for the millionth floor and ride in an elevator 22,000 miles (35,000 km) straight up into space! Propelled by magnetic forces, your elevator car races through the clouds at more than 1,000 miles an hour (1,600 kph) while attached to an amazingly long cable—made of carbon nanotubes 100 times stronger than steel—anchored to a satellite in space. Earth disappears below as you're enveloped in the starry blackness of space. When your elevator ride is over, board a ship to the moon, where you can soar through the sky as you slam dunk a basketball, thanks to low levels of gravity.

DESTINATION 2

A Sightseeing Cruise

Have lots of zero-gravity fun while you cruise to the most fantastic sights in the solar system. Catch extraordinary views of Mars. Continue on to Jupiter, a planet so enormous that if it were hollow, a thousand Earths could fit inside. Stare at Saturn's stunning rings—actually a collection of massive quantities of particles, mostly ice crystals—orbiting the planet. And don't miss spectacular Io, one of Jupiter's many moons. It's covered by lakes and rivers of lava, massive mountains, and volcanoes that spew lava more than 150 miles (240 km) high. Stunning!

DESTINATION **3**

Extreme Martian Adventure

Welcome to the red planet, home to Olympus Mons, the highest mountain in the solar system. It's more than 14 miles (22 km) high. Hike down Valles Marineris, a system of canyons so vast and deep they could swallow several Grand Canyons. When you're ready for more, explore cave systems created by ancient volcanic eruptions. Or visit ice-covered poles on Mars for some unbelievable ski jumping. In the low gravity, you'll sail above the slope for so long you might just think you're flying.

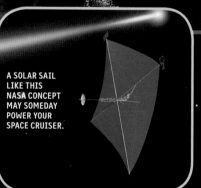

A SOLAR SAIL LIKE THIS NASA CONCEPT MAY SOMEDAY POWER YOUR SPACE CRUISER.

COOL CLICK

To learn more about the future of space travel, go online to NASA's website. nasa.gov

Research Like a Pro

There is so much information on the Internet. How do you find what you need and make sure it's accurate?

Be Specific

To come up with the most effective key-words, write down what you're looking for in the form of a question, and then circle the most important words in that sentence. Those are the keywords to use in your search. And for best results use words that are specific rather than general.

Research

Research on the Internet involves "looking up" information using a search engine (see list below). Type one or two keywords—words that describe what you want to know more about—and the search engine will provide a list of websites that contain information pertinent to your topic.

Trustworthy Sources

When conducting Internet research, be sure the website you use is reliable and the information it provides can be trusted. Sites produced by well-known, established organizations, companies, publications, educational institutions, or the government are your best bet.

Don't Copy

Avoid Internet plagiarism. Take careful notes and cite the websites you use to conduct research (see p. 99 for "Don't Be a Copycat").

HELPFUL AND SAFE SEARCH ENGINES FOR KIDS

Google Safe Search	squirrelnet.com/search/Google_SafeSearch.asp
Yahooligans	kids.yahoo.com
Superkids	super-kids.com
Ask Kids	askkids.com
Kids Click	kidsclick.org
AOL Kids	kids.aol.com

COOL CLICKS

Looking for a good science fair project idea? Go online. sciencebuddies.org. Or read about a science fair success. kids.nationalgeographic.com/stories/spacescience/snowfences

ACE YOUR SCIENCE FAIR

You can learn a lot about science from books, but to really experience it firsthand, you need to get into the lab and "do" some science. Whether you're entering a science fair or just want to learn more on your own, there are many scientific projects you can do. So put on your goggles and lab coat, and start experimenting.

Most likely, the topic of the project will be up to you. So be sure to choose something that you find interesting.

THE BASIS OF ALL SCIENTIFIC INVESTIGATION AND DISCOVERY IS THE SCIENTIFIC METHOD. CONDUCT THE EXPERIMENT USING THESE STEPS:

Observation/Research—Ask a question or identify a problem.

Hypothesis—Once you've asked a question, do some thinking and come up with some possible answers.

Experimentation—How can you determine if your hypothesis is correct? You test it. You perform an experiment. Make sure the experiment you design will produce an answer to your question.

Analysis—Gather your results, and use a consistent process to carefully measure the results.

Conclusion—Do the results support your hypothesis?

Report Your Findings—Communicate your results in the form of a paper that summarizes your entire experiment.

Bonus!

Take your project one step further. Your school may have an annual science fair, but there are also local, state, regional, and national science fair competitions. Compete with other students for awards, prizes, and scholarships!

EXPERIMENT DESIGN
Here are three types of experiments you can do.

MODEL KIT—a display, such as an "erupting volcano" model. Simple and to the point.

DEMONSTRATION—shows the scientific principles in action, such as a tornado in a wind tunnel.

INVESTIGATION—the home run of science projects, and just the type of project for science fairs. This kind demonstrates proper scientific experimentation and uses the scientific method to reveal answers to questions.

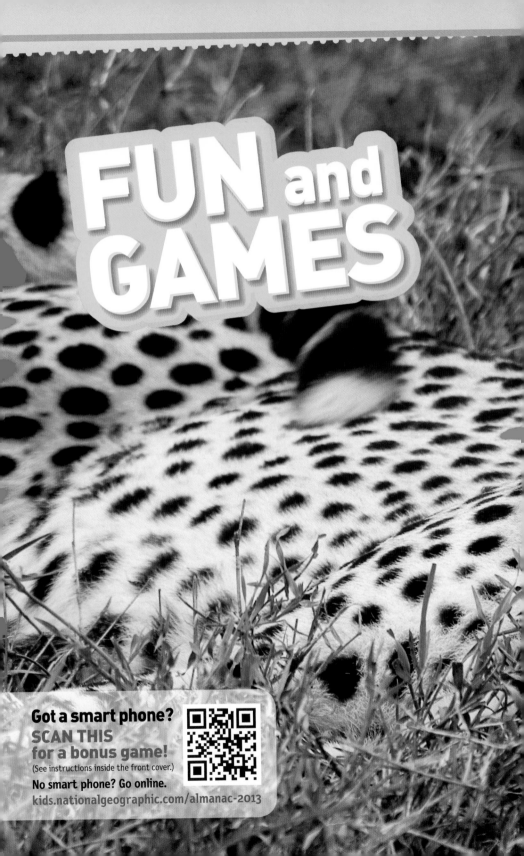

FUN and GAMES

Got a smart phone?
SCAN THIS
for a bonus game!
(See instructions inside the front cover.)

No smart phone? Go online.
kids.nationalgeographic.com/almanac-2013

SPLASH DOWN

START!

Slide your way through this water park without splashing down into the wrong pool. You want to end up in the big wave pool to meet up with your friends. ANSWER ON P. 338

Laugh Out Loud

"MY DOG DELETED MY HOMEWORK FROM MY HARD DRIVE!"

"THANKS, MOM. BUT CAN I SUPERSIZE THAT?"

"KIDS THESE DAYS . . . ALWAYS LOOKING FOR THE EASY WAY OUT!"

Just Joking

Green tree frog

KNOCK, KNOCK.
Who's there?
Annie.
Annie who?
Annie body home?

Q Why did the **police** stake out the baseball field?

A They heard that players were stealing bases.

Q Why couldn't the teddy bear eat his dessert?

A He was stuffed.

You've **got** to be joking...

Q What do you get if **your parakeet** flies into the **blender?**

A Shredded tweet.

CUSTOMER: Waitress! Will my pancakes be long?
WAITRESS: No sir, I expect they'll be round, as usual.

We Gave It a Swirl

Use the clues below to figure out which animals appear in these swirled pictures. ANSWERS ON P. 338

1

HINT! Pink never goes out of style for this leggy creature.

3

HINT! These teddy bear look-alikes aren't really bears.

4

HINT! This gentle giant likes to *moo*-ve in a herd.

2

HINT! Falsely known as a master of camouflage, this animal may actually change color to communicate, not to blend in.

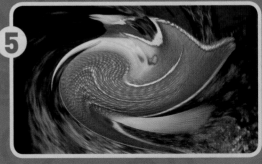

5

HINT! This animal doesn't mind spending its entire life in a school.

A spring rain isn't the only surprise in this town square. Find at least ten things that are wrong in this scene. ANSWERS ON P. 338

169

Just Joking

KNOCK, KNOCK.

Who's there?
Doris.
Doris who?
Doris open.
Come on in.

Gentoo penguin

Q How do you catch a squirrel?

A Climb a tree and act like a nut!

Say this fast three times:

Which **wristwatch** is a **Swiss** **wristwatch?**

Q What did the cheeseburger name its daughter?

A Patty!

Q How do you **communicate** with a fish?

A Drop it a line.

Q Why didn't the duck doctor have any patients?

A Everyone knew he was a quack.

Q Why couldn't **anyone** find the deck **of cards?**

A They got lost in the shuffle.

TONGUE TWISTER!

Say this fast three times:

Friendly Frank flipped five fine flapjacks.

Q What did the **bee say** to the **flower?**

A Hey, bud. When do you open?

171

For even more fun, go online.
kids.nationalgeographic.com/
kids/games/

COOL CLICK

Funny FILL-IN
Movie Madness

Ask someone to give you words to fill in the blanks in this story without showing it to him or her. Then read out loud for a laugh.

I've always wanted to be a famous movie director like ＿＿＿＿＿＿＿＿. So I decided to
famous person

make a home movie called *Pirates of the* ＿＿＿＿＿＿＿＿. The heroes, played by
name of body of water

my friend ＿＿＿＿＿＿ and my ＿＿＿＿＿ pet ＿＿＿＿＿＿, would rescue
friend's name adjective type of bird

a(n) ＿＿＿＿＿＿ treasure from a(n) ＿＿＿＿＿＿ pirate ship. My friends and I
adjective adjective

built a(n) ＿＿＿＿＿ -foot-tall ship out of ＿＿＿＿＿＿＿＿＿＿ and
number item stored in a garage, plural

＿＿＿＿＿＿＿＿＿＿, and glued all of the pieces together with ＿＿＿＿＿＿＿.
object in nature, plural sticky food

As the ship "set sail" in the ＿＿＿＿＿＿＿＿＿ in my ＿＿＿＿＿＿, I looked
something that holds water part of a house

through the lens of my ＿＿＿＿＿＿＿＿ and yelled, "Action!" ＿＿＿＿＿＿＿＿
electronic gadget same friend's name

jumped onto the ship and started battling a(n) ＿＿＿＿＿＿＿ pirate, played by
adjective

＿＿＿＿＿＿＿. Everything went perfectly. I was just about to yell, "Cut!" when we
family member

heard a(n) ＿＿＿＿＿＿ bubbling sound. Suddenly there was ＿＿＿＿＿ everywhere.
adjective liquid

We hadn't noticed that the ＿＿＿＿＿＿＿ had been ＿＿＿＿＿ holes in
same bird as above verb ending in -ing

the ship while we were filming. I tried to plug at least ＿＿＿＿＿ holes with
big number

＿＿＿＿＿＿＿, but it was no use. With a loud ＿＿＿＿＿, the ship started sinking
gooey substance noise

as fast as a(n) ＿＿＿＿＿＿！ My next command? "Abandon ship!"
something heavy

174

SIGNS
OF THE TIMES

Seeing isn't always believing. Two of these funny signs are not real. Can you figure out which two are fake?

ANSWERS ON P. 338

3
DUMP
CLEAN DIRT
HERE ➡
SEE 910

5
45TH
PARALLEL
HALFWAY BETWEEN
THE EQUATOR AND
THE NORTH POLE
PASS
WITH
CARE

4
W 37 ST

1
212
Boring ↗

2
SURFER
X-ING

6
LARGE
WEDGIE
$ 5.99

7
SIGN NOT
IN USE

8
MOLDE BAKERI

9
SLIDE
AREA

What in the World?

ALOHA SPIRIT
These photographs show close-up and faraway views of things you could see in Hawaii. Unscramble the letters to identify what's in each picture.

ANSWERS ON P. 338

EPPIEPLSNA

_____

SELI

_____

TOCNCOU

_____

AIWAAHIN SIRHT

_____

ESA REUTLT

_____

NVLAOOC

_____

DAUSRFOBR

_____

EKUULLE

_____

Scout It Out

The Animal Jam characters want to explore Coral Canyon. Before they head out on their adventure, help them collect their camping gear.

1. backpack
2. compass
3. flashlight
4. map
5. sleeping bag
6. canteen
7. binoculars
8. lantern
9. walkie-talkie
10. first-aid kit
11. hiking boots
12. sunglasses
13. camera
14. climbing rope
15. skillet
16. bicycle

ANSWERS ON P. 338

EXPLORE!

NATIONAL GEOGRAPHIC KIDS' virtual world online.
AnimalJam.com
*see special code below

*Enter the special code
NGKIDSROX for a bonus!
AnimalJam.com

Just Joking

Orca

Q Who helps killer whales that need braces?

A The orca-dontist.

TONGUE TWISTER!

Say this fast three times:

Stu **chews** shoes.

Q What asks **no** **questions** but must be **answered?**

A Doorbell.

Q What happened to the frog that parked illegally?

A He was toad away.

You've **got** to be joking…

Q What does **lightning put on** during **rainy weather?**

A Thunder wear.

Laugh Out Loud

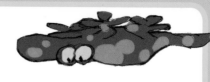

TRY OUR HOPPY MEALS

"I DON'T CARE
IF YOU ARE A GECKO...
YOU CAN'T HANG AROUND
THE HOUSE ALL DAY!"

PEANUT BUTTER
SCHOOL

"OK, SPIKE. IT'S YOUR TURN
TO BE THE DOG!"

The BARGAIN Hunt

YARD SALE TODAY!

FREE PUPPIES TO A GOOD HOME

BOARD GAMES

NO RISK

Find 12 items for sale that start with the letter w.
ANSWERS ON P. 338

180

Funny FILL-IN
Running Wild

Ask someone to give you words to fill in the blanks in this story without showing it to him or her. Then read it out loud for a laugh.

My pet _____ (type of animal) is always getting into trouble. His name is _____ (cartoon character) and all of the neighbors know him. Most days you can find him chewing on _____ (your neighbor's name)'s _____ (something valuable). But I don't know what got into him yesterday. I had just taken him out for his morning _____ (action verb) when a(n) _____ (animal) leaped out from behind a(n) _____ (large object). _____ (same cartoon character) jumped _____ (large number) feet in the air! Then his _____ (something soft) puffed up and he started to _____ (sound made by an animal) really loudly. He took off _____ (verb ending in –ing) at about _____ (large number) miles an hour. Luckily he had stepped in _____ (something mushy) and left a trail of _____ (adjective) _____ (animal body part) prints all the way to the nearest _____ (name of a store). By the time I got there, three _____ (adjective) employees were chasing my _____ (adjective) pet out of the store. The animal was _____ (action verb ending in –ing) down the street with a brand-new pair of _____ (popular sneakers) on his _____ (animal body part). The next thing I knew, he dashed into _____ (name of a restaurant), jumped onto a(n) _____ (furniture), snatched _____ (food, plural) off a customer's plate, and ran out the back door. I thought I had lost him completely when I walked by _____ (another store). There he was, curled up asleep next to a(n) _____ (different animal) in the window. As _____ (adverb ending in –ly) as I could, I clipped on his _____ (noun) and walked him straight to my _____ (building). Boy, was he in the _____ (animal) house!

181

STUMP
YOUR PARENTS

How eco-friendly are your parents? If they can't answer these questions, maybe *they* should take a lesson in going green. ANSWERS ON P. 338

1 Which of these items can be composted, or turned into natural fertilizer, for your garden?

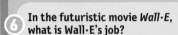

A. eggshells
B. golf balls
C. aluminum foil
D. all of the above

2 What alternative form of transportation does not appear in the Harry Potter book series?

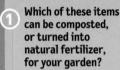

A. a broomstick
B. a hippogriff
C. a skateboard with wings
D. a flying motorcycle

3 What uses the most energy in U.S. homes each year?

A. lighting
B. heating and air-conditioning
C. refrigeration
D. heating water

4 In your lifetime, you will throw away enough trash to fill . . .

A. the Empire State Building.
B. about five trash trucks.
C. six bathtubs.
D. the Grand Canyon.

5 Which of these species is threatened by global warming?

A. koala
B. clownfish
C. arctic fox
D. all of the above

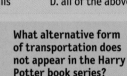

6 In the futuristic movie *Wall·E*, what is Wall·E's job?

A. cleaning up trash left behind by humans
B. planting trees in parks
C. designing eco-friendly tourist destinations
D. sorting bottles at a recycling plant

7 How many degrees has the Earth warmed up in the past 100 years?

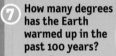

A. 20°F
B. 30°F
C. 1°F
D. 12°F

8 What is most frequently found in beach cleanups?

A. glass
B. pieces of plastic
C. shoes
D. jewelry

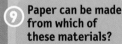

9 Paper can be made from which of these materials?

A. panda droppings
B. hemp
C. wood
D. all of the above

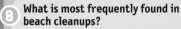
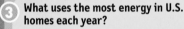

Just for Kicks

GO TIGERS

Have you been in a game like this one? The seven circles below are parts of this crazy scene. Find the spot where each part comes from. ANSWERS ON P. 338

1

7

2 3 4 5 6

Wonders of
Nature

Australia's Great Barrier Reef is a thriving ecosystem that supports more than 1,600 species of fish, such as these orange fairy basslets.

Got a smart phone?
SCAN THIS to experience
the powers of nature!
(See instructions inside the front cover.)

No smart phone? Go online.
kids.nationalgeographic.com/almanac-2013

World Climate

Weather is the condition of the atmosphere—temperature, precipitation, humidity, wind—at a given place at a given time. Climate, however, is the average weather for a particular place over a long period of time. Different places on Earth have different climates, but climate is not a random occurrence. It is a pattern that is controlled by factors such as latitude, elevation, prevailing winds, the temperature of ocean currents, and location on land relative to water. Climate is generally constant, but evidence indicates that human activity is causing a change in the patterns of climate.

Visitors to Norway's Klimapark witness the environmental impact of climate change firsthand. Attractions include an ice tunnel under the Juvfonna ice patch.

GLOBAL CLIMATE ZONES

Climatologists, people who study climate, have created different systems for classifying climates. One often-used system is called the Köppen system, which classifies climate zones according to precipitation, temperature, and vegetation. It has five major categories—Tropical, Dry, Temperate, Cold, and Polar—with a sixth category for locations where high elevations override other factors.

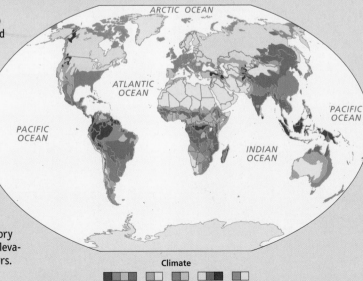

ARCTIC OCEAN

ATLANTIC OCEAN

PACIFIC OCEAN

PACIFIC OCEAN

INDIAN OCEAN

Climate

Tropical Dry Temperate Cold Polar

EXTREME WEATHER

HOTTEST TEMPERATURE ever recorded on Earth: 136°F (57.8°C) in Al'Aziziyah, Libya

COLDEST TEMPERATURE ever recorded on Earth: -128.6°F (-89.2°C) in Vostok Station, Antarctica

HEAVIEST HAIL: 2.25 pounds (1 kg) in Gopalganj District, Bangladesh

MOST RAIN in one hour: 12 inches (30.5 cm) in Holt, Missouri, U.S.A.

Temperature Tips

There are two commonly used temperature scales, **Fahrenheit** (used in the U.S.) and **Celsius** (used in most countries of the world). Although they both measure temperature, the numbers are different. For example, **water freezes at 32°F or 0°C.**

To convert from Fahrenheit to Celsius, subtract 32, then multiply by 5, and divide by 9.

To convert from Celsius to Fahrenheit, multiply by 9, divide by 5, and then add 32.

Example: If water boils at 100°C, and we want to know what temperature that is in Fahrenheit, we'd use the second formula:
100°C x 9 = 900
900 ÷ 5 = 180
180 + 32 = 212°F

CLIMATE CHANGE

Earth's climate history has been a story of ups and downs, with warm periods followed by periods of bitter cold. The early part of the 20th century was marked by colder than average temperatures (see graph below), followed by a period of gradual and then steady increase. Scientists are concerned that the current warming trend is more than a natural cycle. One sign of change is the melting of glaciers in Greenland and Antarctica. If glaciers continue to melt, areas of Florida (shown above in red) and other coastal land will be underwater.

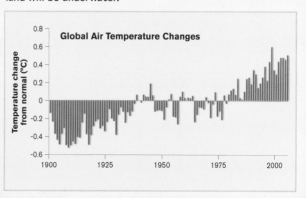

Global Air Temperature Changes

Freaky Weather

Nature can be unbelievably powerful. A major earthquake can topple huge buildings and bring down entire mountainsides. Hurricanes, blizzards, and tornadoes can paralyze major cities. But as powerful as these natural disasters are, here are five other episodes of wacky weather that will really *blow* you away!

1 GAS ATTACK

When a volcano erupts, a glowing sea of lava often flows down its sides, destroying everything in its path. The volcano can also produce a deadly pyroclastic flow, which is a cloud of gas and rock that may reach temperatures above 1,000°F (538°C). The dangerous flow crashes down the side of a volcano like an avalanche, reaching speeds of more than 50 miles an hour (80 kph).

You head outside after a snowstorm and see dozens of log- or drum-shaped snowballs. These rare creations are called snow rollers, formed when wet snow falls on icy ground, so snow can't stick to it. Pushed by strong winds, the snow rolls into logs. Maybe this is nature's way of saying it's time for a snowball fight.

SNOWBALL FACTORY 2

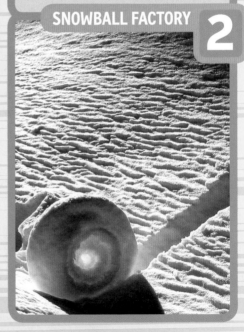

3 MYSTERY WAVES

Imagine you're on an ocean liner when a wall of water ten stories tall races toward you like an unstoppable freight train. It's a rogue wave, also called a freak wave, which can appear without any warning at any time in the open sea. These waves were once considered myths, but scientists now know they are very real—and very dangerous to even the largest ships.

GREAT BALLS OF FIRE 4

During a thunderstorm, a glowing ball the size of your head suddenly appears. It hovers a few feet above the ground, drops down, dances across the yard, and then darts up into the air before it fades away. This freaky phenomenon is ball lightning. Sometimes it disappears with a small explosion. Some scientists think that when normal lightning strikes the ground, it vaporizes a mineral called silicon found in soil. This silicon forms a kind of bubble that burns in the oxygen around it.

5 THE MOTHER OF ALL TORNADOES

The fastest wind speed ever recorded—318 miles (512 km) an hour—occurred during a tornado near Oklahoma City, Oklahoma, U.S.A., in 1999. Scientists classify tornadoes by the damage they can do. With wind speeds of 70 miles (113 km) an hour, a tornado can tear branches from trees. A tornado with wind speeds more than 300 miles (483 km) an hour has the power to derail train cars, tear grass from the ground, and even rip pavement from the street.

Natural Disasters

Every world region has its share of natural disasters—the mix just varies from place to place. The Ring of Fire—grinding tectonic plate boundaries that follow the coasts of the Pacific Ocean—shakes with volcanic eruptions and earthquakes. Lives and livelihoods here and along other oceans can be swept away by tsunamis. North America's heartland endures blizzards in winter and tornadoes that can strike in spring, summer, or fall. Tropical cyclones batter many coastal areas in Asia and Australia with ripping winds, torrents of rain, and huge storm surges along their deadly paths.

HURRICANE

HURRICANES IN 2013

HELLO, MY NAME IS . . .

Hurricane names come from six official international lists. The names alternate between male and female. When a storm becomes a hurricane, a name from the list is used, in alphabetical order. Each list is reused every six years. A name "retires" if that hurricane caused a lot of damage or many deaths.

Andrea
Barry
Chantal
Dorian
Erin
Fernand
Gabrielle
Humberto
Ingrid
Jerry
Karen
Lorenzo
Melissa
Nestor
Olga
Pablo
Rebekah
Sebastien
Tanya
Van
Wendy

A monster storm with 150-mile-an-hour (240 kph) winds churns west across the Atlantic Ocean. Scientists at the National Hurricane Center in Miami have tracked it for days using satellite images. Now they're worried it may threaten the United States.

It's time for the "hurricane hunters" to go to work! All ships and airplanes have been warned away from this monster. But two four-engine airplanes head toward the storm. Their mission? To collect data inside the hurricane that will tell meteorologists where the storm is going, when it will get there, and how violent it will be.

The word "hurricane" comes from Huracan, the god of big winds and evil spirits once worshipped by the Maya people of Central America. These superstrong storms—which usually last about nine days—are the most destructive during their first 12 hours onshore, when high winds can topple homes and cause major flooding.

To help people prepare for a hurricane that's hustling to shore, the U.S. National Oceanic and Atmospheric Administration (NOAA) sends out the "hurricane hunters," who fly straight into the storm to determine characteristics such as temperature, air pressure, wind speed, and wind direction. It's a dangerous job, but by mission's end, the hunters' work will help to keep everyone in the hurricane's path safe.

Scale of Hurricane Intensity

CATEGORY	ONE	TWO	THREE	FOUR	FIVE
DAMAGE	Minimal	Moderate	Extensive	Extreme	Catastrophic
WINDS	74–95 mph (119–153 kph)	96–110 mph (154–177 kph)	111–130 mph (178–209 kph)	131–155 mph (210–249 kph)	Over 155 mph (249+ kph)
(DAMAGE refers to wind and water damage combined.)					

Tornado!

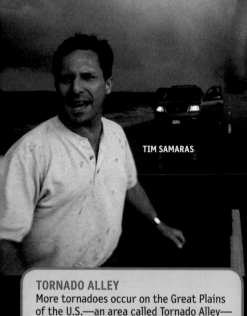

TIM SAMARAS

Most people take shelter when a tornado's coming. Not Tim Samaras. The former National Geographic Emerging Explorer chases the deadly storms, spending every May and June driving across the United States' Tornado Alley in search of the next twister. His mission? To find out why tornadoes form so he can predict them and give people earlier warnings to take shelter before a storm hits.

Samaras and other tornado chasers and meteorologists typically use weather measurement probes to collect data from the twisters. When placed directly in the twister's violent path, the probes record factors like humidity, pressure,

TORNADO ALLEY
More tornadoes occur on the Great Plains of the U.S.—an area called Tornado Alley—than in any other place on Earth.

temperature, wind speed, and direction. This information is crucial to determining how violent a twister may become—and how it may impact the people and places in its path.

Samaras's job is full of thrills and scary moments. When a tornado with more than 200-mile-an-hour (322 km) winds swept through Manchester, South Dakota, U.S.A., Samaras recalls "debris flying overhead, telephone poles were snapped and flung 300 yards (274 m) through the air, roads ripped from the ground, and the town of Manchester literally sucked into the clouds."

Tornado Safety Tips

GO DEEP
Ride out the storm in your basement. If you don't have a basement, go to a closet, bathroom, or small room in the center of your house.

TAKE COVER
If you're outside, run into the closest house or building. Once indoors, get under heavy furniture or a mattress and protect your head.

GET LOW
If you're stuck outside, lie flat in a ditch or low spot, or crouch near a building.

BE ALERT
Don't go outside if there is a tornado watch or warning.

Triple DISASTER

A SIGHTSEEING SHIP IS WASHED ONTO A TWO-STORY BUILDING IN OTSUCHI, IWATE PREFECTURE, JAPAN.

FUKUSHIMA DAIICHI NUCLEAR PLANT SUFFERED SIGNIFICANT DAMAGE AND IS NOT EXPECTED TO REOPEN.

On the morning of March 11, 2011, life in Sendai, Japan, was operating as usual: People rushed off to work, children scrambled to get to school, and fishermen cast their lines into the Pacific Ocean. But by nightfall, this coastal town was almost unrecognizable. When a 9.0-magnitude earthquake—one of the biggest recorded in history—struck off the coast of Honshu, Japan, that afternoon, it triggered a tsunami that all but destroyed parts of eastern Japan. This devastating domino effect sent waves as high as 30 feet (9 m) crashing onto the coast and into towns like Sendai, and badly damaged a nuclear power station in Fukushima, which released dangerous levels of radiation into the environment. Up to 50 aftershocks followed the initial quake, many of them with a magnitude greater than 6.0. All told, more than 15,000 lives were lost as a result of these devastating natural disasters.

Not every underwater earthquake triggers a tsunami. Seismologists say major tsunamis can only be caused by earthquakes measuring greater than 7.0. Location plays a factor, too: About 90 percent of all tsunamis occur in the Pacific Ocean, and the closer to shore the earthquake is, the more powerful—and destructive—the tsunami.

Bet you didn't know

In the open ocean, a **tsunami** sometimes travels as fast as **a jet plane**.

The 2011 quake in Japan was **so powerful, it moved the island** of Honshu **eight feet** (2.4 m).

Wildfire!

A severe drought, high winds, and record-high temps created a recipe for disaster in the wildfire-prone Australian state of Victoria. These conditions fueled more than 400 wildfires raging through the state, destroying homes and wiping out entire towns. All told, the "Black Saturday" bushfires of February 2009 scorched more than 1,500 square miles of farms, forests, and towns. The black, billowing smoke was so thick, it could be seen from space. Collectively, these fires remain the worst wildfires Australia has ever seen.

How do wildfires start? Most often, they're sparked by a careless act by a human, such as leaving a campfire unattended or irresponsibly disposing of a cigarette. Some are deliberately set. Some are ignited by lightning strikes or fallen power lines. However they begin, wildfires can quickly rage out of control, especially when conditions are hot and arid, as they were in Victoria. The extra-dry trees and grass were extremely flammable and created a swift-moving fire that burned through acre upon acre almost without warning.

Highly trained forest firefighters are equipped and experienced to fight huge forest fires. Some, called smokejumpers, actually parachute into a remote area to battle the blaze. But no matter how many firefighters and gallons of water are doused on the flames, it usually takes a break in the weather to finally beat a wildfire. The Victoria fires continued to rage until cooler temperatures and rain offered relief. About a month after the fires ignited, the flames were finally extinguished.

NAT GEO EXPLORER

Mark Thiessen: Wildfire Photographer

What he does:
Takes photographs from the front lines of wildfires every summer.

Most amazing moment:
Photographing a wildfire in Idaho, U.S.A. "To our left is a huge wall of flame that's coming in our direction. The flames start to twirl together and you get this 30-foot [9-m]-tall fire tornado. It's so fascinating, but also so dangerous."

THIESSEN'S PHOTO OF A FIRE-FIGHTER DRIVING THROUGH FLAMES THAT JUMPED THE ROAD IN MONTANA, U.S.A.

Biomes

A BIOME, OFTEN CALLED A MAJOR LIFE ZONE, is one of the natural world's major communities where plants and animals adapt to their specific surroundings. Biomes are classified depending on the predominant vegetation, climate, and geography of a region. They can be divided into six major types: forest, fresh water, marine, desert, grassland, and tundra. Each biome consists of many ecosystems.

Biomes are extremely important. Balanced ecological relationships among biomes help to maintain the environment and life on Earth as we know it. For example, an increase in one species of plant, such as an invasive one, can cause a ripple effect throughout the whole biome.

Since biomes can be fragile in this way, it is important to protect them from negative human activity, such as deforestation and pollution. We must work to conserve these biomes and the unique organisms that live within them.

FOREST

The forest biomes have been evolving for about 420 million years. Today, forests occupy about one-third of Earth's land area. There are three major types of forests: tropical, temperate, and boreal (taiga). Forests are home to a diversity of plants, some of which may hold medicinal qualities for humans, as well as thousands of unseen and undiscovered animal species. Forests can also absorb carbon dioxide, a greenhouse gas, and give off oxygen.

FRESH WATER

Most water on Earth is salty, but freshwater ecosystems include lakes, ponds, wetlands, rivers, and streams—all of which usually contain less than one percent salt concentration. The countless animal and plant species that live in a freshwater biome vary from continent to continent, but include algae, frogs, turtles, fish, and the larvae of many insects. Throughout the world, people use food, medicine, and other resources from this biome.

MARINE

The marine biome covers almost three-fourths of Earth's surface, making it the largest habitat on our planet. The five oceans make up the majority of the salt-water marine biome. Coral reefs are considered to be the most biodiverse of any of the biome habitats. The marine biome is home to more than one million plant and animal species. Some of the largest animals on Earth, such as the blue whale, live in the marine biome.

DESERT

Covering about one-fifth of Earth's surface, deserts are places where precipitation is less than 10 inches (25 cm) per year. Although most deserts are hot, there are other kinds as well. The four major kinds of deserts in the world include: hot, semi-arid, coastal, and cold. Far from being barren wastelands, deserts are biologically rich habitats with a vast array of animals and plants that have adapted to the harsh conditions there.

GRASSLAND

Biomes called grasslands are characterized by having grasses instead of large shrubs or trees. Grasslands generally have precipitation for only about half to three-fourths of the year. If it were more, they would become forests. Widespread around the world, grasslands can be divided into two types: tropical (savannas) and temperate. Grasslands are home to some of the largest land animals on Earth, such as elephants, hippopotamuses, rhinoceroses, and lions.

TUNDRA

The coldest of all biomes, tundras are characterized by an extremely cold climate, simple vegetation, little precipitation, poor nutrients, and short growing seasons. There are two types of tundra: arctic and alpine. A very fragile environment, tundras are home to few kinds of vegetation. Surprisingly, though, there are quite a few animal species that can survive the tundra's extremes, such as wolves, caribou, and even mosquitoes.

HOW DOES Your Garden GROW?

The plant kingdom is more than 300,000 organisms strong, growing all over the world: on top of mountains, in the sea, in frigid temperatures—everywhere. Without plants, life on Earth would not be able to survive. Plants provide food and oxygen for animals and humans.

Three characteristics make plants distinct:

1 Most have chlorophyll (a green pigment that makes photosynthesis work and turns sunlight into energy), while some are parasitic.

2 They cannot change their location on their own.

3 Their cell walls are made from a stiff material called cellulose.

Photosynthesis

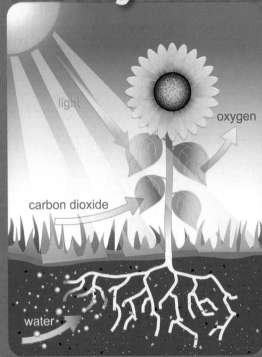

light

oxygen

carbon dioxide

water

Plants are lucky—they don't have to hunt or shop for food. Most use the sun to produce their own food. In a process called photosynthesis, the plant's chloroplast (the part of the plant where the chemical chlorophyll is located) captures the sun's energy and combines it with carbon dioxide from the air and nutrient-rich water from the ground to produce a sugar called glucose. Plants burn the glucose for energy to help them grow. As a waste product, plants emit oxygen, which humans and other animals need to breathe. When animals breathe, we exhale carbon dioxide, which the plants then use for more photosynthesis—it's all a big, finely tuned system. So the next time you pass a lonely houseplant, give it thanks for helping you live.

Try This!

Ask for a parent's help and permission before you start these projects.

GROW AN INDOOR HERB GARDEN

Amp up your food's flavor and help the environment with an at-home herb garden. You'll love watching these plants grow, and by growing your own, you'll cut back on the pollution released into the atmosphere when trucks transport food to stores. Brings a new meaning to "going green"!

YOU WILL NEED

• Empty recyclable cans • Sandpaper • Scissors • Scrap construction paper or wrapping paper • Glue • Stickers, markers, or ribbons • Small stones or marbles • Potting soil • Herb seeds • Water • Wooden craft sticks • Labels

WHAT TO DO

1. Remove can labels and wash and dry the empty cans. With an adult's help, use sandpaper to carefully smooth any rough edges inside the open cans.

2. Cut enough scrap paper or wrapping paper to fit around the outside of the cans and glue it in place. Decorate the paper with stickers, markers, or ribbons.

3. Place a layer of small stones or marbles in the bottom of the cans for drainage. Add potting soil until the cans are three-quarters full. Pat down the soil.

4. Gently press a few seeds into the dirt and cover them with soil. Lightly water the seeds and put your herb containers in a sunny spot.

5. Attach labels to wooden craft sticks and position them in the cans.

6. Your herbs should sprout within a week to ten days.

What foods go best with my herbs?
Basil: pizza, spaghetti
Cilantro: salsa
Dill: veggie dip
Mint: iced tea
Oregano: tomato sauce
Parsley: potatoes, stuffing
Rosemary: chicken
Thyme: meatballs

WORLD WATER

Earth's most precious resource

More than two-thirds of Earth is covered by water, but fresh water, which many plants and animals—including humans—need to survive, makes up less than 3 percent of all the water on Earth. Much of this fresh water is trapped deep underground or frozen in ice sheets and glaciers. Of the small amount of water that is fresh, less than one percent is available for human use.

Unfortunately, human activity often puts great stress on vital watersheds. For example, Brazil has approved the construction of large dams on the Amazon River. Although the dams will provide water and electricity, they will alter the natural flow of water in this giant watershed. In the United States, heavy use of chemical fertilizers and pesticides has created toxic runoff that threatens the health of the Mississippi River watershed.

Access to clean fresh water is critical for human health. But in many places, safe water is scarce due to population pressure and pollution.

Water Facts

One gallon (3.8 L) of water weighs about 8.34 pounds (3.8 kg).

Over the course of 100 years, a water molecule will spend an average of 98 years in the ocean. The rest of the time it's either ice, in lakes and rivers, or in the atmosphere.

Water consists of two hydrogen atoms and one oxygen atom bonded together by an electrical charge.

If all the world's water were fit into a gallon jug, only about one tablespoon (0.5 fl oz) of it would be okay for us to drink.

What does it take for water to be "salty"? Not much! Water with one thousand parts per million or more of dissolved solids is considered saline.

Why does ice float? Water is one of the few substances that is less dense as a solid than a liquid.

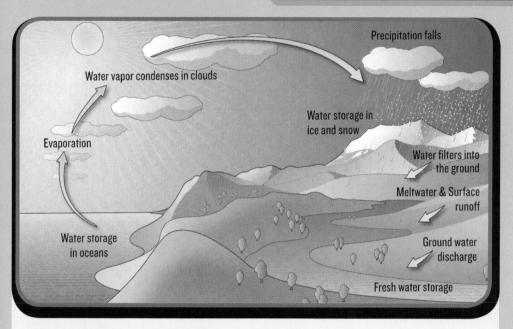

Precipitation falls

Water vapor condenses in clouds

Water storage in ice and snow

Evaporation

Water filters into the ground

Meltwater & Surface runoff

Water storage in oceans

Ground water discharge

Fresh water storage

WATER CYCLE

The amount of water on Earth is more or less constant—only the form changes. As the sun warms Earth's surface, liquid water is changed to water vapor in a process called **evaporation.** Plants lose water from the surface of leaves in a process called **transpiration.** As water vapor rises into the air, it cools and changes form again. This time it becomes clouds in a process called **condensation.** Water droplets fall from the clouds as **precipitation,** which then travels as groundwater or runoff back to the lakes, rivers, and oceans, where the cycle (shown above) starts all over again.

NAT GEO EXPLORER

Enric Sala: Marine Ecologist

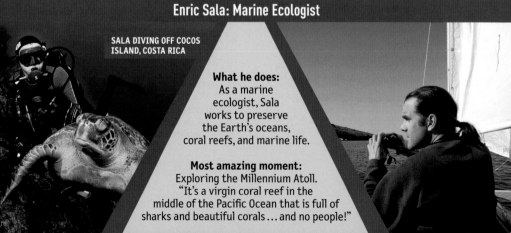

SALA DIVING OFF COCOS ISLAND, COSTA RICA

What he does:
As a marine ecologist, Sala works to preserve the Earth's oceans, coral reefs, and marine life.

Most amazing moment:
Exploring the Millennium Atoll. "It's a virgin coral reef in the middle of the Pacific Ocean that is full of sharks and beautiful corals... and no people!"

THE OC

PACIFIC OCEAN

STATS

Surface area
65,436,200 sq mi (169,479,000 sq km)

Earth's water area
47 percent

Greatest depth
Challenger Deep
(in the Mariana Trench)
-36,070 ft (-10,994 m)

Surface temperatures
Summer high: 90°F (32°C)
Winter low: 28°F (-2°C)

Tides
Highest: 30 ft (9 m) near Korean peninsula
Lowest: 1 ft (0.3 m) near Midway Islands

GEO WHIZ

Some rocks on the bottom of the Pacific Ocean are around 200 million years old.

The ocean's name comes from the Latin *Mare Pacificum*, meaning "peaceful sea," but earthquakes and volcanic activity along its coasts occasionally generate powerful waves called tsunamis, which can cause death and destruction when they slam ashore.

Two out of every three fish harvested on the planet come from the Pacific Ocean.

It would take a stack of more than 24 Empire State Buildings to equal the depth of the Challenger Deep in the western Pacific, the deepest point among all of the oceans.

Cool creatures: giant Pacific octopus, bottlenose whale, clownfish, great white shark

ATLANTIC OCEAN

STATS

Surface area
35,338,500 sq mi (91,526,300 sq km)

Earth's water area
25 percent

Greatest depth
Puerto Rico Trench
-28,232 ft (-8,605 m)

Surface temperatures
Summer high: 90°F (32°C)
Winter low: 28°F (-2°C)

Tides
Highest: 52 ft (16 m)
Bay of Fundy, Canada
Lowest: 1.5 ft (0.5 m)
Gulf of Mexico and Mediterranean Sea

GEO WHIZ

The Mid-Atlantic Ridge, the underwater mountain range that runs 12,240 miles (19,700 km) south from Iceland, is twice as long as the Andes Mountains in South America.

The Atlantic Ocean is about half the size of the Pacific, but it's growing. Spreading along the Mid-Atlantic Ridge—an undersea mountain range—allows molten rock from the Earth's interior to escape and form new ocean floor.

The Atlantic Ocean is believed to have been created about 150 million years ago when a supercontinent split apart.

Cool creatures: blue whale, Atlantic spotted dolphin, sea turtle

EANS

INDIAN OCEAN

STATS

Surface area
28,839,800 sq mi (74,694,800 sq km)

Earth's water area
21 percent

Greatest depth
Java Trench
-23,376 ft (-7,125 m)

Surface temperatures
Summer high: 93°F (34°C)
Winter low: 28°F (-2°C)

Tides
Highest: 36 ft (11 m)
Lowest: 2 ft (0.6 m)
Both along Australia's west coast

GEO WHIZ

The Indian Ocean is the youngest ocean, not reaching its current configuration until just 36 million years ago.

The Bay of Bengal, off the coast of India, is sometimes called Cyclone Alley because of the large number of tropical storms that occur there each year between May and November.

The Indian Ocean is home to the Kerguelen Plateau, an underwater volcanic landmass that's three times the size of Japan.

The Red Sea, an extension of the Indian Ocean along the Arabian Peninsula, is one of the saltiest bodies of water on Earth. Its high salinity is due to a rapid evaporation rate.

Cool creatures: humpback whale, Portuguese man-of-war, dugong (sea cow)

ARCTIC OCEAN

STATS

Surface area
5,390,000 sq mi (13,960,100 sq km)

Earth's water area
4 percent

Greatest depth
Molloy Deep
-18,599 ft (-5,669 m)

Surface temperatures
Summer high: 41°F (5°C)
Winter low: 28°F (-2°C)

Tides
Less than 1 ft (0.3 m)
variation throughout the ocean

GEO WHIZ

Unlike other oceans, where temperatures vary greatly depending on the season and location, the entire Arctic Ocean remains around the freezing point year round.

The geographic North Pole lies roughly in the middle of the Arctic Ocean under 13,000 feet (3,962 m) of water.

Many of the features on the Arctic Ocean floor are named for early Arctic explorers and bordering landmasses.

About 2,700 billion tons (2,400 billion t) of ice drifts out of the Arctic Ocean every year.

While the Arctic Ocean is covered by sea ice both in the summer and in the winter, scientists believe global warming will cause the summer ice to vanish in just a few decades.

Cool creatures: beluga whale, orca, harp seal, narwhal

To see the major oceans and bays in relation to landmasses, look at the map on pages 262 and 263.

Coral Reefs

Just below the surface of the Caribbean Sea's crystal-clear water, miles of vivid corals shoot off in fantastic shapes that shelter tropical fish of every color. Coral reefs account for a quarter of all life in the ocean and are often called the rain forests of the sea. Like big apartment complexes, coral reefs provide a tough limestone skeleton for fish, shrimp, clams, and other organisms to live in—and plenty of food for them to eat, too.

And how does the coral get its color? It's all about the algae that cling to its limestone polyps. Algae and coral live together in a mutually helpful relationship. The coral provides a home to the algae and helps the algae convert sunlight to food that it uses. But as beautiful as coral reefs are, they are also highly sensitive. A jump of even two degrees in water temperature makes the reef rid itself of the algae, leaving the coral with a sickly, bleached look. Pollution is another threat; it can poison the sensitive corals. Humans pose a threat, too: One clumsy kick from a swimmer can destroy decades of coral growth.

BY THE NUMBERS

25 percent of all marine creatures are supported by coral reefs.

500 million is how many years ago the world's first coral reefs formed.

4 is the number of countries that border the Mesoamerican Barrier Reef: Mexico, Honduras, Belize, and Guatemala.

THE GREAT BARRIER REEF IN AUSTRALIA IS THE BIGGEST LIVING STRUCTURE ON EARTH.

Try This!

CREATE A MOtion OCEAN

Shake the jar and watch waves appear!

YOU WILL NEED
- clear jar with lid
- water
- blue food coloring
- glitter
- baby oil
- plastic floating toy

WHAT TO DO
1. Fill the jar halfway with water.
2. Add drops of food coloring until you like the color you see. Shake in a little glitter.
3. Pour in baby oil until the jar is three-quarters full.
4. Place a floating toy on top of the oil, then screw on the lid tightly.
5. Shake the jar gently to set your ocean in motion.

SPEAK NATURALLY

Oral Reports Made Easy

Does the thought of public speaking start your stomach churning like a tornado? Would you rather get caught in an avalanche than give a speech?

Giving an oral report does not have to be a natural disaster. The basic format is very similar to a written essay. There are two main elements that make up a good oral report—the writing and the presentation. As you write your oral report, remember that your audience will be hearing the information as opposed to reading it. Follow the guidelines below, and there will be clear skies ahead.

TIP: Make sure you practice your presentation a few times. Stand in front of a mirror or have a parent record you so you can see if you need to work on anything, such as eye contact.

Writing Your Material

Follow the steps in the "How to Write a Perfect Essay" section on p. 98, but prepare your report to be spoken rather than written.

Try to keep your sentences short and simple. Long, complex sentences are harder to follow. Limit yourself to just a few key points. You don't want to overwhelm your audience with too much information. To be most effective, hit your key points in the introduction, elaborate on them in the body, and then repeat them once again in your conclusion.

An oral report has three basic parts:

- **Introduction**—This is your chance to engage your audience and really capture their interest in the subject you are presenting. Use a funny personal experience or a dramatic story, or start with an intriguing question.

- **Body**—This is the longest part of your report. Here you elaborate on the facts and ideas you want to convey. Give information that supports your main idea and expand on it with specific examples or details. In other words, structure your oral report in the same way you would a written essay so that your thoughts are presented in a clear and organized manner.

- **Conclusion**—This is the time to summarize the information and emphasize your most important points to the audience one last time.

Preparing Your Delivery

1 Practice makes perfect.
Practice! Practice! Practice! Confidence, enthusiasm, and energy are key to delivering an effective oral report, and they can best be achieved through rehearsal. Ask family and friends to be your practice audience, and ask them for feedback when you're done. Were they able to follow your ideas? Did you seem knowledgeable and confident? Did you speak too slow or too fast, too soft or too loud? The more times you practice giving your report, the more you'll master the material. Then you won't have to rely so heavily on your notes or papers and will be able to give your report in a relaxed and confident manner.

2 Present with everything you've got.
Be as creative as you can. Incorporate videos, sound clips, slide presentations, charts, diagrams, and photos. Visual aids help stimulate your audience's senses and keep them intrigued and engaged. They can also help to reinforce your key points. And remember that when you're giving an oral report, you're a performer. Take charge of the spotlight and be as animated and entertaining as you can. Have fun with it.

Need a good subject?
Go online. kidsblogs.national geographic.com/kidsnews

COOL CLICK

3 **Keep your nerves under control.**

Everyone gets a little nervous when speaking in front of a group. That's normal. But the more preparation you've done—meaning plenty of researching, organizing, and rehearsing—the more confident you'll be. Preparation is the key. And if you make a mistake or stumble over your words, just regroup and keep going. Nobody's perfect, and nobody expects you to be.

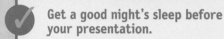

PRESENTATION CHECKLIST

✓ Get a good night's sleep before your presentation.

✓ Have a healthy meal or nutritious snack beforehand.

✓ When you think you're fully prepared, practice it one more time.

✓ Maintain eye contact with your audience throughout your report.

✓ Take a deep breath, relax, and have fun with it.

FUN TIP
Don't rush! Try to speak slowly and deliberately.

FUN TIP
Fighting nerves? As you present, pretend that you're simply having a chat with your best friend.

CONNECTING WORDS

Effective use of connecting words will make your oral report go smoothly. Connecting words help the listener understand as you transition from one idea to the next.
Here are some words you can use to make your oral report flow:

also	next
anyway	nonetheless
consequently	now that
finally	otherwise
furthermore	since
however	still
incidentally	then
instead	therefore
likewise	thus
meanwhile	until
moreover	whether
nevertheless	while

Going Green

A male gorilla in the Democratic Republic of Congo, Africa, soaks in a swamp for hours, repeatedly rinsing and then eating herb roots. Gorillas are an endangered species.

Got a smart phone?
SCAN THIS to discover
more about going green!
(See instructions inside the front cover.)
No smart phone? Go to
kids.nationalgeographic.com/almanac-2013

Trapped by TRASH!

VICTIM: SKUNK
TRASH: YOGURT CONTAINER
PROBLEM: HEAD STUCK

A HOMEOWNER finds a writhing baby skunk in her recycling bin. The skunk has a plastic yogurt container over his head. When the animal tries to push the container off, it won't budge. He claws at his head, struggling to free himself, then tumbles out of the uncovered bin. The panicked little skunk can't see a thing and begins to suffocate.

A PHONE CALL to Wildlife in Crisis, an animal rescue organization in nearby Weston, Connecticut, brings help. Director Dara Reid dispatches caretaker Anna Clark to the woman's home. She wraps the skunk in a towel and then gently tugs the container until the exhausted creature is finally free.

BUT HE'S NOT SAFE. There is no sign of the animal's mother, and this baby skunk is far too young to survive on his own. Wildlife in Crisis feeds him milk and wet cat food until his teeth grow in, and then adds natural foods like berries and worms to his diet. About four months later he's released into the wild.

Animals get trapped every day by the things people carelessly discard. Here are stories of lucky animals that have tangled with trash—and escaped.

VICTIM: SEA LION
TRASH: FISHING LINE
PROBLEM: MOUTH TRAPPED

The sea lion prowls for food off the California shore, sticking his nose in places where fish might hide. When his whiskers snag on some fishing line, he tries to shake it off. But the strong material tangles, wraps around his snout and neck, and eventually traps his mouth shut.

Someone notices the distressed animal and informs the Marine Mammal Center in nearby Sausalito. When the sea lion reappears in a bay, the center's rescue team speeds to the scene. The feisty sea lion eludes them for nearly three weeks.

The worried rescue team sedates him with darts while he rests on a dock. After he becomes sleepy, the team rushes the 260-pound (118-kg) mammal to the center to cut the fishing line, treat his wounds, and feed him. The sea lion eats 100 pounds (45 kg) of herring and is then set free. Hopefully now he steers clear of trash.

FISHING LINE

VICTIM: BALD EAGLE
TRASH: STRING
PROBLEM: WING TANGLED

GETTING BETTER

A young bald eagle is in trouble. When her parents searched for sticks to build the nest, they also found balloon string, fishing line, and other trash. Now the young eagle is tangled in the debris and falls from the nest. The bird hangs four feet (1.2 m) above the ground, breaking her wing in the process.

Dara Reid of Wildlife in Crisis comes to the rescue. She cuts down the suspended eagle and rushes her to the rescue facility. After removing the trash, Reid aligns the bird's broken wing and immobilizes it by bandaging the wing against the eagle's body.

Following 14 months of TLC, the bald eagle is taken to a field. With a helpful heave from Reid, the eagle flaps hard, circles above, and then re-enters the wild—with a perfectly healed wing.

FLYING AGAIN

GLOBAL WARMING

Polar bear on a piece of melting iceberg

Climate Change, Explained

Fact: The world is getting warmer. The global surface temperature has risen by 1.3 °F (.56° C) over the last 100 years, and worldwide, the last decade has been the warmest on record. These are the direct effects of climate change, which refers not only to the increase in the Earth's average temperature (also known as global warming), but also to the long-term effects on winds, rain, and ocean currents. Global warming is the reason glaciers and polar ice sheets are melting—resulting in rising sea levels and shrinking habitats. This makes survival for some animals a big challenge. Warming also means flooding along the coasts and drought for inland areas.

Why are temperatures climbing?

Some of the recent climate changes can be tied to natural causes—such as changes in the sun's intensity, the unusually warm ocean currents of El Niño, and volcanic activity—but human activities are a major factor as well.

Everyday activities that require burning fossil fuels, such as driving gasoline-powered cars, contribute to global warming. These activities produce greenhouse gases, which enter the atmosphere and trap heat. At the current rate, the Earth's global average temperature is projected to rise from 2 to 11.5°F (1 to 6.4°C) by the year 2100, and will get even warmer after that. And as the climate continues to warm, it will unfortunately continue to affect the environment and our society in many ways.

Reduce Your Carbon Footprint

Everything you buy, use, and throw away affects the Earth. Activities such as driving cars and heating or cooling buildings can release greenhouse gases like carbon dioxide into the air. The amount of greenhouse gases produced by your activities is called your carbon footprint. By reducing your footprint, you can help the planet. Here are three ways to do just that.

RIDE A BIKE! Instead of having your mom or dad drive you to a friend's house in the neighborhood, hop on your bike and ride there instead.

PRINT SMART. When you print from the computer, use both sides of the paper. Talk to your teacher about doing the same for classroom print-outs.

GO LOCAL. Talk to your parents about buying local, organic food. Each ingredient in a U.S. meal has traveled an average of 1,500 miles (2,400 km). If everyone ate one meal per week of local, organic food, we'd save 1.1 million barrels of oil every week.

IS THE EARTH Changing Shape?

YES, according to a recent study, which determined that each year, the planet is getting wider around the equator and flatter at the poles. But the shift in size and shape is super-subtle: Experts say that in the past five years or so, the distance around the Earth (also known as the equatorial radius) has grown about one 25th of an inch (one millimeter) per year.

So what's causing the Earth to get bigger—and flatter? Scientists aren't quite sure, but they think it might have something to do with changes in ocean climate. Climate events like El Niño shift where the mass of water is stored among the oceans, in water vapor in the atmosphere, and in soil on the continents. This can result in slight changes of the Earth's gravity field—which may ultimately shift the shape of the planet.

Pollution
Cleaning Up Our Act

So what's the big deal about a little dirt on the planet? Pollution can affect animals, plants, and people. In fact, some studies show that more people die every year from diseases linked to air pollution than from car accidents. And right now nearly one billion of the world's people don't have access to clean drinking water.

A LITTLE POLLUTION = BIG PROBLEMS
You can probably clean your room in a couple of hours. (At least we hope you can!) But you can't shove air and water pollution under your bed or cram them into the closet. Once released into the environment, pollution—whether it's oil leaking from a boat or chemicals spewing from a factory's smokestack—can have a lasting environmental impact.

KEEP IT CLEAN
It's easy to blame things like big factories for pollution problems. But some of the mess comes from everyday activities. Exhaust fumes from cars and garbage in landfills can seriously trash the Earth's health. We all need to pitch in and do some housecleaning. It may mean bicycling more and riding in cars less. Or not dumping water-polluting oil or household cleaners down the drain. Look at it this way: Just as with your room, it's always better not to let Earth get messed up in the first place.

Bottled Up!

Sure, water is good for you. But before you sip, think about how often you use plastic water bottles—and what you're doing with them when you're done. For every six water bottles we use, only one will wind up in a recycling bin. The rest end up in landfills or as litter on land or in rivers, lakes, and oceans, taking many hundreds of years to disintegrate. So, what can you do? Fill up from the tap and drink out of a refillable steel container. And if you do use a plastic bottle, make sure to recycle it.

Declining Biodiversity
Saving All Creatures Great and Small

WILDLIFE
BIODIVERSITY

Insects, Centipedes, and Millipedes

Other Animals

Mammals

Florida manatee

Earth is home to a huge mix of plants and animals—perhaps 100 million species—and scientists have officially identified and named only about 1.9 million so far! Scientists call this healthy mix biodiversity.

THE BALANCING ACT

The bad news is that half of the planet's plant and animal species may be on the path to extinction, mainly because of human activity. People cut down trees, build roads and houses, pollute rivers, overfish, and overhunt. The good news is that many people care. Scientists and volunteers race against the clock every day, working to save wildlife before time runs out. By building birdhouses, planting trees, and following the rules for hunting and fishing, you can be a positive force for preserving biodiversity, too. Every time you do something to help a species survive, you help our planet to thrive.

Habitat Destruction

Living on the Edge

Even though tropical rain forests cover only about 7 percent of the planet's total land surface, they are home to half of all known species of plants and animals. Because people cut down so many trees for lumber and firewood and clear so much land for farms, hundreds of thousands of acres of rain forest disappear every year.

SHARING THE LAND

Wetlands are also important feeding and breeding grounds. People have drained many wetlands, turning them into farm fields or sites for industries. More than half the world's wetlands have disappeared within the past century, squeezing wildlife out. Balancing the needs of humans and animals is the key to lessening habitat destruction.

Toucan

213

World Energy & Minerals

Almost everything people do—from cooking to powering the International Space Station—requires energy. But energy comes in different forms. Traditional energy sources, still used by many people in the developing world, include burning dried animal dung and wood. Industrialized countries and urban centers around the world rely on coal, oil, and natural gas—called fossil fuels because they formed from decayed plant and animal material accumulated from long ago. Fossil fuel deposits, either in the ground or under the ocean floor, are unevenly distributed on Earth, and only some countries can afford to buy them. Fossil fuels are also not renewable, meaning they will run out one day. And unless we find other ways to create energy, we'll be stuck. Without energy we won't be able to drive cars, use lights, or send emails to friends.

TAKING A TOLL

Environmentally speaking, burning fossil fuels isn't necessarily the best choice, either—carbon dioxide from the burning of fossil fuels, as well as other emissions, are contributing to global warming. Concerned scientists are looking at new ways to harness renewable, alternative sources of energy, such as water, wind, and sun.

COOL CLICK To learn more about global trends, go online. nationalgeographic.com/ earthpulse

DIGGING FOR FOSSIL FUELS

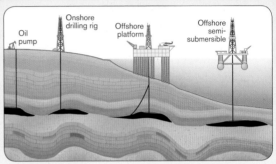

This illustration shows some of the different kinds of onshore and offshore drilling equipment. The type of drilling equipment depends on whether the oil or natural gas is in the ground or under the ocean.

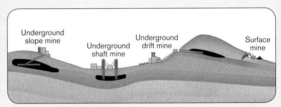

The mining of coal made the industrial revolution possible, and coal still provides a major energy source. Work that was once done by people using picks and shovels is now done with mechanized equipment. This diagram shows some of the various kinds of coal mines currently in use.

WORLD PRIMARY ENERGY SUPPLY

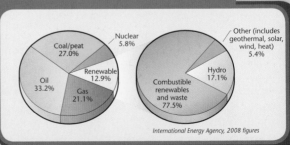

International Energy Agency, 2008 figures

Alternative Power

WIND

Strong winds blowing through California's mountains spin windmill blades on an energy farm, powering giant turbines that generate electricity for the state.

HYDROELECTRIC

Hydroelectric plants, such as Santiago del Estero in Argentina, use dams to harness running water to generate clean, renewable energy.

GEOTHERMAL

Geothermal power, from groundwater heated by molten rock, provides energy for this power plant in Iceland. Swimmers enjoy the warm waters of a lake created by the power plant.

SOLAR

Solar panels on Samso Island in Denmark capture and store energy from the sun, an environmentally friendly alternative to fossil fuels.

BIODIESEL

This Aero L-29 Delfin, nicknamed BioJet 1, was the first jet aircraft powered by 100 percent biodiesel fuel. Biodiesel—which can be made from vegetable oil, animal fats, or french fry grease—is cleaner and emits fewer pollutants than fossil fuels do into the air.

OCEAN ALERT!

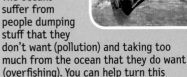

It may seem as if the world's oceans are so vast that nothing could hurt them. Unfortunately, that's not true. The oceans suffer from people dumping stuff that they don't want (pollution) and taking too much from the ocean that they do want (overfishing). You can help turn this problem around.

You probably already know how to help fight water pollution: Participate in stream, river, and beach cleanups; don't litter; and don't dump things into storm drains. But you may not realize that too many fish are taken from the sea. Some overfished species are disappearing, such as shark and the bluefin tuna (above).

Many fish are slow-growing and live decades or even centuries. Chilean sea bass live up to 40 years. Orange roughies can live to be more than 100 years old. And rockfish can live to be 200! When there aren't enough of these slow-growing fish, their species is threatened because the fish often are taken from the sea before they are old enough to reproduce. These species could disappear.

PROTECT THE OCEANS! You can be part of the solution if you choose carefully what fish to eat. Some are okay to eat; others you should avoid because they're overfished or caught in ways that harm the ocean. Ask your parents to consult this guide to some of the best and worst fish choices. Ask a grocer or chef where and how the fish was caught. Saving marine life is hard, but if everyone helps, it will make a difference.

BEST CHOICES

amberjack, greater
barramundi (U.S.)
capelin
clam, Atlantic surf
clam, Geoduck
clam, Manilla-farmed
cockles, New Zealand
crab, Dungeness
crawfish (U.S.)
herring, Atlantic (U.S. and Canada)
hoki
jobfish, Rusty
mackerel, Atlantic
mackerel, chub
mahimahi (pole and troll caught)
mussel, Greenshell (New Zealand)
mussel, Mediterranean

oyster, Eastern
oyster, Pacific
pollock, American
pollock, walleye
salmon, Alaska
sardines—Pacific and Indian
scallops, bay
scallops, Mexican Bat
sea urchin, green (British Columbia)
sea urchin, red (British Columbia)
sea urchin, roe
shrimp, northern
shrimp, pink shrimp, spot (Alaska)
snapper, deep-water
snapper, yellowtail (U.S.)
sole, rock

squid, Argentina
squid, market
tilapia (U.S.)
tuna, albacore (U.S., pole and troll caught)
tuna, albacore (U.S., pole and troll caught, imported)
tuna, Skipjack (pole and troll caught)
tuna, yellowfin (pole and troll caught)

WORST CHOICES

caviar (Caspian Sea)
caviar (U.S. and Canada)
cod, Atlantic (U.S. and Canada, bottom trawl caught)
eel, fresh water–farmed
halibut, Atlantic
orange roughy
oreos

salmon, Atlantic (farmed)
shark (imported)
shrimp (imported wild caught)
tuna, Atlantic bluefin
yellowtail (Japanese farmed)

DEFINITIONS

FARMED: fish raised commercially in enclosures
TROLL: to fish with lines towed by a boat
TRAWL: to fish with a cone-shaped net dragged behind a boat

10 COOL THINGS ABOUT WATER

1 WHEN A RIVER OTTER DIVES, its ears and nose close tightly to keep water out.

2 IT TAKES 2,900 GALLONS OF WATER to produce one pair of jeans.

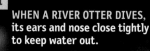

3 THE SNAKE-NECKED turtle, found in marshes and shallow waters of Australia, Indonesia, and New Guinea, smells like a skunk.

5 THE ARMORED CATFISH may look as if it shimmers, but its sheen is actually the reflection of a thin layer of crystals underneath its skin.

4 FRESH WATER MAKES UP LESS THAN **3** PERCENT OF THE EARTH'S WATER.

6 THE RAIN THAT FALLS TODAY IS THE SAME FRESH WATER THAT DINOSAURS DRANK.

7 A BATH USES 75 PERCENT MORE WATER THAN A FIVE-MINUTE SHOWER.

8 DRAGONFLY **LARVAE LIVE** UNDERWATER BEFORE THEY BECOME ADULTS THAT FLY.

9 COLD WATER WEIGHS MORE THAN HOT WATER.

10 A HIPPOPOTAMUS CAN WALK ALONG THE BOTTOMS OF LAKES AND RIVERS.

217

Try This! FUNKY JUNK ART

Who knew recycling could be so much fun?
Check out these ideas for turning junk into awesome art.

1 Bottle Cap Snake

YOU WILL NEED
- 30–50 BOTTLE CAPS
- HAMMER
- AWL
- BOARD (TO HAMMER ON)
- PLASTIC-COATED WIRE
- CRAFT GLUE
- SELF-HARDENING CLAY
- 1 CORK
- 2 PUSHPINS

ASK FOR YOUR PARENTS' HELP AND PERMISSION BEFORE YOU START THESE PROJECTS.

WHAT TO DO
Work with a parent to punch a hole in the center of each bottle cap using a hammer and awl. Do this on a board that is resting on a sturdy surface. Cut a piece of wire that is slightly longer than you want your snake to be. Tie a knot at one end of the wire. String all of the bottle caps on the wire with the tops facing the open end of the wire. Knot the other end of the wire and cut off the excess. Glue a piece of clay to the snake's tail end and twist it into a tail shape. Glue a piece of clay to the opposite end of the snake. Create an indentation with the cork. Let dry. Glue the cork into the clay. Once dry, press push pins into the cork for eyes and some wire into the end of the cork for the tongue. Glue a piece of clay to the cork tip.

Cut up magazines or the Sunday comics and glue the pictures onto construction paper to make a funny collage.

2 Create a Collage

218

③ Toy Mosaic

YOU WILL NEED
- OLD TOYS, COLORED GLASS, STONES, BUTTONS, SHELLS, OR OTHER SMALL ITEMS
- THICK WHITE POSTER BOARD
- CRAFT GLUE
- THICK BLACK POSTER BOARD

WHAT TO DO
Collect small decorative items (see suggestions above) from around your house. Sketch a pattern for your collage on a piece of white poster board. Glue all of the pieces on top of the pattern. Let the glue dry. Cut a piece of heavy black poster board that is two inches wider on all sides than the white poster board. Center the white piece on the black one and glue it in place. Let the glue dry, then put your masterpiece on display for everyone to see.

④ Hang Your Name

Find the letters of your name in old posters or catalogs and cut them out. Glue the letters to cardboard that's covered with paper. Tape your nameplate to your bedroom door.

10 WAYS YOU CAN GO GREEN!

Want to do your part to save the planet? Here are ten things to try today!

1 Use rechargeable batteries, and recycle them when they die to keep harmful metals from entering the environment.

2 Never litter. Trash tossed carelessly outside often winds up in storm drains, which empty into rivers and streams that eventually flow to the oceans.

3 Plant a deciduous (leafy) tree that loses its leaves in the fall on the south side of your home. When it grows tall, its shade will cool your house in the summer. After its leaves fall, sunlight will help warm your house in winter.

4 Reuse or recycle plastic bags. When one ton of plastic bags is reused or recycled, the energy equivalent of 11 barrels of oil is saved!

5 Donate your old clothes and toys to reduce waste.

6 Take shorter showers to save water.

7 Switch off the light every time you leave a room.

8 Participate in cleanup days at your school or at a park—or organize one on your own.

9 Place your desk next to a window and use natural light instead of a lamp.

10 Have a drippy faucet at home? Ask your parents to replace the washer inside it to save water.

GREEN Inventions

KALMIAN AIRCRUISE

BALMIAN

ANCHORED

IN FLIGHT

HOTEL IN THE CLOUDS

The Aircruise is part blimp, part hotel, and totally cool. This futuristic airship—a concept for now—is designed to slowly float through the sky, cruising from New York City to London, England, in 37 hours or Los Angeles, California, to Shanghai, China, in 90 hours. Like a blimp, the Aircruise lifts into the air using hydrogen gas. While aloft, fuel cells and solar power run everything from the lights and TVs to the ship itself. Nearly as tall as the Eiffel Tower, the Aircruise has ten apartments, an open-air deck, dining and recreation areas, and—at the very bottom—a lounge with a glass floor where you can watch birds fly below you.

BOOTS **CHARGE** PHONE

You just saw an awesome movie and have *got* to call your best friend to gab about it. But as you're walking home from the theater, you realize your cell phone is dead. So you slip it into your boot and walk faster. That's the concept behind the Orange Power Wellies: boots that charge your phone. Your feet produce heat as you walk. A thermoelectric module in the boot's sole uses the difference in temperature between your foot and the cold ground to create electricity. The warmer your foot and the chillier the ground, the more power you produce. So keep walking—it'll keep you *and* your phone going.

PHONE GOES HERE

orange

FUTURE OF FLIGHT

In this the airplane of the future? Maybe! NASA is looking ahead 15 to 25 years, hoping to send you into the skies in a quiet, fuel-efficient, eco-friendly aircraft. One possibility is the blended-wing plane, sporting a seamless body for flying effortlessly through the air. The plane's lightweight, aerodynamic design allows it to fly more efficiently than today's planes. Right now, a flight from California to New York can use more than 8,000 gallons of fuel. NASA's goal for the blended-wing aircraft is to cut that amount in half. The first flight may take place around 2025, so fasten your seat belt for greener air travel.

LIGHT THE WAY

GLOW HOME

You just spent a fun day fishing and swimming on the river, and you can't wait to get back to camp for dinner. You could have sworn your campsite was right here ... or was it over there? Don't sweat it: This high-tech tent (not yet available for purchase) lights up to lead you home. Made from a special fabric woven with solar threads, the tent captures energy from the sun and then uses it to power all its tricks. A chip inside your cell phone signals the tent's wireless controller, which in turn triggers the lights to switch on. On chilly nights, the controller can also sense temperature and start heating the groundsheet for you. Now, that's camping in style!

221

GREENHOUSES

LOOK INSIDE!

What: Moveable House

Why it's cool: The Walking House is an agile abode about the size of a large room, with a bed and a small sitting area. Moving in a buglike fashion at speeds of up to 100 feet (60 m) an hour, it uses its six legs to maneuver in every direction.
Eco-friendly features: Power comes straight from the sun—solar panels on the roof catch the rays needed to keep the house chugging along. A wood-burning stove, rainwater-catching system, and composting toilet keep things eco-friendly.

What: Monte-Silo House

Why it's cool: The home is constructed of two metal grain silos, linked together to form an 1,800-square-foot (167-sq-m) living space.
Eco-friendly features: The exterior metal is a recyclable material, while solar heat helps warm up the house during the winter.

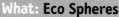

What: **Eco Spheres**

Why it's cool: These wood and fiberglass hanging tree houses are equipped with a working kitchen (but no bathroom!) and sleep four.

Eco-friendly features: What better way to reduce your carbon footprint than living among nature in one of these 11-foot (3.3-m)-wide spheres?

What: **The Orchid House**

Why it's cool: The design of the house resembles a bee orchid, a flower found on the nature reserve in England where it was built. Valued at more than £9 million ($14 million), it's also one of the world's most expensive green homes.

Eco-friendly features: Thanks to an underground geothermal heating pump, the house generates more energy than it consumes.

What: **The Lighthouse**

Why it's cool: It's a net-zero carbon house. The small amount of harmful carbon emissions it releases into the environment is offset by the renewable energy it creates.

Eco-friendly features: The sloped roof catches wind for cooling and ventilation, while solar thermal panels heat water. The large windows have a built-in system to collect and recycle rainwater.

Write a Letter That Gets Results

Knowing how to write a good letter is a useful skill. It will come in handy anytime you want to persuade someone to understand your point of view. Whether you're emailing your congressperson, or writing a letter for a school project or to your grandma, a great letter will help you get your message across. Most important, a well-written letter leaves a good impression.

Check out the example below for the elements of a good letter.

Your address

Date

Salutation
Always use "Dear" followed by the person's name; use Mr. or Mrs. or Dr. as appropriate.

Introductory paragraph
Give the reason you're writing the letter.

Body
The longest part of the letter, which provides evidence that supports your position. Be persuasive!

Closing paragraph
Sum up your argument.

Complimentary closing
Sign off with "Sincerely" or "Thank you."

Your Signature

Christopher Jones
916 Green Street
Los Angeles, CA 90045

March 31, 2013

Dear Mr. School Superintendent,

I am writing to you about how much excess energy our school uses and to offer a solution.

Every day, we leave the computers on in the classroom, the TVs are plugged in all the time, and the lights are on all day. All of this adds up to a lot of wasted energy, which is not only harmful for the Earth as it increases the amount of harmful greenhouse gas emissions into the environment, but it's costly to the school. In fact, I read that schools spend more on energy bills than on computers and textbooks combined!

I am suggesting that we start an Energy Patrol to monitor the use of lighting, air-conditioning, heating, and other energy systems within our school. My idea is to have a group of students dedicated to figuring out ways we can cut back our energy use in the school. We can do room checks, provide reminders to students and teachers to turn off lights and computers, replace old lightbulbs with energy-efficient products, and even reward the classrooms that do the most to save energy.

Above all, I think our school could help the environment tremendously by cutting back on how much energy we use. Let's see an Energy Patrol at our school soon. Thank you.

Sincerely,

Christopher Jones

Christopher Jones

COMPLIMENTARY CLOSINGS

Sincerely, Sincerely yours, Thank you, Regards, Best wishes, Respectfully,

YOU CAN MAKE A DIFFERENCE!

Want to do more to make the world a better place? Have a question or an opinion? Do something about it. Turn your passion for a cause into meaningful action.

DIG DEEPER! Look to newspaper or magazine articles, books, the Internet, and anything else you can get your hands on. Learn about the issue or organization that most inspires you.

GET INVOLVED! The following organizations can connect you to opportunities so you can make a difference:
dosomething.org
globalvolunteers.org
volunteermatch.org

MAKE YOUR VOICE HEARD!
Email, call, or write to politicians or government officials:
congress.org

GO ONLINE TO HELP CARE FOR THE EARTH.
Learn more about environmental issues:
earthday.org
ecokids.ca/pub/kids_home.cfm
kidsplanet.org/defendit/new/
meetthegreens.org
treepeople.org

Collect pennies to help save wild species and wild places:
togethergreen.org/p4p

Start an environmental club at your school:
greenguideforkids.blogspot.com/2008/09/club-green.html

Learn how to start a kitchen compost bin:
meetthegreens.org/episode4/kitchen-composting.html

Reduce paper waste by receiving fewer catalogs:
catalogchoice.org

Learn how to green your school:
nrdc.org/greensquad

LETTER-WRITING TIPS

Before you start writing, think about what you would like to write about.

Use your own words.

Use stationery that is appropriate for the recipient; for example, plain, nice paper for a congressman and maybe a pretty card for your grandma.

When writing by hand, make sure you write neatly.

Follow the elements of a well-written letter at left.

Be creative!

Before you send the letter, read it again and check for spelling errors.

Write neatly on the envelope so that the postal worker can read it easily.

Don't forget the stamp for snail mail.

Want to find out more about how to help look after the planet? See this website:
environment.nationalgeographic.com/environment/green-guide/

COOL CLICKS

GO GREEN!
Save paper and send your letter by email. If you have to print it out, try to use recycled paper.

225

Got a smart phone?
SCAN THIS to travel back in time.
(See instructions inside the front cover.)
No smart phone? Go online.
kids.nationalgeographic.com/almanac-2013

A man rides an elephant in front of the Taj Mahal, in Agra, India. Completed in 1653, this architectural marvel was built by Shah Jahan as a tomb for his wife. Today it is one of India's biggest tourist destinations.

History
Happens

DISCOVERING TUT'S TREASURES

It's pitch-black. His hands trembling, British archaeologist Howard Carter makes a small hole in the tomb's second door. He inserts a candle. Next to him, British millionaire Lord Carnarvon blurts out, "Can you see anything?" After a moment of stunned silence, Carter replies, "Yes, wonderful things."

What Carter sees looks like the inside of a giant treasure chest. Gold gleams everywhere! There are glittering statues, a throne, and fabulous golden beds with posts shaped like the heads of wild animals. Precious items are heaped all over the room.

It's 1922. It has taken years of digging in the Valley of the Kings—a graveyard for ancient Egypt's richest kings—and $500,000 (in today's money) of Lord Carnarvon's cash, but Carter hit the jackpot. He discovered the tomb of Tutankhamun (Tut, for short), who became pharaoh at age nine and died ten years later, around 1323 B.C.

HIDDEN TREASURES

Carter, Lord Carnarvon, and two others enter the cluttered first room, which they call the antechamber. Under a bed with posts in the shape of hippopotamus heads, Lord Carnarvon finds the entrance to another room. Soon known as the annex, this tiny chamber holds more than 2,000 everyday objects. They include boomerangs, shields, a box containing eye makeup, and 116 baskets of food. When Carter clears the annex out later, his workers need to be suspended by ropes to keep from stepping on things.

ANCIENT ROBBERS

The disorder in the annex indicates ancient grave robbers had looted the tomb. They left behind footprints and gold rings wrapped in cloth. Luckily, they'd

The Truth About Tut

For centuries, experts suspected King Tut died in a dramatic fashion, either by a blow to the head or by poisoning. But now, studies reveal that he may have been plagued by poor health. Taking DNA from bones found in Tut's tomb, scientists conducted genetic tests. They also took CT scans. The results showed that Tut likely had malaria, a broken leg, and a bone disorder that caused a club foot—all of which may have led to his death at just 19 years old. And that staff seen in so many images of Tut? It was probably a cane to help the frail pharaoh walk.

Ceremonial instruments of royal authority

Collar on Tut's mummy

Buckle showing King Tut and his queen

Fan

Animal Mummies

Ancient Egyptians were close to the natural world. The ancient Egyptians left paintings and carvings of large animals such as elephants, hippos, leopards, and cheetahs, which were all once common in Egypt—and are still found in the area, but in much smaller numbers. Cats, bulls, and hawks were sacred to the people of ancient Egypt, who believed they embodied the spirit of certain gods and goddesses. When the sacred animals died, the Egyptians would mummify their bodies by wrapping them in linen and give them elaborate burials to honor their deities. Pets were also popular at this time. Although they weren't considered sacred animals, common companions like dogs, cats, and monkeys were just as important to ancient Egyptian society. In fact, they were one of the only ancient cultures to keep animals in their homes, and many Egyptians chose to be buried with them so that they would have companionship in eternity. As a result, scientists have discovered millions of mummified animals in the tombs of ancient Egyptians.

Bighorn sheep mummy

been caught and the tomb resealed. That was more than 3,000 years ago.

The explorers are fascinated by two tall statues in the antechamber showing Tut dressed in gold. The figures seem to be guarding another room. Sweltering in the heat, the group crawls through a hole created by the ancient robbers.

AMAZING DISCOVERY

Before them stands a huge wooden box, or shrine, that glitters with a layer of gold. This room must be Tut's burial chamber! At the very center of the shrine is a carved sarcophagus, or coffin. Inside it are three nested coffins, each one more richly decorated than the one before. Inside the last, made of solid gold, lies the mummy of Tutankhamun. A 22-pound (10-kg) gold mask (page 228, top) covers its head and shoulders. A collar

made from 171 separate gold pieces rests on the mummy's chest, and gold sandals are on its feet.

On one side of the burial chamber is a doorway revealing the fourth room of the tomb—the treasury. Towering over the other objects is a gold-covered shrine guarded by goddesses. It holds Tut's liver, lungs, stomach, and intestines. Each vital organ is preserved, wrapped in linen, and placed in its very own small coffin.

Today, millions of people visit Cairo's Egyptian Museum each year to see Tut's treasures. The ancient Egyptians believed that "to speak the name of the dead is to make them live again." If that is true, Tutankhamun certainly lives on.

Tut's Extreme Makeover

Experts recreated the young king's face using skull measurements from digital images of the mummy. What can't the technology tell us? The color of Tut's eyes and skin, and the shape of his nose.

THE LOST CITY OF POMPEII

When will the volcano that buried this ancient civilization blow again?

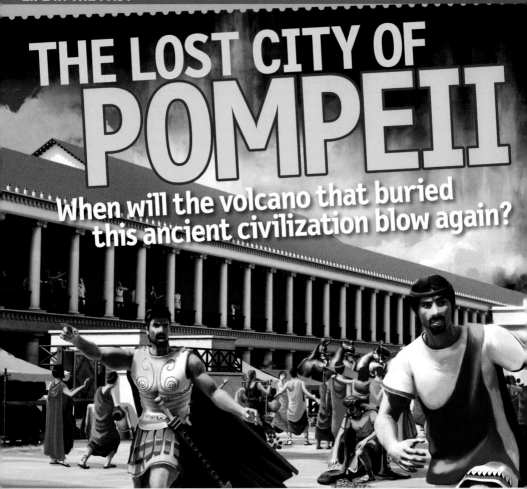

A deafening boom roars through Pompeii's crowded marketplace. The ground shakes violently, throwing the midday shoppers off balance and toppling stands of fish and meat. People start screaming and pointing toward Mount Vesuvius, a massive volcano that rises above the bustling city, located in what is now southern Italy.

Vesuvius has been silent for nearly 2,000 years, but it roars back to life, shooting ash and smoke into the air. Almost overnight, the city and most of its residents have vanished under a blanket of ash and lava.

Now, almost 2,000 years later, scientists agree that Vesuvius is overdue for another major eruption—but no one knows when it will happen. Three million people live in the volcano's shadow, in the modern-day city of Naples, Italy. Correctly predicting when the eruption will take place will mean the difference between life and death for many.

THE SKY IS FALLING

Thanks to excavations that started in 1748 and continue to this day, scientists have been able to re-create almost exactly what happened in Pompeii on that terrible day.

"The thick ash turned everything black," says Pompeii expert Andrew Wallace-Hadrill.

"People couldn't see the sun. All the landmarks disappeared. They didn't have the foggiest idea which way they were going."

Some people ran for their lives, clutching their valuable coins and jewelry. Other people took shelter in their homes. But the debris kept falling. Piles grew as deep as nine feet (2.7 m) in some places, blocking doorways and caving in roofs.

Around midnight, the first of four searing-hot clouds, or surges, of ash, pumice, rock, and toxic gas rushed down the mountainside. Traveling toward Pompeii at up to 180 miles (290 km) an hour, it scorched everything in its path. Around 7 a.m., 18 hours after the

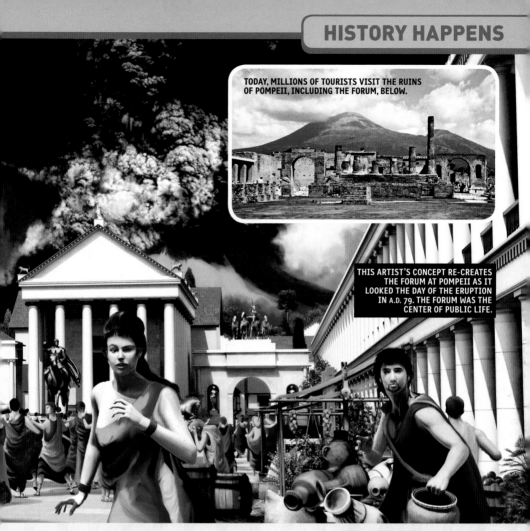

TODAY, MILLIONS OF TOURISTS VISIT THE RUINS OF POMPEII, INCLUDING THE FORUM, BELOW.

THIS ARTIST'S CONCEPT RE-CREATES THE FORUM AT POMPEII AS IT LOOKED THE DAY OF THE ERUPTION IN A.D. 79. THE FORUM WAS THE CENTER OF PUBLIC LIFE.

eruption, the last fiery surge buried the city.

LOST AND FOUND

Visiting the ruins of Pompeii today is like going back in time. The layers of ash actually helped preserve buildings, artwork, and even the forms of bodies. "It gives you the feeling you can reach out and touch the ancient world," Wallace-Hadrill says.

There are kitchens with pots on the stove and bakeries with loaves of bread—now turned to charcoal—still in the ovens. Narrow corridors lead to magnificent mansions with elaborate gardens and fountains. Mosaics, or designs made out of tiles, decorate the walls and floors.

WARNING SIGNS

Pompeii's destruction may be ancient history, but there's little doubt that disaster will strike again. Luckily, people living near Vesuvius today will likely receive evacuation warnings before the volcano blows.

Scientists are closely monitoring Vesuvius for shifts in the ground, earthquakes, and rising levels of certain gases, which could be signs of an upcoming eruption. The Italian government is also working on a plan to help people flee the area in the event of a natural disaster.

CREEPY CASTS

Volcanic ash settled around many of the victims at the moment of death. When the bodies decayed, holes remained inside the solid ash. Scientists poured plaster into the holes to preserve the shapes of the victims.

231

Bet you didn't know

6 incredible facts about the ancient world

1 People **ate noodles** in **CHINA** about **2,000 years** before **people** were eating pasta **in ITALY.**

2 **NOMADS** created **ICE SKATES** made of **bone** at least **4,000** years ago.

Abyssinian cat

3 **SALT was once** considered so valuable that ancient **ROMAN SOLDIERS were paid** partly in the mineral **instead of money.**

4 **CATS** were **domesticated** at least **3,000** years ago in **EGYPT.**

5 Each of the **2.3 million stones** in **EGYPT'S GREAT PYRAMID at GIZA** weighs as much as a pickup truck.

6 **Coins** in ancient China were **mined with holes in the center** so they could be **strung and carried more easily.**

COOL THINGS ABOUT

5 ANCIENT GREECE

ALTHOUGH THEY LIVED MORE THAN 2,000 YEARS AGO, the ancient Greeks were clearly ahead of their time. From science to sports, many Greek traditions are alive and well today. Here are some things that make this civilization stand out.

1 START-UP SCHOOL

In 387 B.C., the Greek philosopher Plato founded the Academy in Athens, which was the earliest example of a modern university. Students (including some women, against the traditions of the time) studied astronomy, biology, math, law, politics, and philosophy. Plato's hope was that the Academy would provide a place for all scholars to work toward better government in the Grecian cities. The Academy would become a center of learning for nearly 1,000 years.

2 OUTDOOR STAGE

The Greeks were among the first to perform plays. These performances sprung from festivals honoring their gods in which men would dress up, act out stories, and sing songs. They built large, outdoor theaters in most of their cities—some big enough to hold 15,000 people! The audience was so far away from the stage that the actors would wear elaborate costumes and sad- or happy-face masks so that people could see each character's expressions no matter where they were sitting.

3 GO LOCAL

Experts believe that ancient Greek civilization was likely begun nearly 4,000 years ago by the Mycenaeans of Crete, a Greek island. The ancient Greek Empire spread from Greece through Europe, and in 800 B.C. the Greeks began splitting their land into hundreds of city-states. Although most Greeks shared the same language and religion, each city-state maintained its own laws, customs, and rulers.

4 SUPERSTITIONS

The ancient Greeks were superstitious people. For instance, they originated the idea that breaking a mirror was bad luck. Believing mirrors showed the will of the gods, they thought a broken mirror meant the gods did not want you to see something unpleasant in your future. They also had unique ideas about food—some ancient Greeks would not eat beans because they believed they contained the souls of the dead.

5 ORIGINAL OLYMPICS

The ancient Greeks held many festivals in honor of their gods, including some serious sports competitions. The most famous took place in Olympia, Greece, starting in 776 B.C. Honoring the god Zeus, this two-day event—which inspired the modern-day Olympic Games—held contests in wrestling, boxing, long jump, javelin, discus, and chariot racing. Winners were given a wreath of leaves, free meals, and the best seats in the theater as prizes.

233

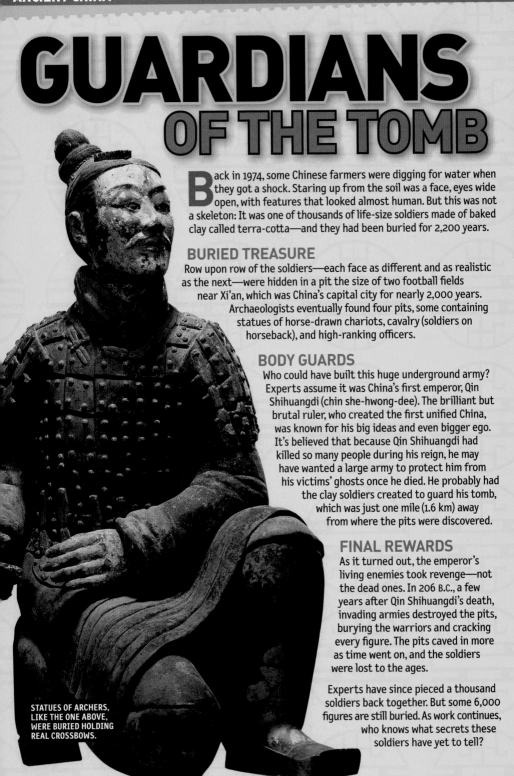

GUARDIANS
OF THE TOMB

Back in 1974, some Chinese farmers were digging for water when they got a shock. Staring up from the soil was a face, eyes wide open, with features that looked almost human. But this was not a skeleton: It was one of thousands of life-size soldiers made of baked clay called terra-cotta—and they had been buried for 2,200 years.

BURIED TREASURE

Row upon row of the soldiers—each face as different and as realistic as the next—were hidden in a pit the size of two football fields near Xi'an, which was China's capital city for nearly 2,000 years. Archaeologists eventually found four pits, some containing statues of horse-drawn chariots, cavalry (soldiers on horseback), and high-ranking officers.

BODY GUARDS

Who could have built this huge underground army? Experts assume it was China's first emperor, Qin Shihuangdi (chin she-hwong-dee). The brilliant but brutal ruler, who created the first unified China, was known for his big ideas and even bigger ego. It's believed that because Qin Shihuangdi had killed so many people during his reign, he may have wanted a large army to protect him from his victims' ghosts once he died. He probably had the clay soldiers created to guard his tomb, which was just one mile (1.6 km) away from where the pits were discovered.

FINAL REWARDS

As it turned out, the emperor's living enemies took revenge—not the dead ones. In 206 B.C., a few years after Qin Shihuangdi's death, invading armies destroyed the pits, burying the warriors and cracking every figure. The pits caved in more as time went on, and the soldiers were lost to the ages.

Experts have since pieced a thousand soldiers back together. But some 6,000 figures are still buried. As work continues, who knows what secrets these soldiers have yet to tell?

STATUES OF ARCHERS, LIKE THE ONE ABOVE, WERE BURIED HOLDING REAL CROSSBOWS.

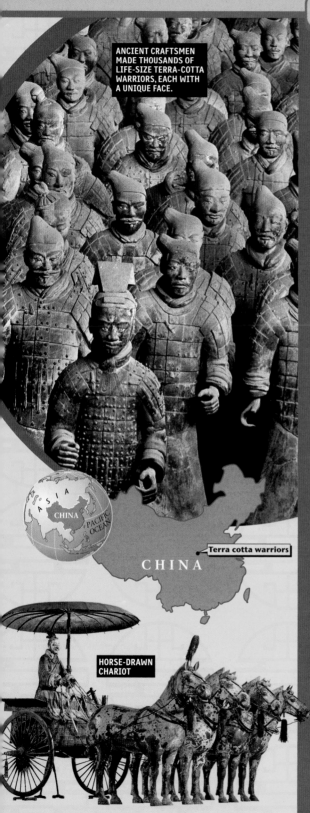

ANCIENT CRAFTSMEN MADE THOUSANDS OF LIFE-SIZE TERRA-COTTA WARRIORS, EACH WITH A UNIQUE FACE.

ASIA

CHINA

PACIFIC OCEAN

Terra cotta warriors

CHINA

HORSE-DRAWN CHARIOT

UNDER
RECONSTRUCTION

Experts have painstakingly rebuilt and restored a thousand terra-cotta warriors found in underground pits near the emperor's tomb. The complex is so vast that excavations may continue for generations.

A warrior's head poking out of the dirt still has traces of red paint. Originally all of the warriors were painted bright colors.

Workers brush dirt away from the collapsed roof that sheltered the terra-cotta warriors.

A toppled terra-cotta warrior lies in its 2,200-year-old underground tomb.

235

The Greatest HEISTS of All Time!

How criminal masterminds pulled off daring thefts— but still got caught.

TRAIN BANDITS

Where: Buckinghamshire, England
Date: August 8, 1963
The Loot: More than £2.6 million ($7 million) in Scottish banknotes from a Royal Mail Train.
The Master Plan: A team of 15 criminals rigs the train signal so the train stops unexpectedly. When it does, they jump into a car filled with mail sacks carrying the money. The thieves transfer the treasure to their vehicle and speed away to their hideout, a farmhouse 27 miles (43 km) away.
The Outcome: A tip leads investigators to the thieves' hideout, where they find stolen mail sacks and fingerprints on everything. Twelve thieves are taken to jail; three are never found.

A DAZZLING CRIME

Where: Antwerp, Belgium
Date: February 16, 2003
The Loot: More than 747,000 euros ($100 million) worth of jewels, gold, and money from a vault under Antwerp's Diamond Center.
The Master Plan: Thieves spend two-and-a-half years planning the robbery. Using hairspray, tape, and Styrofoam boxes, the thieves block the heat, light, and motion sensors so they can't detect the men's body temperatures or movements. They figure out the combination to the vault's three-ton (2.7-t) steel door by installing a tiny hidden camera.
The Outcome: Police discover a bag in the woods with two of the robbers' DNA. Four of the thieves go to jail. The stolen gems are never recovered.

THE ARTFUL CROOK

Where: Paris, France
Date: August 21, 1911
The Loot: The priceless "Mona Lisa"
The Master Plan: A man named Vincenzo Perugia poses as a workman at the Louvre art museum in Paris, grabs the famous painting, and walks past an unmanned guard station with it tucked under his smock.
The Outcome: After hiding the painting in a wooden trunk for two years, Perugia takes it to an art dealer in Florence, Italy—the same city where the "Mona Lisa" was painted by Leonardo da Vinci about 400 years earlier. The suspicious dealer calls the police, who arrest Perugia and return the "Mona Lisa" to the Louvre.

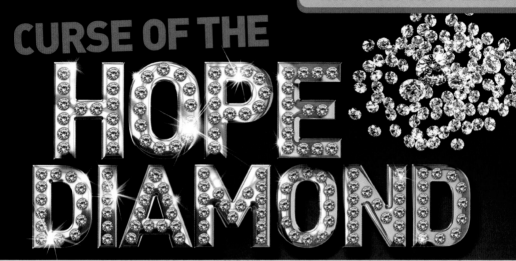

CURSE OF THE HOPE DIAMOND

Is the Hope diamond, one of the world's most valuable jewels, the bearer of bad luck? Legend has it that the stone was stolen from the eye of a sacred statue in India, and Hindu gods cursed the stone to punish the thieves. You decide if the curse is rock solid or just a gem of a tale!

LOSING THEIR HEADS

The French royal family once owned the diamond, but not for too long. After King Louis XVI and his wife, Marie Antoinette, were imprisoned and beheaded during the French Revolution, the government confiscated the stone, which thieves later stole before it was bought by the wealthy Hope family.

LOST HOPE

Lord Francis Hope eventually inherited the diamond, and then his wife left him and he had to sell the pricey stone to help pay off his huge debts. But the gem still bears the Hope family name.

TEMPTING FATE

Millionaire Evalyn McLean bought the diamond in 1911. But luck was not on McLean's side, either. During her lifetime, two of her children died, her husband became mentally ill, and she fell into serious debt.

DOOMED DELIVERY

In 1958 a mailman named James Todd delivered the diamond to its present home—the Smithsonian Institution in Washington, D.C. Within a year Todd's wife died and his house burned down. Was it the curse?

REAL OR FAKE?

"The curse isn't true," says Richard Kurin, author of the book *Hope Diamond: The Legendary History of a Cursed Gem*. It may all just be an eerie coincidence, but one thing's for sure, "The Hope diamond is so valuable because it is a unique stone and because of its famous story," says Kurin.

WHERE DO DIAMONDS COME FROM?

Natural diamonds form about a hundred miles underground and are the hardest known natural substance. Under extreme heat and pressure, carbon atoms are squeezed together into the hard, clear crystals. Volcanic eruptions carry the diamonds toward the Earth's surface, where they are mined for use in industrial tools and sparkly jewelry.

237

SOLVING THE
Ancient Mystery

A s the sun dips below the horizon, a pink glow falls upon a circle of massive stones. Some rise 20 feet (6 m) in the air. Others lie scattered on the field. This gigantic monument, called Stonehenge, has towered above England's Salisbury Plain for 4,500 years—but it's still one of the greatest mysteries on Earth.

Why would ancient people haul hulking stones for miles to this site? And what did this strange prehistoric circle mean to them? We'll probably never know for sure. But one archaeologist's theory may provide answers to these age-old questions.

AN ARTIST'S CONCEPT OF THE COMPLETED STONEHENGE, AROUND 1600 B.C.

THE UNEXPLAINED

For centuries people have been trying to unlock the secrets hidden in these stones. One legend from the 12th century A.D. claimed that giants had placed Stonehenge on a mountain in Ireland, but a wizard named Merlin magically moved it to England.

Later, people guessed Stonehenge was an astronomical observatory because the tallest stones frame the sunrise on the longest day of the year (the summer solstice) and the sunset on the shortest day of the year (the winter solstice).

Other theories have suggested that the site was a place of healing, or a Stone Age "computer" that predicted solar and lunar eclipses, or perhaps a temple to the sun and moon gods.

One thing's for sure: Stonehenge was used as

# of Stonehenge

a cemetery. Experts think that some 200 people are buried on the grounds. But why they were put to rest there is anyone's guess.

AN AMAZING DISCOVERY

Less than two miles (3 km) from Stonehenge, archaeologist Mike Parker Pearson—with support from the National Geographic Society—discovered both the remains of a second, smaller stone circle as well as the ruins of a village that he says may have housed the builders of Stonehenge. Both the stone circle, named "Blue Stonehenge" after the color of the 27 giant stones it once incorporated, and the village are located on a prehistoric site called Durrington Walls. Because of its similar positioning along the River Avon, Parker Pearson suggests that Blue Stonehenge may have been the starting point of a funeral procession that ended at Stonehenge.

STONEHENGE "SUBURB"

If Stonehenge and Bluehenge were for mourning, Durrington Walls may have been for celebrating.

Parker Pearson has unearthed the remains of a cluster of seven village houses and expects to find hundreds more. His team also dug up bones of barbecued pigs and cows—evidence that Stone Age neighbors probably gathered here for feasts. "Durrington Walls may have been like a county fair, where people came to meet, trade, and build Stonehenge," Parker Pearson says.

Is it possible that when leaders at the site died, their bodies were transported from Bluehenge to Stonehenge for burial? Parker Pearson is digging for more clues to prove his theory. For now it seems that the history of Stonehenge will never be written in stone.

ATLANTIC OCEAN

UNITED KINGDOM

EUROPE

Stonehenge

AFRICA

239

WAR!

Since the beginning of time, different countries, territories, and cultures have feuded with each other over land, power, and politics. Major military conflicts include the following wars:

1095–1291 THE CRUSADES
Starting late in the 11th century, these wars over religion were fought in the Middle East for nearly 200 years.

1337–1453 HUNDRED YEARS' WAR
France and England battled over rights to land for more than a century before the French eventually drove the English out in 1453.

1754–1763 FRENCH AND INDIAN WAR (part of Europe's Seven Years' War)
A nine-year war between the British and French for control of North America.

1775–1783 AMERICAN REVOLUTION
Thirteen British colonies in America united to reject the rule of the British government and to form the United States of America.

1861–1865 AMERICAN CIVIL WAR
Occurred when the northern states (the Union) went to war with the southern states, which had seceded, or withdrew, to form the Confederate States of America. Slavery was one of the key issues in the Civil War.

1910–1920 MEXICAN REVOLUTION
The people of Mexico revolted against the rule of dictator President Porfirio Díaz, leading to his eventual defeat and to a democratic government.

1914–1918 WORLD WAR I
The assassination of Austria's Archduke Ferdinand by a Serbian nationalist sparked this wide-spreading war. The U.S. entered after Germany sunk the British ship *Lusitania,* killing more than 120 Americans.

1918–1920 RUSSIAN CIVIL WAR
A conflict pitting the Communist Red Army against the foreign-backed White Army. The Red Army won after four hostile years, leading to the establishment of the Union of Soviet Socialist Republics (U.S.S.R.) in 1922.

1936–1939 SPANISH CIVIL WAR
Aid from Italy and Germany helped the Nationalists gain victory over the Communist-supported Republicans. The war resulted in the loss of more than 300,000 lives and increased tension in Europe leading up to World War II.

1939–1945 WORLD WAR II
This massive conflict in Europe, Asia, and North Africa involved many countries that aligned with the two sides: the Allies and the Axis. After the bombing of Pearl Harbor in Hawaii in 1941, the U.S. entered the war on the side of the Allies. More than 50 million people died during the war.

1946–1949 CHINESE CIVIL WAR
Also known as the "War of Liberation," this pitted the Communist and Nationalist parties in China against each other. The Communists won.

1950–1953 KOREAN WAR
Kicked off when the Communist forces of North Korea, with backing from the Soviet Union, invaded their democratic neighbor to the south. A coalition of 16 countries from the United Nations stepped in to support South Korea.

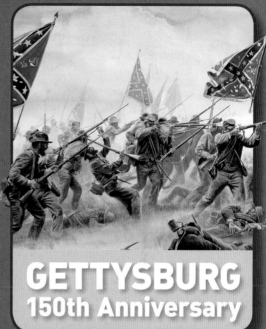

GETTYSBURG
150th Anniversary

1950s–1975 VIETNAM WAR
Fought between the Communist North, supported by its allies including China, and the government of South Vietnam, supported by the United States and other anticommunist nations.

1967 SIX-DAY WAR
A battle for land between Israel and the states of Egypt, Jordan, and Syria. The outcome resulted in Israel's gaining control of coveted territory, including the Gaza Strip and the West Bank.

1990–1991 PERSIAN GULF WAR
When Iraq invaded the country of Kuwait over oil conflicts, a coalition of 32 nations stepped in to destroy Iraq's forces.

1991–PRESENT
SOMALI CIVIL WAR
Began when Somalia's last president, a dictator named Mohamed Siad Barre, was overthrown. The war has led to years of fighting and anarchy.

2001–PRESENT
WAR IN AFGHANISTAN
After attacks in the United States by the terrorist group al-Qaeda, a coalition of more than 40 countries invaded Afghanistan to find Osama bin Laden and other al-Qaeda members. Bin Laden was killed in a U.S. covert operation in 2011.

2003–2011 WAR IN IRAQ
A coalition led by the U.S., and including Britain, Australia, and Spain, invaded Iraq over suspicions that Iraq had weapons of mass destruction.

THE YEAR WAS 1863. The country was embroiled in the Civil War as the Confederacy fought for its independence from the United States. And throughout the first three days of July, soldiers from the Union's Army of the Potomac and the Confederate's Army of Northern Virginia met in Gettysburg, Pennsylvania. Over the course of those three days, casualties numbered about 51,000 as the Union forces eventually defeated the Confederates, making the Battle of Gettysburg the bloodiest battle of the Civil War.

More than 150 years after the Civil War began, the site of this epic clash—known as a turning point that shifted the outcome of the war in the Union's favor—has been well preserved and still remains mostly unchanged. Each year, thousands of visitors roam Gettysburg's flat, grassy fields and view the monuments established to remember this history—and to honor those who lost their lives in one of the most unforgettable battles ever fought on North American soil.

The Constitution & the Bill of Rights

The United States Constitution was written in 1787 by a group of political leaders from the 13 states that made up the U.S. at the time. Thirty-nine men, including Benjamin Franklin and James Madison, signed the document to create a national government. While some feared the creation of a strong federal government, all 13 states eventually ratified, or approved, the Constitution, making it the law of the land. The Constitution has three major parts: the preamble, the articles, and the amendments.

THE PREAMBLE outlines the basic purposes of the government: *We the People of the United States, in order to form a more perfect Union, establish justice, insure domestic tranquility, provide for the common defense, promote the general welfare, and secure the blessings of liberty to ourselves and our posterity, do ordain and establish this Constitution for the United States of America.*

SEVEN ARTICLES outline the powers of Congress, the President, and the court system:

Article I outlines the legislative branch—the Senate and the House of Representatives—and its powers and responsibilities.

Article II outlines the executive branch—the Presidency—and its powers and responsibilities.

Article III outlines the judicial branch—the court system—and its powers and responsibilities.

Article IV describes the individual states' rights and powers.

Article V outlines the amendment process.

Article VI establishes the Constitution as the law of the land.

Article VII gives the requirements for the Constitution to be approved.

THE AMENDMENTS, or additions to the Constitution, were put in later as needed. In 1791, the first ten amendments, known as the Bill of Rights, were added. Since then another 17 amendments have been added. This is the Bill of Rights:

1st Amendment: guarantees freedom of religion, speech, and the press, and the right to assemble and petition

2nd Amendment: discusses the militia and the right of people to bear arms

3rd Amendment: prohibits the military or troops from using private homes without consent

4th Amendment: protects people and their homes from search, arrest, or seizure without probable cause or a warrant

5th Amendment: grants people the right to have a trial and prevents punishment before prosecution; protects private property from being taken without compensation

6th Amendment: guarantees the right to a speedy and public trial

7th Amendment: guarantees a trial by jury in certain cases

8th Amendment: forbids "cruel and unusual punishments"

9th Amendment: states that the Constitution is not all-encompassing and does not deny people other, unspecified rights

10th Amendment: grants the powers not covered by the Constitution to the states and the people

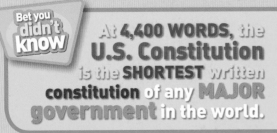

Bet you didn't know

At 4,400 WORDS, the U.S. Constitution is the SHORTEST written constitution of any MAJOR government in the world.

A Pennsylvania GENERAL ASSEMBLY CLERK HANDWROTE the Constitution for $30.

GEORGE
WASHINGTON'S
REAL LOOK

WITH HELP FROM SCIENCE, THESE WAX FIGURES SOLVE THE MYSTERY OF WHAT THE FIRST U.S. PRESIDENT LOOKED LIKE.

Did George Washington really look like the portrait on the dollar bill, which appears above? Without photos, no one knew for sure. So officials at Mount Vernon, Washington's Virginia estate, called the experts. Using scientific methods, they accurately recreated Washington at the ages of 19, 45 (big picture), and 57. Here's how they gave Washington a makeover.

FACE In 1785, artist Jean Antoine Houdon created a mask of Washington after laying plaster-soaked gauze over his face. The mask was a near-perfect match of Washington's face, so scientists scanned it into a computer to create a 3-D image (right) that accurately showed Washington's facial features.

HAIR Because Washington often powdered his hair, not many people knew what his real hair color was. That's why experts examined Washington's hair samples (left, in center) and written descriptions by people who knew him. That confirmed once and for all that the President had reddish-brown hair.

Washington, age 19

JAW Washington started losing his teeth around age 24, which meant that his jaw changed shape over time. To determine what Washington's jawline would have looked like at 19, anthropologist Jeffrey Schwartz examined two sets of Washington's false teeth, which were scanned into a computer.

The result? Turns out the real George Washington was thinner than many artists portrayed him. And his face was actually broader and longer than how it looks on the dollar bill. "Basically," Schwartz says, "no one portrait represents him faithfully from head to toe."

Washington, age 57

243

Branches of Government

The **UNITED STATES GOVERNMENT** is divided into three branches: **executive**, **legislative**, and **judicial**. The system of checks and balances is a way to control power and to make sure one branch can't take the reins of government. For example, most of the President's actions require the approval of Congress. Likewise, the laws passed in Congress must be signed by the President before they can take effect.

White House

Executive Branch

The Constitution lists the central powers of the President: to serve as Commander in Chief of the armed forces; make treaties with other nations; grant pardons; inform Congress on the state of the union; and appoint ambassadors, officials, and judges. The executive branch includes the President and the governmental departments. Originally there were three departments—State, War, and Treasury. Today there are 15 departments (see chart below).

Theodore Roosevelt had the West Wing built onto the White House in 1902 so he could have a quiet place to work. It now houses the official offices of the President and senior members of the Executive Office staff.

Government of the United States

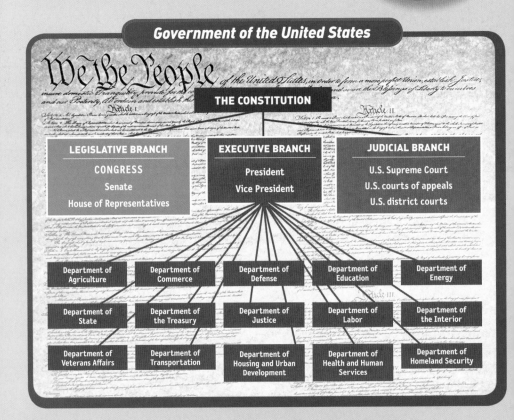

THE CONSTITUTION

LEGISLATIVE BRANCH

CONGRESS

Senate

House of Representatives

EXECUTIVE BRANCH

President

Vice President

JUDICIAL BRANCH

U.S. Supreme Court

U.S. courts of appeals

U.S. district courts

Department of Agriculture	Department of Commerce	Department of Defense	Department of Education	Department of Energy
Department of State	Department of the Treasury	Department of Justice	Department of Labor	Department of the Interior
Department of Veterans Affairs	Department of Transportation	Department of Housing and Urban Development	Department of Health and Human Services	Department of Homeland Security

Legislative Branch

The U.S. Capitol in Washington, D.C.

This branch is made up of Congress—the Senate and the House of Representatives. The Constitution grants Congress the power to make laws. Congress is made up of elected representatives from each state. Each state has two representatives in the Senate, while the number of representatives in the House is determined by the size of the state's population. Washington, D.C., and the territories elect non-voting representatives to the House of Representatives. The Founding Fathers set up this system as a compromise between big states—which wanted representation based on population—and small states—which wanted all states to have equal representation rights.

Judicial Branch

The judicial branch is composed of the federal court system—the U.S. Supreme Court, the courts of appeals, and the district courts. The Supreme Court is the most powerful court. Its motto is "Equal Justice Under Law." This influential court is responsible for interpreting the Constitution and applying it to the cases that it hears. The decisions of the Supreme Court are absolute—they are the final word on any legal question.

The U.S. Supreme Court Building in Washington, D.C.

There are nine justices on the Supreme Court. They are appointed by the President of the United States and confirmed by the Senate.

Bet you didn't know

It's Against the Law to:

DYE OR COLOR the feathers and fur of baby chicks, ducklings, and rabbits in California.

RIDE A SLED that's pulled by a car in Portland, Oregon.

PLAY PINBALL if you're a kid in South Carolina.

RIDE A BIKE with your hands off the handlebars in Sun Prairie, Wisconsin.

WAKE UP A BEAR to take its picture in Alaska.

BRING A SKUNK into the state of Tennessee.

HONK YOUR HORN in front of a sandwich shop at night in Little Rock, Arkansas.

HOOT LOUDLY after 11 p.m. on weekdays in Athens, Georgia.

RIDE A HORSE faster than ten miles an hour (16 kph) in the streets of Indianapolis, Indiana.

OWN MORE THAN FOUR DOGS in Cheyenne, Wyoming.

The President of the United States is the chief of the executive branch, the Commander in Chief of the U.S. armed forces, and head of the federal government. Elected every four years, the President is the highest policymaker in the nation. The 22nd Amendment (1951) says that no person may be elected to the office of President more than twice. There have been 44 Presidencies and 43 Presidents.

JAMES MONROE
5th President of the United States ★ 1817–1825

BORN April 28, 1758, in Westmoreland County, VA
POLITICAL PARTY Democratic-Republican
NO. OF TERMS two
VICE PRESIDENT Daniel D. Tompkins
DIED July 4, 1831, in New York, NY

GEORGE WASHINGTON
1st President of the United States ★ 1789–1797

BORN Feb. 22, 1732, in Pope's Creek, Westmoreland County, VA
POLITICAL PARTY Federalist
NO. OF TERMS two
VICE PRESIDENT John Adams
DIED Dec. 14, 1799, at Mount Vernon, VA

JOHN QUINCY ADAMS
6th President of the United States ★ 1825–1829

BORN July 11, 1767, in Braintree (now Quincy), MA
POLITICAL PARTY Democratic-Republican
NO. OF TERMS one
VICE PRESIDENT John Caldwell Calhoun
DIED Feb. 23, 1848, at the U.S. Capitol, Washington, DC

JOHN ADAMS
2nd President of the United States ★ 1797–1801

BORN Oct. 30, 1735, in Braintree (now Quincy), MA
POLITICAL PARTY Federalist
NO. OF TERMS one
VICE PRESIDENT Thomas Jefferson
DIED July 4, 1826, in Quincy, MA

ANDREW JACKSON
7th President of the United States ★ 1829–1837

BORN March 15, 1767, in the Waxhaw region, NC and SC
POLITICAL PARTY Democrat
NO. OF TERMS two
VICE PRESIDENTS 1st term: John Caldwell Calhoun
2nd term: Martin Van Buren
DIED June 8, 1845, in Nashville, TN

THOMAS JEFFERSON
3rd President of the United States ★ 1801–1809

BORN April 13, 1743, at Shadwell, Goochland (now Albemarle) County, VA
POLITICAL PARTY Democratic-Republican
NO. OF TERMS two
VICE PRESIDENTS 1st term: Aaron Burr
2nd term: George Clinton
DIED July 4, 1826, at Monticello, Charlottesville, VA

MARTIN VAN BUREN
8th President of the United States ★ 1837–1841

BORN Dec. 5, 1782, in Kinderhook, NY
POLITICAL PARTY Democrat
NO. OF TERMS one
VICE PRESIDENT Richard M. Johnson
DIED July 24, 1862, in Kinderhook, NY

JAMES MADISON
4th President of the United States ★ 1809–1817

BORN March 16, 1751, at Belle Grove, Port Conway, VA
POLITICAL PARTY Democratic-Republican
NO. OF TERMS two
VICE PRESIDENTS 1st term: George Clinton
2nd term: Elbridge Gerry
DIED June 28, 1836, at Montpelier, Orange County, VA

WILLIAM HENRY HARRISON
9th President of the United States ★ 1841

BORN Feb. 9, 1773, in Charles City County, VA
POLITICAL PARTY Whig
NO. OF TERMS one (cut short by death)
VICE PRESIDENT John Tyler
DIED April 4, 1841, in the White House, Washington, DC

JOHN TYLER

10th President of the United States ★ *1841–1845*
BORN March 29, 1790, in Charles City County, VA
POLITICAL PARTY Whig
NO. OF TERMS one (partial)
VICE PRESIDENT none
DIED Jan. 18, 1862, in Richmond, VA

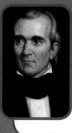

JAMES K. POLK

11th President of the United States ★ *1845–1849*
BORN Nov. 2, 1795, near Pineville, Mecklenburg County, NC
POLITICAL PARTY Democrat
NO. OF TERMS one
VICE PRESIDENT George Mifflin Dallas
DIED June 15, 1849, at Nashville, TN

ZACHARY TAYLOR

12th President of the United States ★ *1849–1850*
BORN Nov. 24, 1784, in Orange County, VA
POLITICAL PARTY Whig
NO. OF TERMS one (cut short by death)
VICE PRESIDENT Millard Fillmore
DIED July 9, 1850, in the White House, Washington, DC

MILLARD FILLMORE

13th President of the United States ★ *1850–1853*
BORN Jan. 7, 1800, in Cayuga County, NY
POLITICAL PARTY Whig
NO. OF TERMS one (partial)
VICE PRESIDENT none
DIED March 8, 1874, in Buffalo, NY

FRANKLIN PIERCE

14th President of the United States ★ *1853–1857*
BORN Nov. 23, 1804, in Hillsborough (now Hillsboro), NH
POLITICAL PARTY Democrat
NO. OF TERMS one
VICE PRESIDENT William Rufus De Vane King
DIED Oct. 8, 1869, in Concord, NH

JAMES BUCHANAN

15th President of the United States ★ *1857–1861*
BORN April 23, 1791, in Cove Gap, PA
POLITICAL PARTY Democrat
NO. OF TERMS one
VICE PRESIDENT John Cabell Breckinridge
DIED June 1, 1868, in Lancaster, PA

ABRAHAM LINCOLN

16th President of the United States ★ *1861–1865*
BORN Feb. 12, 1809, near Hodgenville, KY
POLITICAL PARTY Republican (formerly Whig)
NO. OF TERMS two (assassinated)
VICE PRESIDENTS 1st term: Hannibal Hamlin
2nd term: Andrew Johnson
DIED April 15, 1865, in Washington, DC

ANDREW JOHNSON

17th President of the United States ★ *1865–1869*
BORN Dec. 29, 1808, in Raleigh, NC
POLITICAL PARTY Democrat
NO. OF TERMS one (partial)
VICE PRESIDENT none
DIED July 31, 1875, in Carter's Station, TN

Presidential Nicknames

"His Rotundity" John Adams
"Fiddlin' Thomas" Thomas Jefferson
"The Short Sir" James Madison
"The Old Man" William Henry Harrison
"Honest Abe" Abraham Lincoln
"Uncle Jumbo" Grover Cleveland
"Big Bill" William Howard Taft
"Ike" Dwight David Eisenhower
"JFK" John Fitzgerald Kennedy
"President Squeak" Jimmy Carter
"The Gipper" Ronald Reagan
"Bubba" William Jefferson Clinton
"Dubya" George Walker Bush

ULYSSES S. GRANT

18th President of the United States ★ 1869–1877

BORN April 27, 1822, in Point Pleasant, OH
POLITICAL PARTY Republican
NO. OF TERMS two
VICE PRESIDENTS 1st term: Schuyler Colfax
2nd term: Henry Wilson
DIED July 23, 1885, in Mount McGregor, NY

RUTHERFORD B. HAYES

19th President of the United States ★ 1877–1881

BORN Oct. 4, 1822, in Delaware, OH
POLITICAL PARTY Republican
NO. OF TERMS one
VICE PRESIDENT William Almon Wheeler
DIED Jan. 17, 1893, in Fremont, OH

JAMES A. GARFIELD

20th President of the United States ★ 1881

BORN Nov. 19, 1831, near Orange, OH
POLITICAL PARTY Republican
NO. OF TERMS one (assassinated)
VICE PRESIDENT Chester A. Arthur
DIED Sept. 19, 1881, in Elberon, NJ

CHESTER A. ARTHUR

21st President of the United States ★ 1881–1885

BORN Oct. 5, 1829, in Fairfield, VT
POLITICAL PARTY Republican
NO. OF TERMS one (partial)
VICE PRESIDENT none
DIED Nov. 18, 1886, in New York, NY

GROVER CLEVELAND

22nd and 24th President of the United States 1885–1889 ★ 1893–1897

BORN March 18, 1837, in Caldwell, NJ
POLITICAL PARTY Democrat
NO. OF TERMS two (nonconsecutive)
VICE PRESIDENTS 1st administration:
Thomas Andrews Hendricks
2nd administration:
Adlai Ewing Stevenson
DIED June 24, 1908, in Princeton, NJ

BENJAMIN HARRISON

23rd President of the United States ★ 1889–1893

BORN Aug. 20, 1833, in North Bend, OH
POLITICAL PARTY Republican
NO. OF TERMS one
VICE PRESIDENT Levi Parsons Morton
DIED March 13, 1901, in Indianapolis, IN

WILLIAM MCKINLEY

25th President of the United States ★ 1897–1901

BORN Jan. 29, 1843, in Niles, OH
POLITICAL PARTY Republican
NO. OF TERMS two (assassinated)
VICE PRESIDENTS 1st term:
Garret Augustus Hobart
2nd term:
Theodore Roosevelt
DIED Sept. 14, 1901, in Buffalo, NY

THEODORE ROOSEVELT

26th President of the United States ★ 1901–1909

BORN Oct. 27, 1858, in New York, NY
POLITICAL PARTY Republican
NO. OF TERMS one, plus balance of McKinley's term
VICE PRESIDENTS 1st term: none
2nd term: Charles Warren Fairbanks
DIED Jan. 6, 1919, in Oyster Bay, NY

WILLIAM HOWARD TAFT

27th President of the United States ★ 1909–1913

BORN Sept. 15, 1857, in Cincinnati, OH
POLITICAL PARTY Republican
NO. OF TERMS one
VICE PRESIDENT James Schoolcraft Sherman
DIED March 8, 1930, in Washington, DC

WOODROW WILSON

28th President of the United States ★ 1913–1921

BORN Dec. 29, 1856, in Staunton, VA
POLITICAL PARTY Democrat
NO. OF TERMS two
VICE PRESIDENT Thomas Riley Marshall
DIED Feb. 3, 1924, in Washington, DC

WARREN G. HARDING

29th President of the United States ★ 1921–1923
BORN Nov. 2, 1865, in Caledonia
(now Blooming Grove), OH
POLITICAL PARTY Republican
NO. OF TERMS one (died while in office)
VICE PRESIDENT Calvin Coolidge
DIED Aug. 2, 1923, in San Francisco, CA

HARRY S. TRUMAN

33rd President of the United States ★ 1945–1953
BORN May 8, 1884, in Lamar, MO
POLITICAL PARTY Democrat
NO. OF TERMS one, plus balance of
Franklin D. Roosevelt's term
VICE PRESIDENTS 1st term: none
2nd term:
Alben William Barkley
DIED Dec. 26, 1972, in Independence, MO

CALVIN COOLIDGE

30th President of the United States ★ 1923–1929
BORN July 4, 1872, in Plymouth, VT
POLITICAL PARTY Republican
NO. OF TERMS one, plus balance of
Harding's term
VICE PRESIDENTS 1st term: none
2nd term:
Charles Gates Dawes
DIED Jan. 5, 1933, in Northampton, MA

DWIGHT D. EISENHOWER

34th President of the United States ★ 1953–1961
BORN Oct. 14, 1890, in Denison, TX
POLITICAL PARTY Republican
NO. OF TERMS two
VICE PRESIDENT Richard M. Nixon
DIED March 28, 1969,
in Washington, DC

HERBERT HOOVER

31st President of the United States ★ 1929–1933
BORN Aug. 10, 1874,
in West Branch, IA
POLITICAL PARTY Republican
NO. OF TERMS one
VICE PRESIDENT Charles Curtis
DIED Oct. 20, 1964, in New York, NY

JOHN F. KENNEDY

35th President of the United States ★ 1961–1963
BORN May 29, 1917, in Brookline, MA
POLITICAL PARTY Democrat
NO. OF TERMS one (assassinated)
VICE PRESIDENT Lyndon B. Johnson
DIED Nov. 22, 1963,
in Dallas, TX

FRANKLIN D. ROOSEVELT

32nd President of the United States ★ 1933–1945
BORN Jan. 30, 1882, in Hyde Park, NY
POLITICAL PARTY Democrat
NO. OF TERMS four (died while in office)
VICE PRESIDENTS 1st & 2nd terms: John
Nance Garner; 3rd term:
Henry Agard Wallace;
4th term: Harry S. Truman
DIED April 12, 1945,
in Warm Springs, GA

LYNDON B. JOHNSON

36th President of the United States ★ 1963–1969
BORN Aug. 27, 1908,
near Stonewall, TX
POLITICAL PARTY Democrat
NO. OF TERMS one, plus balance of
Kennedy's term
VICE PRESIDENTS 1st term: none
2nd term: Hubert
Horatio Humphrey
DIED Jan. 22, 1973, near San Antonio, TX

TRAVELING IN STYLE

CALVIN COOLIDGE cruised **on a** PRESIDENTIAL YACHT called the *Mayflower.*

BARACK OBAMA's limousine, a special-made Cadillac complete with **eight inches of** ARMOR PLATING, is nicknamed "The Beast."

AIR FORCE ONE, also known as THE PRESIDENTIAL JET, has three levels and is equipped with an operating room with life-saving equipment in case of an emergency.

JOHN F. KENNEDY became the **first President to pilot** a JET AIRCRAFT, a modified Boeing 707.

RICHARD NIXON
37th President of the United States ★ 1969–1974
BORN Jan. 9, 1913, in Yorba Linda, CA
POLITICAL PARTY Republican
NO. OF TERMS two (resigned)
VICE PRESIDENTS 1st term & 2nd term (partial): Spiro Theodore Agnew; 2nd term (balance): Gerald R. Ford
DIED April 22, 1994, in New York, NY

GERALD R. FORD
38th President of the United States ★ 1974–1977
BORN July 14, 1913, in Omaha, NE
POLITICAL PARTY Republican
NO. OF TERMS one (partial)
VICE PRESIDENT Nelson Aldrich Rockefeller
DIED Dec. 26, 2006, in Rancho Mirage, CA

JIMMY CARTER
39th President of the United States ★ 1977–1981
BORN Oct. 1, 1924, in Plains, GA
POLITICAL PARTY Democrat
NO. OF TERMS one
VICE PRESIDENT Walter Frederick (Fritz) Mondale

RONALD REAGAN
40th President of the United States ★ 1981–1989
BORN Feb. 6, 1911, in Tampico, IL
POLITICAL PARTY Republican
NO. OF TERMS two
VICE PRESIDENT George H. W. Bush
DIED June 5, 2004, in Los Angeles, CA

GEORGE H. W. BUSH
41st President of the United States ★ 1989–1993
BORN June 12, 1924, in Milton, MA
POLITICAL PARTY Republican
NO. OF TERMS one
VICE PRESIDENT James Danforth (Dan) Quayle III

BILL CLINTON
42nd President of the United States ★ 1993–2001
BORN Aug. 19, 1946, in Hope, AR
POLITICAL PARTY Democrat
NO. OF TERMS two
VICE PRESIDENT Albert Gore, Jr.

GEORGE W. BUSH
43rd President of the United States ★ 2001–2009
BORN July 6, 1946, in New Haven, CT
POLITICAL PARTY Republican
NO. OF TERMS two
VICE PRESIDENT Richard Bruce Cheney

BARACK OBAMA
44th President of the United States ★ 2009–present
BORN August 4, 1961, in Honolulu, HI
POLITICAL PARTY Democrat
VICE PRESIDENT Joseph Biden

Presidential Firsts

FIRST TO BE PHOTOGRAPHED: James Polk

FIRST TO RIDE IN A CAR WHILE IN OFFICE: Theodore Roosevelt

FIRST TO APPEAR ON TELEVISION: Franklin Delano Roosevelt

FIRST TO HAVE A STEPMOTHER: Millard Fillmore

FIRST LEFT-HANDED PRESIDENT: James Garfield

FIRST TO APPEAR ON A STAMP: George Washington

FAST FACT

Benjamin Harrison had the White House wired for electricity, but he never touched a light switch for fear of getting shocked!

The Indian Experience

American Indians are indigenous to North and South America—they are the people who were here before Columbus and other European explorers came to these lands. They lived in nations, tribes, and bands across both continents. For decades following the arrival of Europeans in 1492, American Indians clashed with the newcomers who had ruptured the Indians' way of living.

Tribal Land

During the 19th century, both United States legislation and military action restricted the movement of American Indians, forcing them to live on reservations and attempting to dismantle tribal structures. For centuries Indians were often displaced or killed, or became assimilated into the general U.S. population. In 1924 the Indian Citizenship Act granted citizenship to all American Indians. Unfortunately, this was not enough to end the social discrimination and mistreatment that many Indians have faced. Today, American Indians living in the U.S. still face many challenges.

Healing the Past

Many members of the 560-plus recognized tribes in the United States live primarily on reservations. Some tribes have more than one reservation, while others have none. Together these reservations make up less than 3 percent of the nation's land area. The tribal governments on reservations have the right to form their own governments and enforce laws, similar to individual states. Many feel that this sovereignty is still not enough to right the wrongs of the past: They hope for a change in the U.S. government's relationship with American Indians.

A Navajo man in traditional costume, Monument Valley, Arizona/Utah, U.S.A.

More than 44,000 American Indians served in the U.S. armed forces in World War II.

More than 173,000 people live on the Navajo reservation in Arizona, New Mexico, and Utah—making it the largest reservation in the U.S.A.

CIVIL RIGHTS

The Little Rock Nine study during the weeks when they were blocked from school.

Although the Constitution protects the civil rights of American citizens, it has not always been able to protect all Americans from persecution or discrimination. During the first half of the 20th century, many Americans, particularly African Americans, were subjected to widespread discrimination and racism. By the mid-1950s, many people were eager to end the bonds of racism and bring freedom to all men and women.

The civil rights movement of the 1950s and 1960s sought to end the racial discrimination against African Americans, especially in the southern states. The movement wanted to restore the fundamentals of economic and social equality to those who had been oppressed.

The Little Rock Nine

September 4, 1957, marked the first day of school at Little Rock Central High in Little Rock, Arkansas. But this was no ordinary back-to-school scene: Armed soldiers surrounded the entrance, awaiting the arrival of Central's first-ever African-American students. The welcome was not warm, however, as the students—now known as the Little Rock Nine—were refused entry into the school by the soldiers and a group of protesters, angry about the potential integration. This did not deter the students, and they gained the support of President Dwight D. Eisenhower to eventually earn their right to go to an integrated school. Today, the Little Rock Nine are still considered civil rights icons for challenging a racist system—and winning!

Key Events in the Civil Rights Movement

1954	The Supreme Court case *Brown* v. *Board of Education* declares school segregation illegal.
1955	Rosa Parks refuses to give up her bus seat to a white passenger and spurs a bus boycott.
1957	The Little Rock Nine help to integrate schools.
1960	Four black college students begin sit-ins at a restaurant in Greensboro, North Carolina.
1961	Freedom Rides to southern states begin as a way to protest segregation in transportation.
1963	Martin Luther King, Jr., leads the famous March on Washington.
1964	The Civil Rights Act, signed by President Lyndon B. Johnson, prohibits discrimination based on race, color, religion, sex, and national origin.
1967	Thurgood Marshall becomes the first African American to be named to the Supreme Court.
1968	President Lyndon B. Johnson signs the Civil Rights Act of 1968, which prohibits discrimination in the sale, rental, and financing of housing.

Champions of Civil Rights: Prominent figures who emerged from the civil rights movement included Rosa Parks, John F. Kennedy, Malcolm X, and Martin Luther King, Jr. Here's more about these powerful leaders.

ROSA PARKS 1913 (Alabama, U.S.A.) – 2005 (Michigan, U.S.A.)

After refusing to give up her bus seat to a white passenger, activist Parks sparked a 381-day boycott of the city bus line in Montgomery, Alabama. This eventually led to the 1956 Supreme Court ruling declaring segregation illegal on public buses, giving Parks the unofficial title of "The Mother of the Modern-Day Civil Rights Movement."

Did you know? At the time of her arrest, Parks was 42 and on her way home from work as a seamstress. Aside from being arrested, she was fined $14 for refusing to give up her seat.

JOHN F. KENNEDY 1917 (Massachusetts, U.S.A.) – 1963 (Texas, U.S.A.)

As President, Kennedy used executive orders and pleas to the public to show his support of civil rights. This included sending 400 U.S. Marshals to Alabama in 1961 to protect the "Freedom Riders," a group of men and women who boarded buses, trains, and planes to the deep South to test the 1960 U.S. Supreme Court ruling outlawing racial segregation. Kennedy was assassinated during a presidential motorcade in Dallas, Texas, on November 22, 1963.

Did you know? Kennedy was the first U.S. President born in the 20th century.

MALCOLM X 1925 (Nebraska, U.S.A.) – 1965 (New York, U.S.A.)

A preacher and talented public speaker, Malcolm X believed that people would be set free of racism by working together, and encouraged his African-American followers to be proud of their race. He also advocated peace and unity among all people, regardless of the color of their skin. While giving a speech in Harlem, New York, Malcolm X was shot and killed by three members of the Nation of Islam, the religious organization he once belonged to.

Did you know? Malcolm X was born with the last name "Little," but changed it to "X" once he joined the Nation of Islam.

MARTIN LUTHER KING, JR. 1929 (Georgia, U.S.A.) – 1968 (Tennessee, U.S.A.)

Civil rights leader Dr. Martin Luther King, Jr., born in Atlanta, Georgia, in 1929, never backed down in his stand against racism. He dedicated his life to achieving equality and justice for Americans of all colors. From a family of preachers, King experienced racial prejudice early in life. As an adult fighting for civil rights, his speeches, marches, and mere presence motivated people to fight for justice for all. His March on Washington in 1963 was one of the largest activist gatherings in our nation's history. King was assassinated by James Earl Ray on April 4, 1968.

Did you know? The year 2013 marks the 50th anniversary of King's March on Washington.

WOMEN
Fighting for Equality

EQUALITY OF RIGHTS UNDER THE LAW SHALL NOT BE DENIED OR ABRIDGE
BY THE UNITED STATES OR BY ANY STATE ON ACCOUNT OF SEX

Women march for equality
in Washington, D.C.

Today, women make up about half of the country's workforce. But a little over a century ago, less than 20 percent worked outside the home. In fact, they didn't even have the right to vote!

That changed in the mid-1800s when women, led by pioneers like Elizabeth Cady Stanton and Susan B. Anthony, started speaking up about inequality. They organized public demonstrations, gave speeches, published documents, and wrote newspaper articles to express their ideas. In 1848, about 300 people attended the Seneca Falls Convention in New York to address the need for equal rights. By the late 1800s, the National American Woman Suffrage Association had made great strides toward giving women the freedom to vote. One by one, states began allowing women to vote. By 1920, the U.S. Constitution was amended, giving women across the country the ability to cast a vote during any election.

But the fight for equality did not end there. In the 1960s and 1970s, the women's rights movement experienced a rebirth, as feminists protested against injustices in areas such as the workplace and in education.

While these efforts enabled women to make great strides in our society, the efforts to even the playing field among men and women continue today.

New Zealand gave women the right to vote in 1893, becoming the world's first country to do so.

Sri Lanka elected its first female prime minister in 1960.

Girls at a suffrage meeting, ca 1920

Key Events in Women's History

1848: **Elizabeth Cady Stanton** and **Lucretia Mott** organize the Seneca Falls Convention in New York. Attendees rally for equitable laws, equal educational and job opportunities, and the right to vote.

1920: **The 19th Amendment,** guaranteeing women the right to vote, is ratified.

1964: **Title VII,** which prohibits employment discrimination on the basis of sex, is successfully amended.

1966: **The National Organization for Women** (NOW), the largest feminist organization in the United States, is founded by women, including writer Betty Friedan; Rev. Pauli Murray, the first African-American female Episcopal priest; and Shirley Chisholm, the first African-American woman to run for president of the United States.

1971: **Gloria Steinem** heads up the National Women's Political Caucus, which encourages women to be active in government. She also launches *Ms.*, a magazine about women's issues.

1972: Congress approves **the Equal Rights Amendment** (ERA), proposing that women and men have equal rights under the law. It is ratified by 35 of the necessary 38 states, and is still not part of the U.S. Constitution.

1981: President Ronald Reagan appoints **Sandra Day O'Connor** as the first female Supreme Court justice.

1984: Democrat **Geraldine Ferraro** is nominated as a major party's first female vice-presidential candidate.

1996: **Madeleine Albright** is appointed the first female Secretary of State.

2005: **Condoleezza Rice** becomes the first African-American woman to be appointed Secretary of State.

Amelia Bloomer Changes Style

While women were fighting for equal rights in the 19th century, they were doing so wearing confining corsets and layers of heavy petticoats underneath their dresses. But thanks to women's rights activist Amelia Bloomer, women's clothing eventually became a lot more comfortable. Bloomer, who tackled pressing women's issues in her newspaper *The Lily*, suggested a new style of looser tops and skirts that stopped at the knee with a pair of pants underneath. The style stuck—and short pants worn under a skirt or dress are still known as "bloomers" to this day.

Woman in bloomers

Madame President

Though no woman has ever been elected President of the United States, dozens have thrown their hats in the ring. Victoria Woodhull was the first in 1872. And in recent years, some women have nearly reached the coveted position. For example, in her 2008 run for the Democratic nomination for U.S. President, Hillary Rodham Clinton came closer to winning the nomination of a major political party in the United States than any other woman had. That same year, Sarah Palin—the governor of Alaska—ran for Vice President on the Republican ticket alongside presidential contender John McCain. And in the 2012 U.S. presidential election, Minnesota Congresswoman Michele Bachmann was an early frontrunner for the Republican nomination. So when will a woman become the first female President of the United States? Only time will tell!

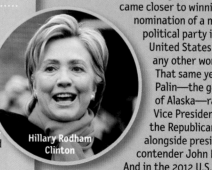

Hillary Rodham Clinton

Brilliant Biographies

Author
J. K. Rowling

A biography is the story of a person's life. It can be a brief summary or a long book. Biographers—those who write biographies—use many different sources to learn about their subjects. You can write your own biography of a famous person whom you find inspiring.

How to Get Started

Choose a subject you find interesting. If you think Cleopatra is cool, you have a good chance of getting your reader interested, too. If you're bored by ancient Egypt, your reader will be snoring after your first paragraph.

Your subject can be almost anyone: an author, an inventor, a celebrity, a politician, or a member of your family. To find someone to write about, ask yourself these simple questions:

1. Whom do I want to know more about?
2. What did this person do that was special?
3. How did this person change the world?

Do Your Research

- Find out as much about your subject as possible. Read books, news articles, and encyclopedia entries. Watch video clips and movies, and search the Internet. Conduct interviews, if possible.
- Take notes, writing down important facts and interesting stories about your subject.

Writing the Biography

- Come up with a title. Include the person's name.
- Write an introduction. Consider asking a probing question about your subject.
- Include information about the person's childhood. When was this person born? Where did he or she grow up? Whom did he or she admire?
- Highlight the person's talents, accomplishments, and personal attributes.
- Describe the specific events that helped to shape this person's life. Did this person ever have a problem and overcome it?
- Write a conclusion. Include your thoughts about why it is important to learn about this person.
- Once you have finished your first draft, revise and then proofread.

Here's a **SAMPLE BIOGRAPHY** of **J. K. Rowling, author of the** *Harry Potter* **series. Of course, there is so much more for you to discover, and write about on your own!**

J. K. Rowling—Author

Joanne "Jo" Rowling was born on July 31, 1965, in Gloucestershire, England, the oldest of two children to her mother, Anne, and father, Peter James.

Joanne grew up writing fantasy stories and reading them to her younger sister, Dianne. But she did not set out to be a writer. She studied French at the University of Exeter and worked as both a researcher for Amnesty International, a nonprofit organization, and as a teacher. It wasn't until she was stuck on a delayed train between Manchester and London that the idea for *Harry Potter* popped into her head. She began writing as soon as she returned to her home in London, but it took six years before the book was completed and eventually published.

Rowling lives in Scotland with her husband, Neil, daughters Jessica and Mackenzie, and son, David. She finished the final novel in the *Harry Potter* series in 2007, but she continues to write and remains one of the world's most well-known—and wealthiest—authors.

REVEAL YOUR SOURCES

A bibliography is a list of all the sources you used to get information for your essay, such as books, magazine articles, interviews, and websites. It is included at the end of your essay or report.

The bibliography should list sources in alphabetical order by author's last name. If a source doesn't have an author, then it should be alphabetized by title.

BOOK

Author (last name, first name). *Title*. City of publisher: publisher, date of publication.

Ex: Allen, Thomas B. *George Washington, Spymaster*. Washington, D.C.: National Geographic, 2004.

ENCYCLOPEDIA

Author (last name, first name) (if given). "Article title." *Name of Encyclopedia*. Edition. Volume. City of publisher: publisher, date of publication.

Ex: "Gerbil." *The Encyclopedia Britannica*. 15th ed. Vol. 5. Chicago: Encyclopedia Britannica, 2007.

MAGAZINE/NEWSPAPER ARTICLE

Author (last name, first name). "Article title." *Name of magazine*. Date: page numbers.

Ex: Elder, Scott. "Great Migrations." *NATIONAL GEOGRAPHIC KIDS*. Nov. 2010: pp. 20–25.

DVD/FILM

Title of film. Director's name. Year of original film's release. Format. Name of distributor, year, video/DVD/etc. produced.

Ex: *Lewis & Clark: Great Journey West*. Dir. Bruce Neibaur. 2002. Large-format film. National Geographic, 2002.

INTERVIEW

Person interviewed (last name, first name). Type of interview (personal, telephone, email, etc.). Date of interview.

Ex: Hiebert, Fredrik. Personal interview. April 28, 2011.

WEBSITE

Author (last name, first name) (if given). *Title of the site*. Editor. Date and/or version number. Name of sponsoring institution. Date of access. <URL>.

Ex: Hora, Reenita Malhotra. *Diwali, India's Festival of Light*. 2008. National Geographic. May 12, 2011. kids.nationalgeographic.com/kids/stories/peopleplaces/diwali.

TIP:

If you keep track of all your sources as you use them, compiling the information to create your bibliography can be done in a snap.

COOL CLICK

Want to find out more about sources and books? The Library of Congress has a great website.
loc.gov/families

A moose stands in the shadow of Mount McKinley, also called Denali. Located in Alaska, U.S.A., Mount McKinley is the tallest mountain in North America.

Geography
Rocks

Got a smart phone?
**SCAN THIS to improve
your geography I.Q.**
(See instructions inside the front cover.)
No smart phone? Go online.
kids.nationalgeographic.com/almanac-2013

THE POLITICAL WORLD

Earth's land area is made up of seven continents, but people have divided much of the land into smaller political units called countries. Australia is a continent made up of a single country, and Antarctica is set aside for scientific research. But the other five continents include almost 200 independent countries. The political map shown here depicts boundaries—imaginary lines created by treaties—that separate countries. Some boundaries, such as the one between the United States and Canada, are very stable and have been recognized for many years.

AUSTRIA ❶
BELGIUM ❷
BOSNIA & HERZEGOVINA ❸
CROATIA ❹
CZECH REPUBLIC ❺
HUNGARY ❻
KOSOVO ❼
LUXEMBOURG ❽
MACEDONIA ❾
MONTENEGRO ❿
NETHERLANDS ⓫
SERBIA ⓬
SLOVAKIA ⓭
SLOVENIA ⓮
SWITZERLAND ⓯

ARCT

Queen Elizabeth Is.

Chukchi Sea

Beaufort Sea

RUSSIA

Alaska (U.S.)

60°

Bering Sea

Gulf of Alaska

Great Bear Lake

Great Slave Lake

Baffin Bay

Greenland (Denmark)

Greenla

ARCTIC CI

ICELAND

Labrador Sea

Hudson Bay

C A N A D A

Lake Winnipeg

Great Lakes

Great Salt Lake

U N I T E D   S T A T E S

UNI
KINGI

IRELANI

FRA

PORT.

MORO(

30°

Hawai'i (U.S.)

TROPIC OF CANCER

Gulf of Mexico

MEXICO

BAHAMAS

CUBA

HAITI

DOMINICAN REP.

Puerto Rico (U.S.)

Western Sahara (Morocco)

MAURITANIA

CAPE VERDE

ST. KITTS & NEVIS
ANTIGUA & BARBUDA
Guadeloupe (France)
DOMINICA
Martinique (France)
BARBADOS
ST. VINCENT & THE GRENADINES
TRINIDAD AND TOBAGO

SENEGAL

GAMBIA

GUINEA-BISSAU

BELIZE
JAMAICA

Caribbean Sea

ST. LUCIA
GRENADA

GUATEMALA
EL SALVADOR   HONDURAS
NICARAGUA

COSTA RICA

PANAMA

VENEZUELA

GUYANA

French Guiana (France)

GUINEA

SIERRA LEONE

LIBERIA

COLOMBIA

SURINAME

CÔTE D'IVOIRE (IVORY COAST)

EQ. GUINE

PACIFIC

EQUATOR   150°   120°   90°

0°

KIRIBATI

O C E A N

Galápagos Islands (Ecuador)

ECUADOR

PERU

B R A Z I L

SAO TO
PRINC

Marquesas Islands (France)

SAMOA

American Samoa (U.S.)

French Polynesia (France)

BOLIVIA

PARAGUAY

ATLANTIC

TONGA

TROPIC OF CAPRICORN

OCEAN

URUGUAY

30°

CHILE

ARGENTINA

0   miles   2000

0   kilometers   3000

Winkel Tripel Projection

Chatham Is. (N.Z.)

Falkland Islands (U.K.)

Tierra del Fuego

Strait of Magellan

Drake Passage

ANTA

60°

Weddell Sea

More cool geography online. kids.nationalgeographic.com/kids/places

Ross Sea

A   N

COOL CLICK

Other boundaries, such as the one between Ethiopia and Eritrea in northeast Africa, are relatively new and still disputed. Countries come in all shapes and sizes. Russia and Canada are giants; others, such as Luxembourg, are small. Some countries are long and skinny—look at Chile in South America! Still other countries—such as Indonesia and Japan in Asia—are made up of groups of islands. The political map is a clue to the diversity that makes Earth so fascinating.

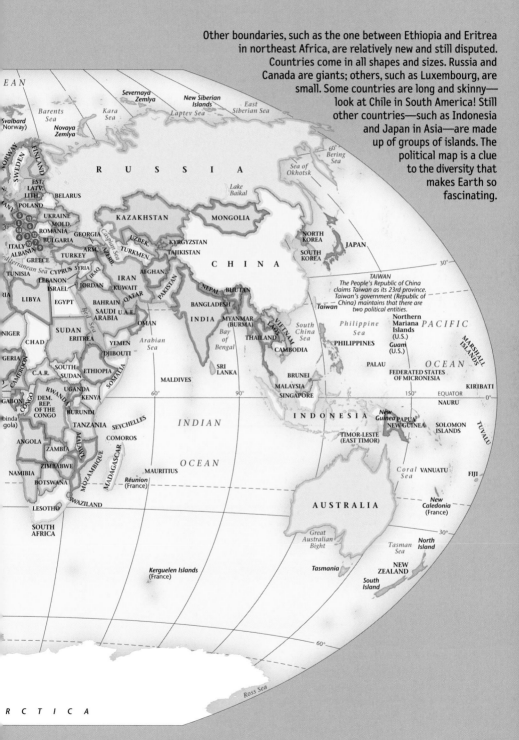

TAIWAN
The People's Republic of China claims Taiwan as its 23rd province. Taiwan's government (Republic of China) maintains that there are two political entities.

THE PHYSICAL WORLD

Earth is dominated by large landmasses called continents—seven in all—and by an interconnected global ocean that is divided into four parts by the continents. More than 70 percent of Earth's surface is covered by oceans, and the remaining 30 percent is made up of land areas.

Different landforms give variety to the surface of the continents. The Rockies and the Andes mark the western edge of the Americas, and the Himalaya tower above southern Asia. The Plateau of Tibet forms the rugged core of Asia, while

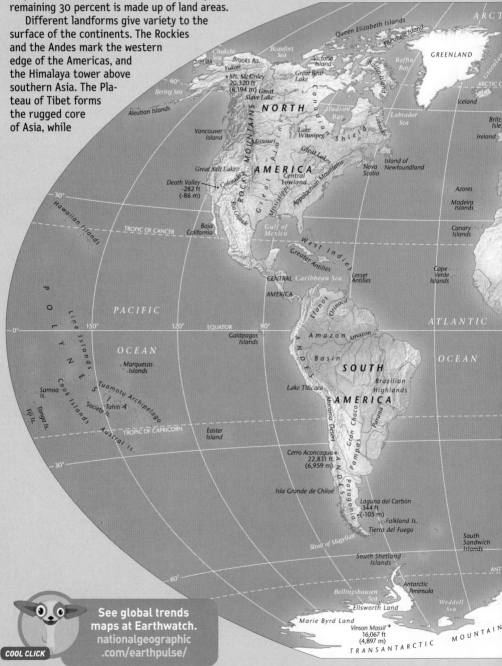

See global trends maps at Earthwatch.
nationalgeographic
.com/earthpulse/

COOL CLICK

the Northern European Plain extends from the North Sea to the Ural Mountains. Much of Africa is a plateau, and dry plains cover large areas of Australia. Mountains rise more than 16,000 feet (4,877 m) above Antarctica's massive ice sheets. Mountains and trenches make the ocean floors as varied as any continent. A mountain chain called the Mid-Atlantic Ridge runs the length of the Atlantic Ocean. In the western Pacific, trenches drop deep into the ocean floor.

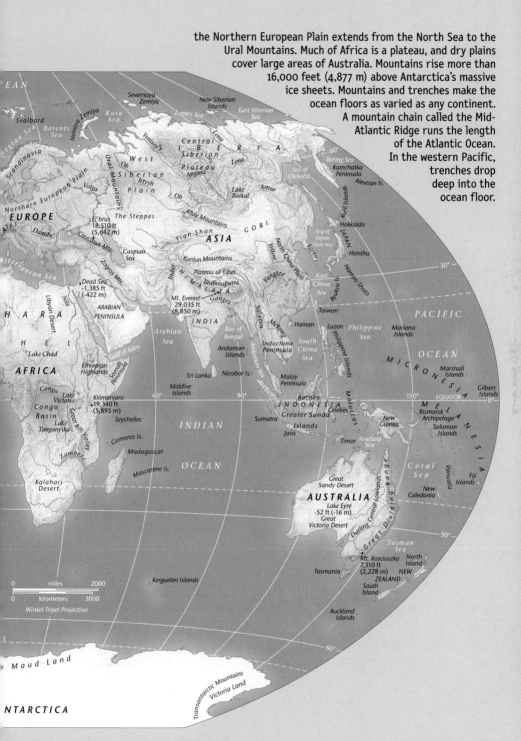

EAN

Svalbard
Scandinavia
Barents Sea
Novaya Zemlya
Severnaya Zemlya
New Siberian Islands
East Siberian Sea
Laptev Sea
Kara Sea
Yenisey
Lena
Central Siberian Plateau
S I B E R I A
West Siberian Plain
Ob
Irtysh
Ural Mountains
Volga
Northern European Plain
EUROPE
Alps
Danube
The Steppes
El'brus 18,510 ft (5,642 m)
Black Sea
Caucasus Mts.
Zagros Mts.
Caspian Sea
Dead Sea -1,385 ft (-422 m)
ARABIAN PENINSULA
Mediterranean Sea
S A H A R A
S A H E L
Libyan Desert
Nile
Lake Chad
Ethiopian Highlands
Gulf of Aden
Somali Peninsula
AFRICA
Congo
Lake Victoria
Congo Basin
Lake Tanganyika
Great Rift Valley
Zambezi
Kalahari Desert
Kilimanjaro 19,340 ft (5,895 m)
Seychelles
Comoros Is.
Madagascar
Mascarene Is.
Arabian Sea
Lena
Angara
Lake Baikal
Ob
Amur
Altay Mountains
Tian Shan
ASIA
GOBI
Kunlun Mountains
Plateau of Tibet
Indus
Brahmaputra
Ganges
Mt. Everest 29,035 ft (8,850 m)
HIMALAYA
INDIA
Sri Lanka
Maldive Islands
Nicobar Is.
Andaman Islands
Bay of Bengal
Salween
Mekong
Yellow
Yangtze
North China Plain
Korea
Sea of Okhotsk
Kamchatka Peninsula
Bering Sea
Kuril Islands
Aleutian Is.
Hokkaido
Sea of Japan (East Sea)
JAPAN
Honshu
Nampo Shoto
East China Sea
Taiwan
Hainan
Luzon
Philippine Islands
South China Sea
Indochina Peninsula
Malay Peninsula
Philippine Sea
Mariana Islands
PACIFIC
OCEAN
MICRONESIA
Marshall Islands
Gilbert Islands
EQUATOR
INDIAN OCEAN
Sumatra
Java
Greater Sunda Islands
INDONESIA
Celebes
Borneo
Moluccas
New Guinea
Timor
Arafura Sea
MELANESIA
Bismarck Archipelago
Solomon Islands
Vanuatu
Fiji Islands
New Caledonia
Coral Sea
Kerguelen Islands
Great Sandy Desert
AUSTRALIA
Lake Eyre -52 ft (-16 m)
Great Victoria Desert
Darling
Central Lowlands
Great Dividing Range
Tasman Sea
Mt. Kosciuszko 7,310 ft (2,228 m)
Tasmania
North Island
NEW ZEALAND
South Island
Auckland Islands

0 miles 2000
0 kilometers 3000
Winkel Tripel Projection

Maud Land
Transantarctic Mountains
Victoria Land
NTARCTICA

60°
30°
0°
30°
60°
60°
90°
150°

263

KINDS OF MAPS

Maps are special tools that geographers use to tell a story about Earth. Maps can be used to show just about anything related to places. Some maps show physical features, such as mountains or vegetation. Maps can also show climates or natural hazards and other things we cannot easily see. Other maps illustrate different features on Earth—political boundaries, urban centers, and economic systems.

AN IMPERFECT TOOL

Maps are not perfect. A globe is a scale model of Earth with accurate relative sizes and locations. Because maps are flat, they involve distortions of size, shape, and direction. Also, cartographers—people who create maps— make choices about what information to include. Because of this, it is important to study many different types of maps to learn the complete story of Earth. Three commonly found kinds of maps are shown on this page.

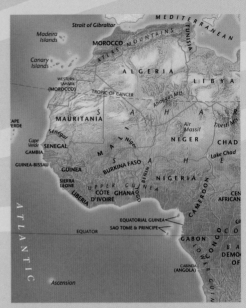

PHYSICAL MAPS. Earth's natural features—landforms, water bodies, and vegetation—are shown on physical maps. The map above uses color and shading to illustrate mountains, lakes, rivers, and deserts of western Africa. Country names and borders are added for reference, but they are not natural features.

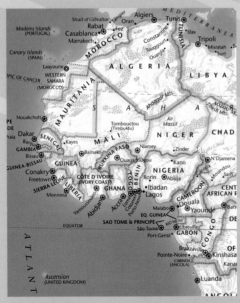

POLITICAL MAPS. These maps represent characteristics of the landscape created by humans, such as boundaries, cities, and place-names. Natural features are added only for reference. On the map above, capital cities are represented with a star inside a circle, while other cities are shown with black dots.

THEMATIC MAPS. Patterns related to a particular topic or theme, such as population distribution, appear on these maps. The map above displays the region's climate zones, which range from tropical wet (bright green) to tropical wet and dry (light green) to semiarid (dark yellow) to arid or desert (light yellow).

GEOGRAPHIC FEATURES

From roaring rivers to parched deserts, from underwater canyons to jagged mountains, Earth is covered with beautiful and diverse environments. Here are examples of the most common types of geographic features found around the world.

DESERT
Deserts are land features created by climate, specifically by a lack of water. Here, a camel caravan crosses the Sahara in North Africa.

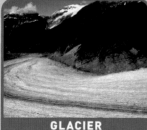

VALLEY
Valleys, cut by running water or moving ice, may be broad and flat or narrow and steep, such as the Indus River Valley in Ladakh, India (above).

RIVER
As a river moves through flatlands, it twists and turns. Above, the Rio Los Amigos winds through a rain forest in Peru.

MOUNTAIN
Mountains are Earth's tallest landforms, and Mount Everest (above) rises highest of all, at 29,035 feet (8,850 m) above sea level.

GLACIER
Glaciers—"rivers" of ice—such as Alaska's Hubbard Glacier (above) move slowly from mountains to the sea. Global warming is shrinking them.

CANYON
Steep-sided valleys called canyons are created mainly by running water. Buckskin Gulch (above) is the deepest slot canyon in the American Southwest.

WATERFALL
Waterfalls form when a river reaches an abrupt change in elevation. Above, Kaieteur Falls, in Guyana, has a sheer drop of 741 feet (226 m).

AFRICA

The massive continent of Africa, where humankind began millions of years ago, is second only to Asia in size. The 54 independent countries of Africa are home to a wide variety of cultures and traditions. In many areas traditional tribal life is still very common, such as among the Maasai people of Kenya and Tanzania.

Maasai women in native costume

From Arabic and Nubian, to Zulu and Sandawe, some 1,600 languages are spoken in Africa—more than on any other continent.

Although rich in natural resources, from oil and coal to gemstones and precious metals, Africa is the poorest continent, long plagued by outside interference, corruption, and disease.

Africa spans nearly as far from west to east as it does from north to south. The Sahara—the world's largest desert—covers Africa's northern third, while bands of grassland, tropical rain forest, and more desert lie to the south. The rain forests of Africa are home to half of the continent's animal species. Wild creatures, such as lions, roam sub-Saharan Africa, and water-loving hippos live near the great lakes of this large continent.

The first great civilization in Africa arose 6,000 years ago on the banks of the lower Nile. Today, though the continent is still largely rural, Africans increasingly migrate to booming cities such as Cairo, Egypt; Lagos, Nigeria; and Johannesburg, South Africa.

355 FEET (108 M) HEIGHT OF VICTORIA FALLS, THE LARGEST WATERFALL IN AFRICA

11 NUMBER OF OFFICIAL LANGUAGES IN THE COUNTRY OF SOUTH AFRICA

1 NUMBER OF HUMPS ON AFRICA'S ARABIAN CAMELS; BACTRIAN CAMELS IN ASIA HAVE TWO

Downtown Johannesburg in South Africa

A ZEBRA'S TEETH KEEP GROWING FOR ITS ENTIRE LIFE • LIKE HUM

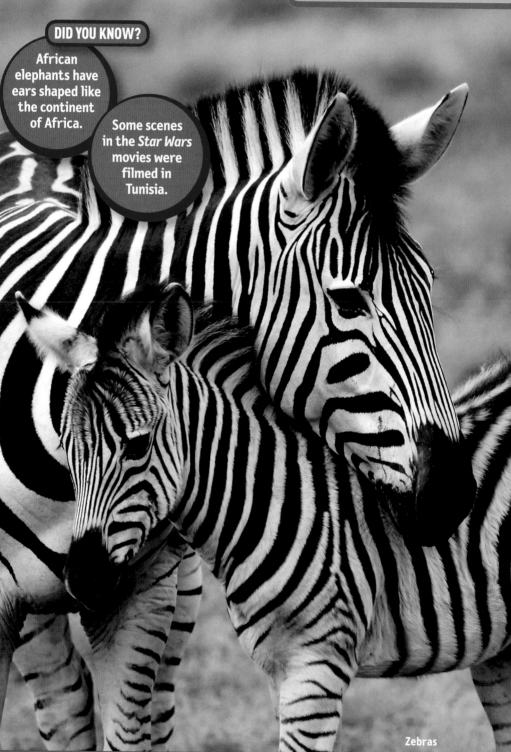

DID YOU KNOW?

African elephants have ears shaped like the continent of Africa.

Some scenes in the *Star Wars* movies were filmed in Tunisia.

Zebras

NGERPRINTS, NO TWO ZEBRAS' STRIPES ARE EXACTLY THE SAME

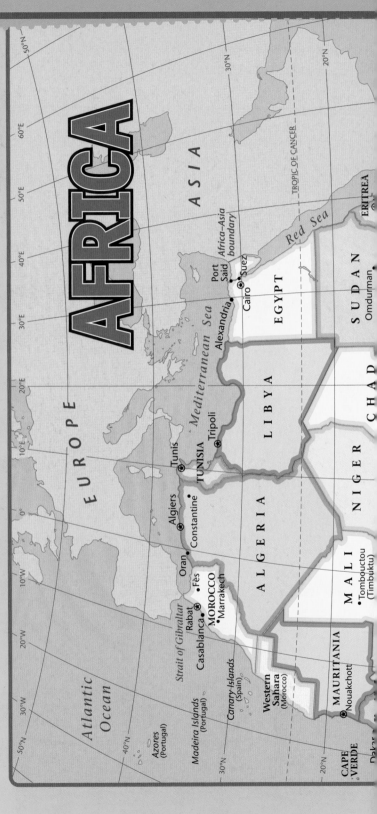

PHYSICAL

LAND AREA
11,608,000 sq mi
(30,065,000 sq km)

LOWEST POINT
Lake Assal, Djibouti
-512 ft (-156 m)

LARGEST LAKE
Victoria
26,800 sq mi
(69,500 sq km)

HIGHEST POINT
Kilimanjaro, Tanzania
19,340 ft (5,895 m)

LONGEST RIVER
Nile
4,241 mi (6,825 km)

POLITICAL

POPULATION
1,051,506,000

LARGEST METROPOLITAN AREA
Cairo, Egypt
Pop. 10,903,000

LARGEST COUNTRY
Algeria
919,595 sq mi
(2,381,741 sq km)

MOST DENSELY POPULATED COUNTRY
Mauritius 1,631 people
per sq mi (630 per sq km)

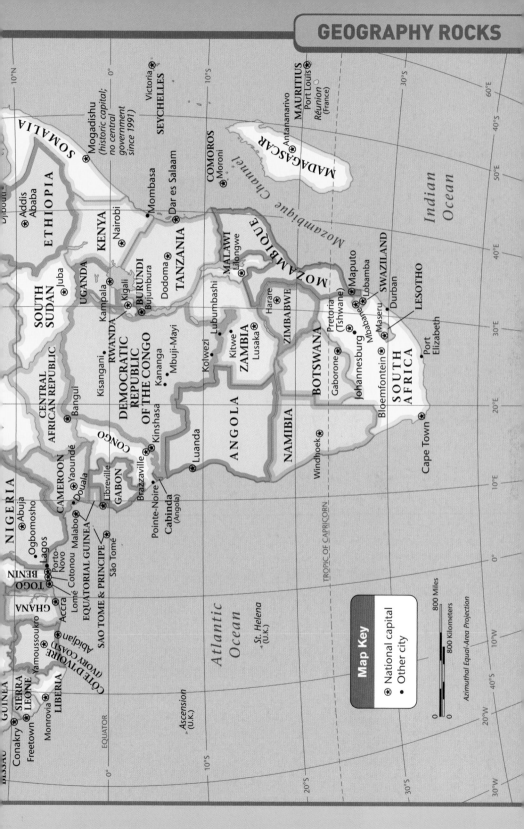

SEYCHELLES
Victoria ⊛

MAURITIUS ⊛
Port Louis
Réunion ○
(France)

COMOROS ⊛
Moroni

Antananarivo ⊛

MADAGASCAR

Mozambique Channel

Indian
Ocean

Mogadishu ⊛
(historic capital;
no central
government
since 1991)

SOMALIA ⊛

Djibouti

Addis ⊛
Ababa

ETHIOPIA

Mombasa ●

Dar es Salaam ⊛

KENYA
Nairobi ⊛

Juba ●

UGANDA
Kampala ●

Kigali ⊛
RWANDA
BURUNDI
Bujumbura ⊛

TANZANIA
Dodoma ⊛

MALAWI
Lilongwe ⊛

Harare ⊛

ZIMBABWE

MOZAMBIQUE

Maputo ⊛
Lobamba
SWAZILAND

Mbabane ⊛

Pretoria
(Tshwane) ⊛

Durban ●

LESOTHO
Maseru ⊛

Johannesburg ●

Bloemfontein ⊛

Port
Elizabeth ●

SOUTH
AFRICA

Cape Town ⊛

SOUTH
SUDAN

CENTRAL
AFRICAN REPUBLIC

Bangui ⊛

Kisangani ●

DEMOCRATIC
REPUBLIC
OF THE CONGO

Kananga ●
Mbuji-Mayi ●

Lubumbashi ●

Kolwezi ●
Kitwe ●
Lusaka ⊛
ZAMBIA

BOTSWANA

Gaborone ⊛

NAMIBIA

Windhoek ⊛

ANGOLA

Luanda ⊛

CONGO

Brazzaville ⊛

Kinshasa ⊛

Pointe-Noire ●

Cabinda
(Angola)

GABON
Libreville ⊛

Yaoundé ⊛
Douala ●

CAMEROON

São Tomé ●

SAO TOME & PRINCIPE

EQUATORIAL GUINEA
Malabo ⊛

NIGERIA
Abuja ⊛

Ogbomosho ●
Lagos ●
Porto-
Novo ⊛
BENIN
Cotonou ●
Lomé ⊛
TOGO

GHANA
Accra ⊛

Yamoussoukro ⊛
CÔTE D'IVOIRE
(IVORY COAST)
Abidjan ●

LIBERIA
Monrovia ⊛

SIERRA
LEONE
Freetown ⊛

GUINEA
Conakry ⊛

BISSAU

Atlantic
Ocean

St. Helena
(U.K.)

Ascension
(U.K.)

EQUATOR

TROPIC OF CAPRICORN

Azimuthal Equal-Area Projection

0°
10°S
20°S
30°S
40°S

10°N
0°
10°S
20°S
30°S

0°
10°E
20°E
30°E
40°E
50°E
60°E

30°W
20°W
10°W
0°

Map Key

⊛ National capital
● Other city

800 Miles

800 Kilometers

0

0

ANTARC

This frozen continent may be an interesting place to see, but unless you're a penguin, you probably wouldn't want to hang out in Antarctica for long. The fact that it's the coldest, windiest, and driest continent helps explain why humans never colonized this ice-covered land surrounding the South Pole.

No country actually owns Antarctica. Dozens of countries work together to study and care for its barren landscape. Antarctica is the only continent without a permanent population. Photographers and tourists visit. Scientists live there temporarily to study such things as weather, environment, and wildlife.

Visitors can observe several species of penguins that breed in Antarctica, including the emperor penguin. Antarctica's shores also serve as breeding grounds for six kinds of seals. And the surrounding waters provide food for whales.

People and animals share Antarctica. But there are still places on this vast, icy continent that have yet to be explored.

3 MILES (4.8 KM)	DEPTH OF THICKEST ICE COVERING THE CONTINENT
200 MPH (322 KMP)	TOP SPEED OF WIND GUSTS IN PARTS OF ANTARCTICA
70	NUMBER OF LAKES HIDDEN UNDER ANTARCTIC ICE

WEDDELL SEALS CAN DIVE DOWN 2,000 FEET (610 M)

TICA

DID YOU KNOW?

Antarctica was located near the Equator hundreds of millions of years ago.

It hasn't rained for at least 800,000 years in parts of Antarctica.

Emperor penguins

Weddell seal

HEY CAN SWIM BY THE TIME THEY ARE TWO WEEKS OLD

271

PHYSICAL

LAND AREA
5,100,000 sq mi
(13,209,000 sq km)

HIGHEST POINT
Vinson Massif
16,067 ft (4,897 m)

LOWEST POINT
Bentley Subglacial
Trench
-8,383 ft (-2,555 m)

COLDEST PLACE
Plateau Station, annu-
al average tempera-
ture -70°F (-56.7°C)

**AVERAGE
PRECIPITATION ON
THE POLAR PLATEAU**
Less than 2 in (5 cm)
per year

POLITICAL

POPULATION
There are no indig-
enous inhabitants,
but there are both
permanent and
summer-only staffed
research stations.

**NUMBER OF
INDEPENDENT
COUNTRIES** 0

**NUMBER OF
COUNTRIES
CLAIMING LAND** 7

**NUMBER OF
COUNTRIES
OPERATING YEAR-
ROUND RESEARCH
STATIONS** 18

**NUMBER OF YEAR-
ROUND RESEARCH
STATIONS** 45

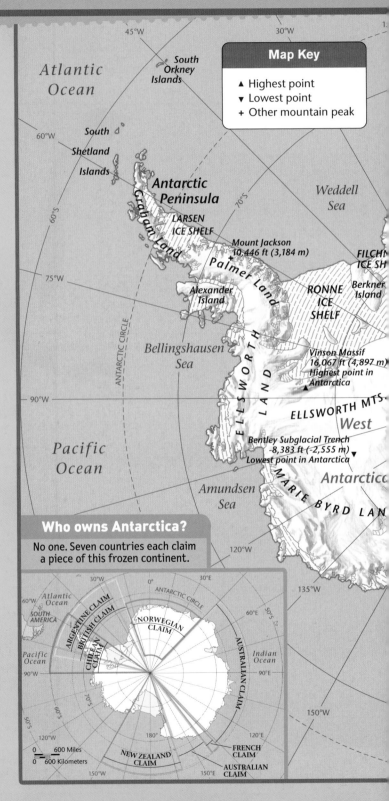

Map Key

▲ Highest point
▼ Lowest point
+ Other mountain peak

*Atlantic
Ocean*

South
Orkney
Islands

South
Shetland
Islands

**Antarctic
Peninsula**

LARSEN
ICE SHELF

Graham Land

Mount Jackson
10,446 ft (3,184 m)

Palmer Land

*Weddell
Sea*

FILCHN
ICE SH

RONNE
ICE
SHELF

Berkner
Island

Alexander
Island

Vinson Massif
16,067 ft (4,897 m)
Highest point in
Antarctica

*Bellingshausen
Sea*

ELLSWORTH LAND

ELLSWORTH MTS

West

Bentley Subglacial Trench
-8,383 ft (-2,555 m)
Lowest point in Antarctica

*Pacific
Ocean*

MARIE BYRD LAN

Antarctic

*Amundsen
Sea*

Who owns Antarctica?

No one. Seven countries each claim
a piece of this frozen continent.

*Atlantic
Ocean*

ANTARCTIC CIRCLE

SOUTH
AMERICA

ARGENTINE CLAIM

BRITISH CLAIM

NORWEGIAN
CLAIM

CHILEAN
CLAIM

*Pacific
Ocean*

*Indian
Ocean*

AUSTRALIAN CLAIM

NEW ZEALAND
CLAIM

FRENCH
CLAIM

AUSTRALIAN
CLAIM

0   600 Miles
0   600 Kilometers

ANTARCTICA

FIMBUL
ICE SHELF

15°E

0°

30°E

45°E

RIISER-LARSEN
ICE SHELF

60°E

ENDERBY
LAND

QUEEN MAUD LAND

Indian
Ocean

Valkyrie
Dome

MacKenzie Bay

75°E

Lambert
Glacier

AMERY ICE SHELF

AMERICAN

HIGHLAND

WEST
ICE SHELF

POLAR PLATEAU

East

90°E

South Pole

Antarctica

SHACKLETON
ICE SHELF

T R A N S A N T A R C T I C   M O U N T A I N S

80°S

105°E

W I L K E S   L A N D

ROSS
ICE
SHELF

Roosevelt
Island

Taylor
Glacier

Ross Island

70°S

Mount Erebus
12,448 ft
(3,794 m)

V I C T O R I A   L A N D

Ross
Sea

120°E

Talos
Dome

60°S

180°

150°E

135°E

*South
Magnetic
Pole (2012)

Indian
Ocean

°W

0

600 Miles

0

600 Kilometers

Azimuthal Equidistant Projection

273

DID YOU KNOW?

Scuba divers can send postcards from a mailbox off the coast of Japan that's nearly 33 feet (10 m) underwater.

The Asian vampire moth, found in Siberia, sometimes drinks the blood of animals.

Downtown Shanghai in eastern China

A MALE ORANGUTAN'S ARMS CAN SPAN 7 FEET (2 M) ACROSS

ASIA

From western Turkey to the eastern tip of Russia, Asia sprawls across nearly 180 degrees of longitude—almost half the globe! It boasts the highest (Mount Everest) and the lowest (the Dead Sea) places on Earth's surface.

Home to more than 40 countries, Asia is the world's largest continent, with more than four billion people. Three out of five people on the planet live here—that's more than live on all the other continents combined.

Asia is a land of contrasts. The continent's expansive rural areas are home to the most farmers in the world. Contemporary, commercial, and sacred cities also cover its vast lands. Asia boasts the most million-plus cities, including Tokyo, Japan; Riyadh, Saudi Arabia; Jakarta, Indonesia; and Beijing, China.

Orangutans

The world's first civilization arose in Sumer, in what is now Iraq. Rich cultures also emerged along rivers in present-day India and China, strongly influencing the world ever since. Asia is also home to a large number of religions, such as Islam, Buddhism, Hinduism, Judaism, and Christianity. Dozens of languages— from Arabic to Xiang—are spoken here.

The Asian economy is growing rapidly. Several Asian nations, such as China and South Korea, are among the top players of the global marketplace.

60	PERCENT OF THE WORLD'S POPULATION THAT LIVES IN ASIA
4,500 MILES (7,242 KM)	LENGTH OF THE GREAT WALL OF CHINA
541 FEET (165 m)	HEIGHT OF THE WORLD'S TALLEST FLAGPOLE, FOUND IN TAJIKISTAN

Mongolian horse rider

BY ORANGUTANS MAY STAY WITH THEIR MOTHERS FOR SIX OR SEVEN YEARS

PHYSICAL

LAND AREA
17,208,000 sq mi
(44,570,000 sq km)

HIGHEST POINT
Mount Everest,
China–Nepal
29,035 ft (8,850 m)

LOWEST POINT
Dead Sea,
Israel–Jordan
-1,385 ft (-422 m)

LONGEST RIVER
Yangtze, China
3,880 mi (6,244 km)

**LARGEST LAKE
ENTIRELY IN ASIA**
Lake Baikal
12,200 sq mi
(31,500 sq km)

POLITICAL

POPULATION
4,216,020,000

**LARGEST
METROPOLITAN AREA**
Tokyo, Japan
Pop. 36,669,000

**LARGEST COUNTRY
ENTIRELY IN ASIA**
China 3,705,405 sq mi
(9,596,960 sq km)

**MOST DENSELY
POPULATED COUNTRY**
Singapore
20,263 people
per sq mi
(7,829 per sq km)

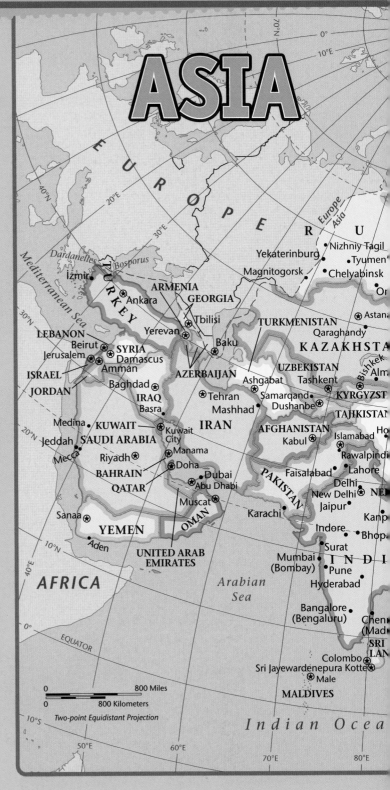

ASIA

EUROPE

Yekaterinburg • Nizhniy Tagil
• Tyumen
Magnitogorsk • Chelyabinsk
Or

Dardanelles
Bosporus
Mediterranean Sea
İzmir
TURKEY
ARMENIA
Ankara
GEORGIA
Tbilisi
TURKMENISTAN
Qaraghandy
• Astana
KAZAKHSTA
Yerevan
LEBANON
Beirut
Jerusalem
SYRIA
Damascus
Amman
AZERBAIJAN
Baku
UZBEKISTAN
Bishkek
ISRAEL
JORDAN
Baghdad
IRAQ
Basra
Ashgabat
Tashkent
Alm
Samarqand
Dushanbe
KYRGYZST
• Tehran
Mashhad
TAJIKISTA
Medina
KUWAIT
Kuwait
City
IRAN
AFGHANISTAN
Kabul
Islamabad
Ho
Jeddah
SAUDI ARABIA
Mecca
Manama
BAHRAIN
QATAR
Riyadh
Doha
Dubai
Abu Dhabi
PAKISTAN
Faisalabad
Rawalpindi
Lahore
Delhi
New Delhi
NE
Jaipur
Sanaa
Muscat
OMAN
Karachi
Kanp
YEMEN
Aden
UNITED ARAB
EMIRATES
Indore
Bhop
AFRICA
Arabian
Sea
Mumbai
(Bombay)
Surat
Pune
I N D I
Hyderabad
Bangalore
(Bengaluru)
Chen
(Mad
SRI
LAN
Colombo
Sri Jayewardenepura Kotte
• Male
MALDIVES
Indian Oce

EQUATOR

0   800 Miles
0   800 Kilometers
Two-point Equidistant Projection

276

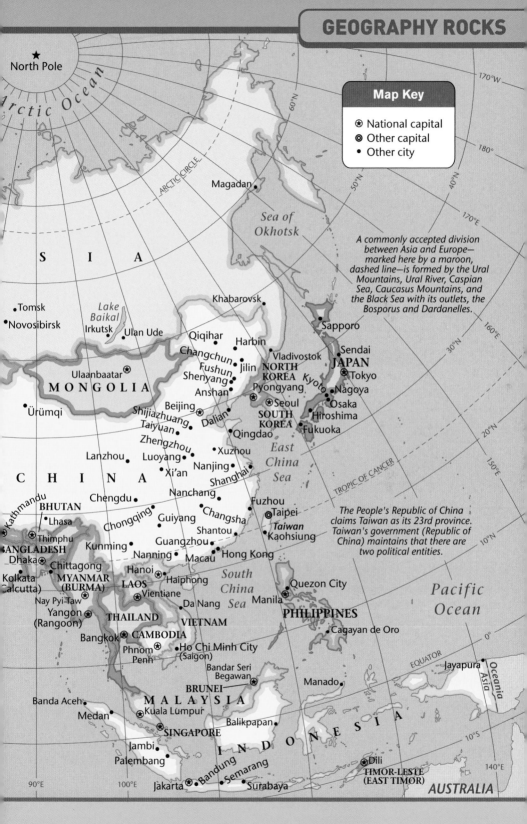

★ North Pole

Arctic Ocean

Map Key

⊛ National capital
◎ Other capital
• Other city

170°W

180°

170°E

60°N

50°N

Magadan

Sea of Okhotsk

A commonly accepted division between Asia and Europe—marked here by a maroon, dashed line—is formed by the Ural Mountains, Ural River, Caspian Sea, Caucasus Mountains, and the Black Sea with its outlets, the Bosporus and Dardanelles.

S I A

ARCTIC CIRCLE

160°E

•Tomsk
•Novosibirsk
Lake Baikal
Irkutsk • Ulan Ude

Khabarovsk

Sapporo

Qiqihar
Changchun
Fushun
Shenyang
Jilin
Harbin

Vladivostok

Sendai
Tokyo
Nagoya
Osaka
Hiroshima
Fukuoka

30°N

JAPAN

Kyoto

Ulaanbaatar ⊛

M O N G O L I A

•Ürümqi

Beijing ⊛
Shijiazhuang
Taiyuan
Zhengzhou
Dalian

NORTH KOREA
Pyongyang ◎
Seoul ⊛
SOUTH KOREA
Qingdao

150°E

20°N

Lanzhou
Luoyang
Xuzhou
Nanjing
Shanghai

East China Sea

C H I N A
Xi'an

Chengdu
Nanchang

Fuzhou

Kathmandu
BHUTAN
•Lhasa
Thimphu ⊛
Chongqing
Guiyang
Changsha
Shantou
Taipei ◎
Taiwan
Kaohsiung

TROPIC OF CANCER

The People's Republic of China claims Taiwan as its 23rd province. Taiwan's government (Republic of China) maintains that there are two political entities.

10°N

ANGLADESH
Dhaka ⊛
Kolkata
Calcutta)
Chittagong
Kunming
MYANMAR (BURMA)
Nanning
Guangzhou
Macau
Hong Kong

Hanoi ⊛
LAOS
Haiphong
Vientiane ⊛

South China Sea

Quezon City

Pacific Ocean

Nay Pyi Taw ⊛
Yangon ⊛
(Rangoon)
THAILAND
Da Nang
VIETNAM
Manila ⊛
PHILIPPINES

0°

Bangkok ⊛
CAMBODIA
Phnom Penh ⊛
Ho Chi Minh City (Saigon)
Cagayan de Oro

EQUATOR

Jayapura •
Oceania
Asia

Banda Aceh•
Medan •
Bandar Seri Begawan ◎
BRUNEI
M A L A Y S I A
Manado•

Kuala Lumpur ⊛
Balikpapan

10°S

⊛ SINGAPORE
Jambi•
Palembang•
I N D O N E S I A
Bandung
Semarang
Surabaya

Dili ◎
TIMOR-LESTE (EAST TIMOR)

140°E

AUSTRALIA

90°E
100°E
Jakarta ⊛

AUSTRA
NEW ZEALAND, AND

This vast region includes Australia—the world's smallest and flattest continent—New Zealand, and a fleet of mostly tiny islands scattered across the Pacific Ocean. Apart from Australia, New Zealand, and Papua New Guinea, Oceania's other 11 independent countries cover about 25,000 square miles (65,000 sq km), an area only slightly larger than half of New Zealand's North Island. Twenty-one other island groups are dependencies of the United States, France, Australia, New Zealand, or the United Kingdom.

Australia has a strong indigenous population of Aborigines but is also heavily influenced by Anglo-Western culture. "Aussies," as Australians like to call themselves, nicknamed their continent the "land down under." That's because the entire continent lies south of, or "under," the Equator. Most Australians live in cities along the coast. But Australia also has huge cattle and sheep ranches. Many ranch children live far from school, and they get their lessons by mail or over the Internet or radio. Their doctors even visit by airplane!

Maori man in traditional dress. Maoris are indigenous people of New Zealand.

Wallaby

WALLABIES CAN SWIM • WHEN THREATENED, A WALLABY WILL THUM

LIA, OCEANIA,

Sydney Opera House,
in Sydney Harbor, Australia

DID YOU KNOW?

People from
New Zealand
are often
referred to
as "Kiwis."

Tonga, in the
South Pacific,
has some 170
islands, but only
36 are
inhabited.

1,429 MILES (2,300 KM)	LENGTH OF AUSTRALIA'S GREAT BARRIER REEF, EARTH'S LARGEST CORAL REEF STRUCTURE
140	NUMBER OF SPECIES OF LAND SNAKES FOUND IN AUSTRALIA, INCLUDING THE INLAND TAIPAN
ABOUT 830	INDIGENOUS LANGUAGES SPOKEN IN PAPUA NEW GUINEA

PHYSICAL

LAND AREA
3,278,000 sq mi
(8,490,000 sq km)

HIGHEST POINT
Mount Wilhelm,
Papua New Guinea
14,793 ft (4,509 m)

LOWEST POINT
Lake Eyre, Australia
-52 ft (-16 m)

LONGEST RIVER
Murray-Darling,
Australia 2,310 mi
(3,718 km)

LARGEST LAKE
Lake Eyre, Australia
3,430 sq mi
(8,884 sq km)

POLITICAL

POPULATION
37,105,000

**LARGEST
METROPOLITAN AREA**
Sydney, Australia
Pop. 4,429,000

LARGEST COUNTRY
Australia
2,969,906 sq mi
(7,692,024 sq km)

**MOST DENSELY
POPULATED COUNTRY**
Nauru
1,256 people per sq
mi (485 per sq km)

Map Key

⊛ National capital
• Other city

30°N
135°E   150°E

Northern Mariana
Islands
(U.S.)
• Capital Hill

15°N

Guam
(U.S.)

M i c r o n

PALAU   Yap   Truk Islands
Islands
• Melekeok   C a r o l i n e   I s l a n d

FEDERATED STATES
OF MICRONESIA

0°

M e l

Oceania–Asia   PAPUA NEW GUINEA
boundary   Honiar
Solomon Island

Port Moresby

15°S   Coral Sea
Islands
Territory
(Australia)

C o r a l   S e a

A U S T R A L I A

• Brisbane

• Perth

Sydney•   Lord Howe
Island
Adelaide•   (Australia)
Canberra ⊛
Melbourne•   Tasm
Sea

Indian
Ocean

Tasmania   •Hobart

45°S

0   800 Miles
0   800 Kilometers

Mercator Projection

120°E   135°E   150°E

65°E   180°   165°W   150°W   135°W

North Pacific Ocean

Midway Is. (U.S.)

TROPIC OF CANCER

Honolulu
Hawai'i (U.S.)
Hilo

Wake Island (U.S.)

Monday | Sunday

Johnston Atoll (U.S.)

15°N

Bikini Atoll

MARSHALL ISLANDS

Ratak Chain

Balik Chain

Majuro

Kingman Reef (U.S.)

Palmyra Atoll (U.S.)

M **i** **c** **r** **o** **n** **e** **s** **i** **a**

Howland Island (U.S.)

Tarawa

Gilbert Islands

Baker Island (U.S.)

Kiritimati

EQUATOR   0°

Line Islands

Yaren
NAURU

Jarvis I. (U.S.)

Phoenix Is.

K I R I B A T I

SOLOMON ISLANDS

TUVALU

Funafuti

Tokelau (N.Z.)

Marquesas Islands

Santa Cruz Islands

M **e** **l** **a** **n** **e** **s** **i** **a**

Wallis and Futuna Is. (France)

SAMOA
Apia

American Samoa (U.S.)

Cook Islands (N.Z.)

Tuamotu Archipelago

15°S

VANUATU

Suva
FIJI

TONGA

Pago Pago

Society Is.

Papeete

P **o** **l** **y** **n** **e** **s** **i** **a**

Niue (N.Z.)

French Polynesia (France)

Port Vila
Nouméa

Nuku'alofa

Avarua

Austral Is.

TROPIC OF CAPRICORN

New Caledonia (France)

Norfolk Island (Australia)

South Pacific Ocean

Pitcairn Island (U.K.)

30°S

Kermadec Islands (N.Z.)

Auckland

NEW ZEALAND

Wellington

Christchurch

Chatham Island (N.Z.)

AUSTRALIA, NEW ZEALAND, AND OCEANIA

Date Line

45°S

65°E   180°   165°W   150°W   135°W

EUROPE

A cluster of islands and peninsulas jutting west from Asia, Europe is bordered by the Atlantic and Arctic Oceans and more than a dozen seas. These bodies of water are linked to inland areas by canals and navigable rivers such as the Rhine and the Danube. The continent boasts a bounty of landscapes. Sweeping west from the Ural Mountains in Russia and Kazakhstan is the fertile Northern European Plain. Rugged uplands form part of Europe's western coast, while the Alps shield Mediterranean lands from frigid northern winds.

Europe is geographically small but is home to more than 700 million people in almost 50 countries, representing a mosaic of cultures, languages, and borders. Some of the most widely spoken languages in Europe include German, French, Italian, Spanish, Polish, Russian, and Dutch.

Here, first Greek and then Roman civilizations laid Europe's cultural foundation. Its colonial powers built vast empires, while its inventors and thinkers revolutionized world industry, economy, and politics. Today, the 27-member European Union seeks to unite the continent's diversity.

Ukrainian girl in traditional dress

55 DAYS	HOW LONG IT TOOK A MAN TO WALK FROM VIENNA, AUSTRIA, TO PARIS, FRANCE— ON HIS HANDS
44 PERCENT	AMOUNT OF EUROPEAN LAND COVERED BY FORESTS
78 MILLION	NUMBER OF FOREIGN TOURISTS VISITING FRANCE EACH YEAR

Alpine ibex

THE ALPINE IBEX IS A TYPE OF WILD GOAT • MALE IBEXES HAVE CURVE[D]

DID YOU KNOW?

The word *Europe* is believed to have come from the mythological Greek princess, Europa.

Europe's five oldest countries are San Marino, France, Bulgaria, Denmark, and Portugal.

La Sagrada Familia, in Barcelona, Spain, was designed by renowned architect Antoni Gaudí.

PHYSICAL

LAND AREA
3,841,000 sq mi
(9,947,000 sq km)

HIGHEST POINT
El'brus, Russia
18,510 ft (5,642 m)

LOWEST POINT
Caspian Sea
-92 ft (-28 m)

LONGEST RIVER
Volga, Russia
2,290 mi
(3,685 km)

**LARGEST LAKE
ENTIRELY IN
EUROPE**
Ladoga, Russia
6,835 sq mi
(17,703 sq km)

POLITICAL

POPULATION
740,936,000

**LARGEST
METROPOLITAN AREA**
Moscow, Russia
Pop. 10,550,000

**LARGEST COUNTRY
ENTIRELY IN
EUROPE**
Ukraine
233,090 sq mi
(603,700 sq km)

**MOST DENSELY
POPULATED COUNTRY**
Monaco
45,000 people per sq
mi (18,000 per sq km)

Map Key

⊛ National capital
• Other city
□ Small country

Reykjavík ⊛
ICELAND

*Norwegian
Sea*

*Faroe Islands
(Denmark)*

ARCTIC CIRCLE

PRIME MERIDIAN

*Shetland
Islands*

Orkney Islands

SCOTLAND

Glasgow
N. IRELAND
Belfast
•Edinburgh

*North
Sea*

IRELAND
Dublin ⊛ **UNITED KINGDOM**
Liverpool •Manchester
WALES Birmingham
Cardiff• ENGLAND
London ⊛ The Hague⊛ •Amsterdam

DENMA

Kiel•

NETH.
Hambu

GERMA

Brussels ⊛
BELGIUM

—LUX.

Frankf•

*Atlantic
Ocean*

⊛ Paris

•Nantes

*Bay of
Biscay*

•Bordeaux

Munich
LIECH.
Zürich•
Bern•
SWITZ.

Lyon•

Oporto•

Bilbao•

•Valladolid

•Toulouse

MONACO
•Marseille

PORTUGAL

ANDORRA
•Zaragoza

Nice□

Milan
•Turin Venic
•Genoa
SAN
MARINO

Lisbon ⊛
Madrid ⊛

SPAIN
Valencia•

Barcelona•

*Corsica
(France)*

VATICAN
CITY□
Rome•

ITA

Seville• Murcia•

Málaga•

Gibraltar (U.K.)

*Balearic Is.
(Spain)*

*Sardinia
(Italy)*

M e d i t e r r a n e a

Palerm

0   400 Miles
0   400 Kilometers

Azimuthal Equidistant Projection

AFRICA

Valle
MA

Barents Sea

• Murmansk

Asia
Europe

ASIA

• Arkhangel'sk

R U S S I A

EUROPE

N O R W A Y

S W E D E N

FINLAND

• Helsinki

St. Petersburg

• Ufa

Stockholm

Tallinn ⊛

ESTONIA

• Yaroslavl'

• Kazan'

eborg

Baltic Sea

Rīga •

LATVIA

• Tver'

• Nizhniy Novgorod

enhagen

LITHUANIA

Vitsyebsk •

Moscow ⊛

• Samara

• Orenburg

Kaliningrad

(Russia)

Kaunas •

• Vilnius

• Smolensk

Ryazan' •

• Penza

Gdańsk •

⊛ Minsk

• Bryansk

• Saratov

KAZAKHSTAN

rlin

POLAND

BELARUS

Homyel' •

• Kursk

• Warsaw ⊛

Bydgoszcz

Łódź •

⊛ Kiev

• Volgograd

Wrocław •

• Kraków

Poltava

• Kharkiv

• Astrakhan'

Prague

CH REP.

L'viv •

U K R A I N E

Donets'k •

• Rostov

Vinnytsya •

Dnipropetrovs'k

Caspian Sea

SLOVAKIA

MOLDOVA

na ⊛

⊛ Bratislava

TRIA

⊛ Chişinău

Groznyy •

ubljana

⊛ Budapest

HUNGARY

ROMANIA

• Odesa

GEORGIA

Baku

Zagreb

Simferopol'

CROATIA

Belgrade •

Bucharest •

Sevastopol'

AZERBAIJAN

BOSNIA &

EGOVINA

SERBIA

• Varna

Black Sea

Sarajevo

KOSOVO

MONTENEGRO

Prishtina

BULGARIA

Bosporus

Podgorica

⊛ Sofia

oles

Tirana •

⊛ Skopje

MACED.

Istanbul

ALBANIA

• Thessaloniki

T U R K E Y

Messina

Dardanelles

tania

GREECE

⊛ Athens

A commonly accepted division
between Asia and Europe—
marked here by a maroon,
dashed line—is formed by the
Ural Mountains, Ural River, Caspian
Sea, Caucasus Mountains, and
the Black Sea with its outlets, the
Bosporus and Dardanelles.

e a

Crete

Nicosia ⊛

CYPRUS

NORTH AMERICA

A girl in traditional costume at an Oaxaca, Mexico, festival

From the Great Plains of the United States and Canada to the rain forest of Panama, the third-largest continent stretches 5,500 miles (8,850 km), spanning natural environments that support diverse wildlife, ranging from polar bears to jaguars.

North America can be divided into four large regions: the Great Plains, the mountainous West, the Canadian Shield of the Northeast, and the eastern region. Before Columbus even "discovered" the New World, it was a land of abundance for its inhabitants. Cooler, less seasonal, and more thickly forested than today, it contained a wide variety of species. Living off the land, Native Americans spread across these varied landscapes. Although some native groups remain, the majority of North Americans today are descendants of immigrants.

North America is home to many large industrialized cities, including two of the largest metropolitan areas in the world: Mexico City, Mexico, and New York City, New York, U.S.A.

While abundant resources and fast-changing technologies have brought prosperity to Canada and the United States, other North American countries wrestle with the most basic needs. Promise and problems abound across this contrasting realm of 23 countries and more than 540 million people.

Quebec, Canada

BISON ARE THE HEAVIEST LAND ANIMALS IN NORTH AMERIC

MORE THAN 205	THE NUMBER OF ACTIVE VOLCANOES IN NORTH AMERICA
5,525 MILES (8,892 KM)	LENGTH OF THE CANADA–UNITED STATES BORDER, THE WORLD'S LONGEST BOUNDARY BETWEEN TWO NATIONS
2 INCHES (5 CM)	SIZE OF CUBA'S BEE HUMMINGBIRD, THE SMALLEST BIRD IN THE WORLD

DID YOU KNOW?

The Chihuahua, the world's smallest dog, is named for a state in Mexico.

13.3% of Canadians speak only French.

A bison in Yellowstone National Park, western United States

BISON CAN RUN FASTER THAN 30 MILES AN HOUR (48 KPH).

PHYSICAL

LAND AREA
9,449,000 sq mi
(24,474,000 sq km)

HIGHEST POINT
Mount McKinley, Alaska
20,320 ft (6,194 m)

LOWEST POINT
Death Valley, California
-282 ft (-86 m)

LONGEST RIVER
Mississippi–Missouri,
United States
3,780 mi (6,083 km)

LARGEST LAKE
Lake Superior,
U.S.–Canada
31,700 sq mi
(82,100 sq km)

POLITICAL

POPULATION
546,048,000

LARGEST COUNTRY
Canada
3,855,101 sq mi
(9,984,670 sq km)

LARGEST METROPOLITAN AREA
Mexico City, Mexico
Pop. 19,319,000

MOST DENSELY POPULATED COUNTRY
Barbados / 1,651 people
per sq mi (637 per sq km)

Map Key

⊛ National capital
• Other city

EUROPE

Greenland
(Denmark)

ARCTIC CIRCLE

North Pole

Arctic Ocean

C A N A D A

• Edmonton

• Calgary

Vancouver

Alaska
(U.S.)

• Anchorage

ASIA

800 Miles

800 Kilometers

Azimuthal Equidistant Projection

0°
20°W
40°W
60°W
80°N
60°N
160°W
180°
160°E
40°W

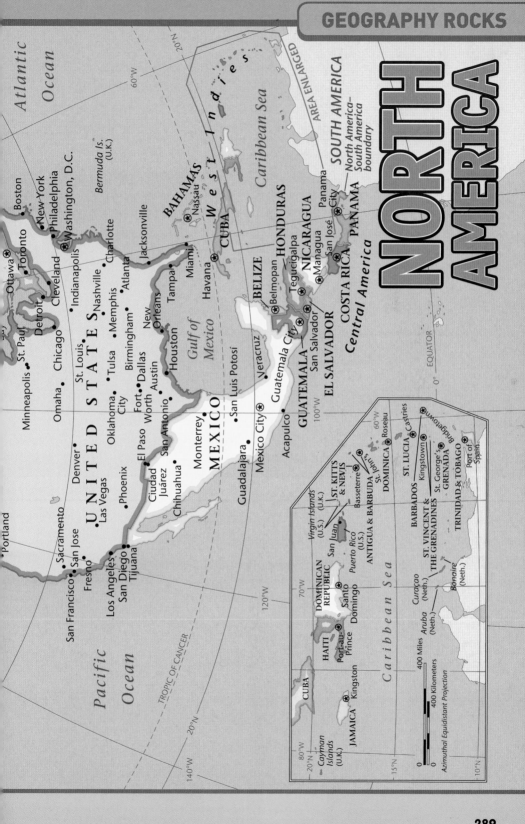

NORTH AMERICA

SOUTH AMERICA

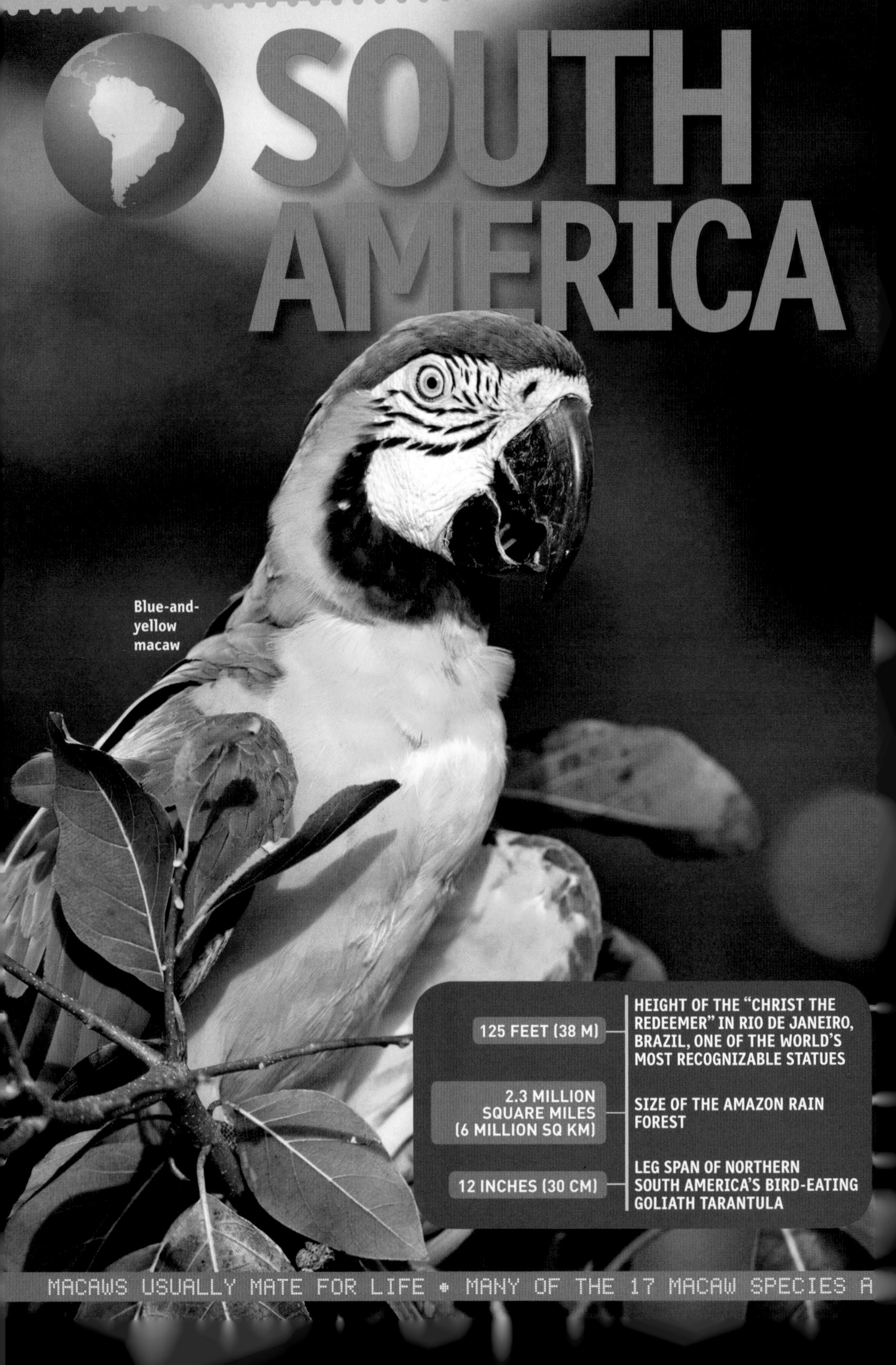

Blue-and-yellow macaw

125 FEET (38 M)	HEIGHT OF THE "CHRIST THE REDEEMER" IN RIO DE JANEIRO, BRAZIL, ONE OF THE WORLD'S MOST RECOGNIZABLE STATUES
2.3 MILLION SQUARE MILES (6 MILLION SQ KM)	SIZE OF THE AMAZON RAIN FOREST
12 INCHES (30 CM)	LEG SPAN OF NORTHERN SOUTH AMERICA'S BIRD-EATING GOLIATH TARANTULA

MACAWS USUALLY MATE FOR LIFE • MANY OF THE 17 MACAW SPECIES A

The 12 countries of South America stretch from the warm waters of the Caribbean to the frigid ocean around Antarctica. The mighty Amazon carries more water than the world's next ten biggest rivers combined, draining a third of the continent. Its basin contains the planet's largest rain forest. The Andes tower along the continent's western edge from Colombia to southern Chile.

The gold-seeking Spaniards conquered the Amerindians when they arrived in the Andes in 1532. Along with the Portuguese, they ruled most of the continent for almost 300 years. The conquest of South America by Europeans took a heavy toll on its indigenous peoples.

Centuries of ethnic blending have woven Amerindian, European, African, and Asian heritages into South America's rich cultural fabric. Today's mix of colonial and indigenous languages demonstrates this unique blend.

Despite its relatively small population and wealth of natural resources, South America today is burdened by economic, social, and environmental problems. But this combination of small population and great resources also means that the continent has nearly unlimited potential.

Peruvian girl in festival costume

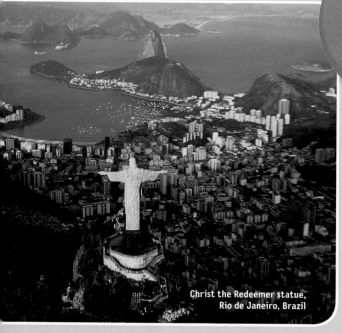

Christ the Redeemer statue, Rio de Janeiro, Brazil

DID YOU KNOW?

With the most World Cup wins, Brazil boasts the world's most successful soccer team.

The earliest inhabitants of Peru arrived there thousands of years ago.

The water and sand in Venezuela's Canaima National Park are tinted red by minerals in the soil.

DANGERED, INCLUDING THE HYACINTH, GREAT GREEN, AND GLAUCOUS MACAWS

PHYSICAL

LAND AREA
6,880,000 sq mi
(17,819,000 sq km)

HIGHEST POINT
Cerro Aconcagua,
Argentina
22,831 ft (6,959 m)

LOWEST POINT
Laguna del Carbón,
Argentina
-344 ft (-105 m)

LONGEST RIVER
Amazon
4,150 mi (6,679 km)

LARGEST LAKE
Lake Maracaibo,
Venezuela: 5,025 sq
mi (13,010.00 sq km)

POLITICAL

POPULATION
396,184,000

LARGEST COUNTRY
Brazil
3,287,612 sq mi
(8,514,877 sq km)

LARGEST METROPOLITAN AREA
São Paulo, Brazil
Pop. 19,960,000

**MOST DENSELY POPULATED
COUNTRY**
Ecuador / 135 people per
sq mi (52 per sq km)

Map Key

⊛ National capital
• Other city

600 Miles
600 Kilometers

Azimuthal Equidistant Projection

EQUATOR

Natal

Fortaleza

Recife

Salvador

Belém

Cayenne
French Guiana
(France)

Paramaribo

SURINAME

Georgetown

GUYANA

Manaus

B R A Z I L

VENEZUELA

Caracás

Valencia

Maracaibo

Barquisimeto

Barranquilla

Caribbean
Sea

*Central
America*

Medellín

Bogotá

Cali

COLOMBIA

Quito

ECUADOR

Guayaquil

Trujillo

Lima

P E R U

*South America–
North America
boundary*

EQUATOR

80°W

70°W

60°W

50°W

10°N

0°

10°S

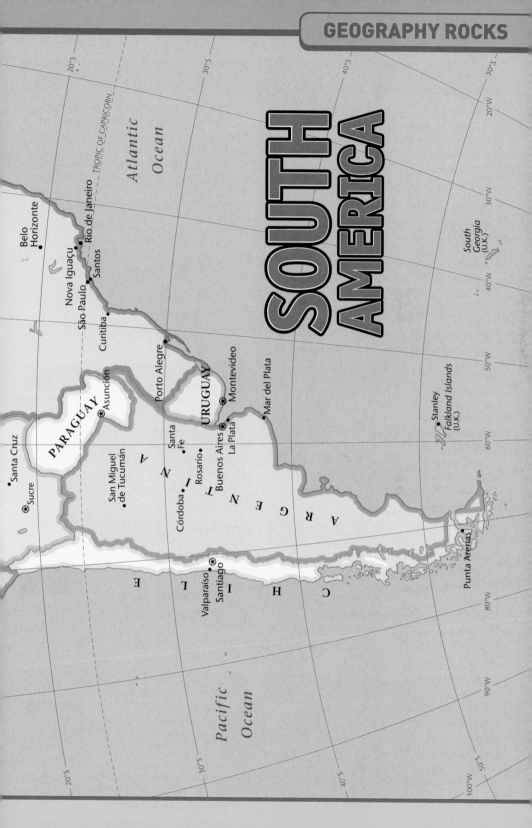

SOUTH AMERICA

Atlantic Ocean

Belo Horizonte
Nova Iguaçu
Rio de Janeiro
São Paulo
Santos
Curitiba
TROPIC OF CAPRICORN

Porto Alegre

PARAGUAY
Asunción

URUGUAY
Montevideo
Mar del Plata

Santa Cruz
Sucre

San Miguel de Tucumán
Santa Fe
Rosario
Córdoba
Buenos Aires
La Plata

A R G E N T I N A

C H I L E

Valparaíso
Santiago

Pacific Ocean

South Georgia (U.K.)

Stanley
Falkland Islands (U.K.)

Punta Arenas

20°S
30°S
40°S
50°S

20°S
30°S

20°W
30°W
40°W
50°W
60°W
80°W
90°W
100°W

40°S
50°S

COUNTRIES OF THE WORLD

The following pages present a general overview of all 195 independent countries recognized by the National Geographic Society, including the newest nation, South Sudan, which gained independence in 2011.

Flags of each independent country symbolize diverse cultures and histories. The statistical data cover highlights of geography and demography and provide a brief overview of each country. They present general characteristics and are not intended to be comprehensive. For example, not every language spoken in a specific country can be listed. Thus, languages shown are the most representative of that area. This is also true of the religions mentioned.

A country is defined as a political body with its own independent government, geographical space, and, in most cases, laws, military, and taxes.

Disputed areas such as Northern Cyprus and Taiwan, and dependencies of independent nations, such as Bermuda and Puerto Rico, are not included in this listing.

Note the color key at the bottom of the pages and the locator map below, which assign a color to each country based on the continent on which it is located. All information is accurate as of press time.

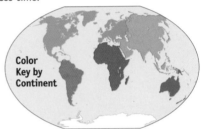

Color Key by Continent

Afghanistan

Area: 251,773 sq mi (652,090 sq km)
Population: 32,358,000
Capital: Kabul, pop. 3,573,000
Currency: afghani
Religions: Sunni Muslim, Shiite Muslim
Languages: Afghan Persian (Dari), Pashto, Turkic languages (primarily Uzbek and Turkmen), Baluchi, 30 minor languages (including Pashai)

Albania

Area: 11,100 sq mi (28,748 sq km)
Population: 3,197,000
Capital: Tirana, pop. 433,000
Currency: lek
Religions: Muslim, Albanian Orthodox, Roman Catholic
Languages: Albanian, Greek, Vlach, Romani, Slavic dialects

Algeria

Area: 919,595 sq mi (2,381,741 sq km)
Population: 35,980,000
Capital: Algiers, pop. 2,740,000
Currency: Algerian dinar
Religion: Sunni Muslim
Languages: Arabic, French, Berber dialects

Andorra

Area: 181 sq mi (469 sq km)
Population: 85,000
Capital: Andorra la Vella, pop. 25,000
Currency: euro
Religion: Roman Catholic
Languages: Catalan, French, Castilian, Portuguese

Angola

Area: 481,354 sq mi (1,246,700 sq km)
Population: 19,638,000
Capital: Luanda, pop. 4,511,000
Currency: kwanza
Religions: indigenous beliefs, Roman Catholic, Protestant
Languages: Portuguese, Bantu, and other African languages

Antigua and Barbuda

Area: 171 sq mi (442 sq km)
Population: 88,000
Capital: St. John's, pop. 27,000
Currency: East Caribbean dollar
Religions: Anglican, Seventh-day Adventist, Pentecostal, Moravian, Roman Catholic, Methodist, Baptist, Church of God, other Christian
Languages: English, local dialects

Argentina

Area: 1,073,518 sq mi
(2,780,400 sq km)
Population: 40,488,000
Capital: Buenos Aires,
pop. 12,988,000
Currency: Argentine peso
Religion: Roman Catholic
Languages: Spanish, English, Italian, German, French

Armenia

Area: 11,484 sq mi
(29,743 sq km)
Population: 3,123,000
Capital: Yerevan, pop. 1,110,000
Currency: dram
Religions: Armenian Apostolic, other Christian
Language: Armenian

Australia

Area: 2,969,906 sq mi
(7,692,024 sq km)
Population: 22,670,000
Capital: Canberra, pop. 384,000
Currency: Australian dollar
Religions: Roman Catholic, Anglican
Language: English

Austria

Area: 32,378 sq mi (83,858 sq km)
Population: 8,418,000
Capital: Vienna, pop. 1,693,000
Currency: euro
Religions: Roman Catholic, Protestant, Muslim
Language: German

Azerbaijan

Area: 33,436 sq mi
(86,600 sq km)
Population: 9,150,000
Capital: Baku, pop. 1,950,000
Currency: Azerbaijani manat
Religion: Muslim
Language: Azerbaijani (Azeri)

Bahamas

Area: 5,382 sq mi (13,939 sq km)
Population: 357,000
Capital: Nassau, pop. 248,000
Currency: Bahamian dollar
Religions: Baptist, Anglican, Roman Catholic, Pentecostal, Church of God
Languages: English, Creole

Bahrain

Area: 277 sq mi (717 sq km)
Population: 1,336,000
Capital: Manama, pop. 163,000
Currency: Bahraini dinar
Religions: Shiite Muslim, Sunni Muslim, Christian
Languages: Arabic, English, Farsi, Urdu

Bangladesh

Area: 55,598 sq mi (143,998 sq km)
Population: 150,685,000
Capital: Dhaka, pop. 14,251,000
Currency: taka
Religions: Muslim, Hindu
Languages: Bangla (Bengali), English

Barbados

Area: 166 sq mi (430 sq km)
Population: 274,000
Capital: Bridgetown, pop. 112,000
Currency: Barbadian dollar
Religions: Anglican, Pentecostal, Methodist, other Protestant, Roman Catholic
Language: English

Belarus

Area: 80,153 sq mi
(207,595 sq km)
Population: 9,472,000
Capital: Minsk, pop. 1,837,000
Currency: Belarusian ruble
Religions: Eastern Orthodox, other (includes Roman Catholic, Protestant, Jewish, Muslim)
Languages: Belarusian, Russian

Belgium

Area: 11,787 sq mi (30,528 sq km)
Population: 10,970,000
Capital: Brussels, pop. 1,892,000
Currency: euro
Religions: Roman Catholic, other (includes Protestant)
Languages: Dutch, French

Belize

Area: 8,867 sq mi (22,965 sq km)
Population: 318,000
Capital: Belmopan, pop. 20,000
Currency: Belizean dollar
Religions: Roman Catholic, Protestant (includes Pentecostal, Seventh-day Adventist, Mennonite, Methodist)
Languages: Spanish, Creole, Mayan dialects, English, Garifuna (Carib), German

Benin

Area: 43,484 sq mi (112,622 sq km)
Population: 9,109,000
Capitals: Porto-Novo, pop. 276,000; Cotonou, pop. 815,000
Currency: Communauté Financière Africaine franc
Religions: Christian, Muslim, Vodoun
Languages: French, Fon, Yoruba, tribal languages

Bhutan

Area: 17,954 sq mi (46,500 sq km)
Population: 708,000
Capital: Thimphu, pop. 89,000
Currencies: ngultrum; Indian rupee
Religions: Lamaistic Buddhist, Indian- and Nepalese-influenced Hindu
Languages: Dzongkha, Tibetan dialects, Nepalese dialects

Bolivia

Area: 424,164 sq mi (1,098,581 sq km)
Population: 10,088,000
Capitals: La Paz, pop. 1,642,000; Sucre, pop. 281,000
Currency: boliviano
Religions: Roman Catholic, Protestant (includes Evangelical Methodist)
Languages: Spanish, Quechua, Aymara

Bosnia and Herzegovina

Area: 19,741 sq mi (51,129 sq km)
Population: 3,843,000
Capital: Sarajevo, pop. 392,000
Currency: konvertibilna marka (convertible mark)
Religions: Muslim, Orthodox, Roman Catholic
Languages: Bosnian, Croatian, Serbian

Botswana

Area: 224,607 sq mi (581,730 sq km)
Population: 2,033,000
Capital: Gaborone, pop. 196,000
Currency: pula
Religions: Christian, Badimo
Languages: Setswana, Kalanga

Brazil

Area: 3,287,612 sq mi (8,514,877 sq km)
Population: 196,655,000
Capital: Brasília, pop. 3,789,000
Currency: real
Religions: Roman Catholic, Protestant
Language: Portuguese

Brunei

Area: 2,226 sq mi (5,765 sq km)
Population: 410,000
Capital: Bandar Seri Begawan, pop. 22,000
Currency: Bruneian dollar
Religions: Muslim, Buddhist, Christian, other (includes indigenous beliefs)
Languages: Malay, English, Chinese

Bulgaria

Area: 42,855 sq mi (110,994 sq km)
Population: 7,476,000
Capital: Sofia, pop. 1,192,000
Currency: lev
Religions: Bulgarian Orthodox, Muslim
Languages: Bulgarian, Turkish, Roma

COLOR KEY ● Africa ● Australia, New Zealand, and Ocean

Burkina Faso

Area: 105,869 sq mi (274,200 sq km)
Population: 16,968,000
Capital: Ouagadougou, pop. 1,777,000
Currency: Communauté Financière Africaine franc
Religions: Muslim, indigenous beliefs, Christian
Languages: French, native African languages

Cambodia

Area: 69,898 sq mi (181,035 sq km)
Population: 14,702,000
Capital: Phnom Penh, pop. 1,519,000
Currency: riel
Religion: Theravada Buddhist
Language: Khmer

Burundi

Area: 10,747 sq mi (27,834 sq km)
Population: 10,216,000
Capital: Bujumbura, pop. 455,000
Currency: Burundi franc
Religions: Roman Catholic, indigenous beliefs, Muslim, Protestant
Languages: Kirundi, French, Swahili

Cameroon

Area: 183,569 sq mi (475,442 sq km)
Population: 20,052,000
Capital: Yaoundé, pop. 1,739,000
Currency: Communauté Financière Africaine franc
Religions: indigenous beliefs, Christian, Muslim
Languages: 24 major African language groups, English, French

You Are There!
Amazon Cruise, Brazil

Picture this: You're on a boat in northeastern Brazil, cruising down a slow-moving river as a lush, green rain forest beckons before you. Below, a massive manatee glides beneath the water's surface. In the distance you hear the telltale screech of a howler monkey. You can only be in one place—the Amazon. This massive rain forest is situated along the 4,150-mile (6,679-km)-long Amazon River. An Amazon cruise is the best way to visit this region. The large boats take you down the river, making stops so you can get out and explore with a guide. Watch for wildlife, trek through the thick jungle, or go fishing (just watch out for piranha!).

● Asia   ● Europe   ● North America   ● South America

297

Canada

Area: 3,855,101 sq mi
(9,984,670 sq km)
Population: 34,468,000
Capital: Ottawa, pop. 1,170,000
Currency: Canadian dollar
Religions: Roman Catholic, Protestant (includes United Church, Anglican), other Christian
Languages: English, French

Cape Verde

Area: 1,558 sq mi (4,036 sq km)
Population: 496,000
Capital: Praia, pop. 125,000
Currency: Cape Verdean escudo
Religions: Roman Catholic (infused with indigenous beliefs), Protestant (mostly Church of the Nazarene)
Languages: Portuguese, Crioulo

Central African Republic

Area: 240,535 sq mi (622,984 sq km)
Population: 4,950,000
Capital: Bangui, pop. 702,000
Currency: Communauté Financière Africaine franc
Religions: indigenous beliefs, Protestant, Roman Catholic, Muslim
Languages: French, Sangho, tribal languages

Chad

Area: 495,755 sq mi (1,284,000 sq km)
Population: 11,536,000
Capital: N'Djamena, pop. 808,000
Currency: Communauté Financière Africaine franc
Religions: Muslim, Catholic, Protestant, animist
Languages: French, Arabic, Sara, more than 120 languages and dialects

Chile

Area: 291,930 sq mi
(756,096 sq km)
Population: 17,268,000
Capital: Santiago, pop. 5,883,000
Currency: Chilean peso
Religions: Roman Catholic, Evangelical
Language: Spanish

China

Area: 3,705,405 sq mi
(9,596,960 sq km)
Population: 1,345,855,000
Capital: Beijing, pop. 12,214,000
Currency: renminbi (yuan)
Religions: Taoist, Buddhist, Christian
Languages: Standard Chinese or Mandarin, Yue, Wu, Minbei, Minnan, Xiang, Gan, Hakka dialects

Colombia

Area: 440,831 sq mi
(1,141,748 sq km)
Population: 46,871,000
Capital: Bogotá, pop. 8,262,000
Currency: Colombian peso
Religion: Roman Catholic
Language: Spanish

Comoros

Area: 863 sq mi (2,235 sq km)
Population: 754,000
Capital: Moroni, pop. 49,000
Currency: Comoran franc
Religion: Sunni Muslim
Languages: Arabic, French, Shikomoro

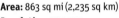

5 cool things about CHILE

1. Chile is one of the few places on the planet where you can find blue lapis stone.

2. Running along the entire length of Chile, the Andes is the longest continental mountain range in the world.

3. Chile is only about 100 miles (160 km) wide from east to west.

4. There are more than 2,000 volcanoes in Chile—only about 100 of them are active.

5. Covering over 20 acres, the largest swimming pool in the world is in Chile.

Congo

Area: 132,047 sq mi (342,000 sq km)
Population: 4,144,000
Capital: Brazzaville, pop. 1,292,000
Currency: Communauté Financière Africaine franc
Religions: Christian, animist
Languages: French, Lingala, Monokutuba, local languages

Costa Rica

Area: 19,730 sq mi (51,100 sq km)
Population: 4,727,000
Capital: San José, pop. 1,416,000
Currency: Costa Rican colón
Religions: Roman Catholic, Evangelical
Languages: Spanish, English

Côte d'Ivoire (Ivory Coast)

Area: 124,503 sq mi (322,462 sq km)
Population: 22,621,000
Capitals: Abidjan, pop. 4,009,000; Yamoussoukro, pop. 808,000
Currency: Communauté Financière Africaine franc
Religions: Muslim, indigenous beliefs, Christian
Languages: French, Dioula, other native dialects

Croatia

Area: 21,831 sq mi (56,542 sq km)
Population: 4,405,000
Capital: Zagreb, pop. 685,000
Currency: kuna
Religions: Roman Catholic, Orthodox
Language: Croatian

Cuba

Area: 42,803 sq mi (110,860 sq km)
Population: 11,240,000
Capital: Havana, pop. 2,140,000
Currency: Cuban peso
Religions: Roman Catholic, Protestant, Jehovah's Witnesses, Jewish, Santería
Language: Spanish

Cyprus

Area: 3,572 sq mi (9,251 sq km)
Population: 1,107,000
Capital: Nicosia, pop. 240,000
Currencies: euro; new Turkish lira in Northern Cyprus
Religions: Greek Orthodox, Muslim, Maronite, Armenian Apostolic
Languages: Greek, Turkish, English

Czech Republic (Czechia)

Area: 30,450 sq mi (78,866 sq km)
Population: 10,546,000
Capital: Prague, pop. 1,162,000
Currency: koruny
Religion: Roman Catholic
Language: Czech

A church in the **CZECH REPUBLIC** has a chandelier made of **HUMAN BONES.**

Democratic Republic of the Congo

Area: 905,365 sq mi (2,344,885 sq km)
Population: 67,823,000
Capital: Kinshasa, pop. 8,401,000
Currency: Congolese franc
Religions: Roman Catholic, Protestant, Kimbanguist, Muslim, syncretic sects, indigenous beliefs
Languages: French, Lingala, Kingwana, Kikongo, Tshiluba

Denmark

Area: 16,640 sq mi (43,098 sq km)
Population: 5,574,000
Capital: Copenhagen, pop. 1,174,000
Currency: Danish krone
Religions: Evangelical Lutheran, other Protestant, Roman Catholic
Languages: Danish, Faroese, Greenlandic, German, English as second language

Djibouti

Area: 8,958 sq mi
(23,200 sq km)
Population: 906,000
Capital: Djibouti, pop. 567,000
Currency: Djiboutian franc
Religions: Muslim, Christian
Languages: French, Arabic, Somali, Afar

Dominica

Area: 290 sq mi (751 sq km)
Population: 73,000
Capital: Roseau, pop. 14,000
Currency: East Caribbean
dollar
Religions: Roman Catholic, Seventh-day Adventist,
Pentecostal, Baptist, Methodist, other Christian
Languages: English, French patois

Dominican Republic

Area: 18,704 sq mi
(48,442 sq km)
Population: 10,010,000
Capital: Santo Domingo,
pop. 2,138,000
Currency: Dominican peso
Religion: Roman Catholic
Language: Spanish

Ecuador

Area: 109,483 sq mi
(283,560 sq km)
Population: 14,666,000
Capital: Quito, pop. 1,801,000
Currency: U.S. dollar
Religion: Roman Catholic
Languages: Spanish, Quechua, other
Amerindian languages

You Are There!

Eiffel Tower, Paris, France

La Tour Eiffel is one of the most famous landmarks on the planet. Millions of visitors flock here each year just to get a glimpse of this 81-story tower, the tallest building in Paris. Originally built as a symbol to welcome visitors to Paris for the 1889 World's Fair, the iron tower was once thought of as an eyesore. But the country of France—and soon, the world—eventually embraced its unique architecture, and today it easily earns the status of the most-visited paid monument in the world.

COLOR KEY ● Africa ● Australia, New Zealand, and Oceania

Egypt

Area: 386,874 sq mi
(1,002,000 sq km)
Population: 82,637,000
Capital: Cairo, pop. 10,903,000
Currency: Egyptian pound
Religions: Muslim (mostly Sunni), Coptic Christian
Languages: Arabic, English, French

Ethiopia

Area: 426,373 sq mi
(1,104,300 sq km)
Population: 87,118,000
Capital: Addis Ababa,
pop. 2,863,000
Currency: birr
Religions: Christian, Muslim, traditional
Languages: Amharic, Oromigna, Tigrinya, Guaragigna

El Salvador

Area: 8,124 sq mi (21,041 sq km)
Population: 6,227,000
Capital: San Salvador,
pop. 1,534,000
Currency: U.S. dollar
Religions: Roman Catholic, Protestant
Languages: Spanish, Nahua

Fiji

Area: 7,095 sq mi (18,376 sq km)
Population: 852,000
Capital: Suva, pop. 174,000
Currency: Fijian dollar
Religions: Christian (Methodist, Roman Catholic,
Assembly of God), Hindu (Sanatan), Muslim (Sunni)
Languages: English, Fijian, Hindustani

Equatorial Guinea

Area: 10,831 sq mi (28,051 sq km)
Population: 720,000
Capital: Malabo, pop. 128,000
Currency: Communauté
Financière Africaine franc
Religions: Christian (predominantly Roman Catholic),
pagan practices
Languages: Spanish, French, Fang, Bubi

Finland

Area: 130,558 sq mi
(338,145 sq km)
Population: 5,387,000
Capital: Helsinki, pop. 1,107,000
Currency: euro
Religion: Lutheran Church of Finland
Languages: Finnish, Swedish

Eritrea

Area: 45,406 sq mi (117,600 sq km)
Population: 5,939,000
Capital: Asmara, pop. 649,000
Currency: nakfa
Religions: Muslim, Coptic Christian, Roman Catholic,
Protestant
Languages: Afar, Arabic, Tigre, Kunama, Tigrinya, other
Cushitic languages

France

Area: 210,026 sq mi
(543,965 sq km)
Population: 63,305,000
Capital: Paris, pop. 10,410,000
Currency: euro
Religions: Roman Catholic, Muslim
Language: French

Estonia

Area: 17,462 sq mi (45,227 sq km)
Population: 1,340,000
Capital: Tallinn, pop. 399,000
Currency: euro
Religions: Evangelical Lutheran, Orthodox
Languages: Estonian, Russian

Gabon

Area: 103,347 sq mi (267,667 sq km)
Population: 1,534,000
Capital: Libreville, pop. 619,000
Currency: Communauté Financière
Africaine franc
Religions: Christian, animist
Languages: French, Fang, Myene, Nzebi, Bapounou/
Eschira, Bandjabi

COOL CLICK

Want to see interactive maps and videos of the countries? Go online to National Geographic.
travel.nationalgeographic.com/travel/countries/

Greece

Area: 50,949 sq mi (131,957 sq km)
Population: 11,329,000
Capital: Athens, pop. 3,252,000
Currency: euro
Religion: Greek Orthodox
Languages: Greek, English, French

Gambia

Area: 4,361 sq mi (11,295 sq km)
Population: 1,778,000
Capital: Banjul, pop. 436,000
Currency: dalasi
Religions: Muslim, Christian
Languages: English, Mandinka, Wolof, Fula, other indigenous vernaculars

Grenada

Area: 133 sq mi (344 sq km)
Population: 105,000
Capital: St. George's, pop. 40,000
Currency: East Caribbean dollar
Religions: Roman Catholic, Anglican, other Protestant
Languages: English, French patois

Georgia

Area: 26,911 sq mi (69,700 sq km)
Population: 4,329,000
Capital: Tbilisi, pop. 1,115,000
Currency: lari
Religions: Orthodox Christian, Muslim, Armenian-Gregorian
Languages: Georgian, Russian, Armenian, Azeri, Abkhaz

Guatemala

Area: 42,042 sq mi (108,889 sq km)
Population: 14,740,000
Capital: Guatemala City, pop. 1,075,000
Currency: quetzal
Religions: Roman Catholic, Protestant, indigenous Maya beliefs
Languages: Spanish, 23 official Amerindian languages

Germany

Area: 137,847 sq mi (357,022 sq km)
Population: 81,755,000
Capital: Berlin, pop. 3,438,000
Currency: euro
Religions: Protestant, Roman Catholic, Muslim
Language: German

Guinea

Area: 94,926 sq mi (245,857 sq km)
Population: 10,232,000
Capital: Conakry, pop. 1,597,000
Currency: Guinean franc
Religions: Muslim, Christian, indigenous beliefs
Languages: French, ethnic languages

Ghana

Area: 92,100 sq mi (238,537 sq km)
Population: 24,966,000
Capital: Accra, pop. 2,269,000
Currency: Ghana cedi
Religions: Christian (Pentecostal/Charismatic, Protestant, Roman Catholic, other), Muslim, traditional beliefs
Languages: Asante, Ewe, Fante, Boron (Brong), Dagomba, Dangme, Dagarte (Dagaba), Akyem, Ga, English

Guinea-Bissau

Area: 13,948 sq mi (36,125 sq km)
Population: 1,610,000
Capital: Bissau, pop. 302,000
Currency: Communauté Financière Africaine franc
Religions: indigenous beliefs, Muslim, Christian
Languages: Portuguese, Crioulo, African languages

Guyana

Area: 83,000 sq mi (214,969 sq km)
Population: 757,000
Capital: Georgetown, pop. 132,000
Currency: Guyanese dollar
Religions: Christian, Hindu, Muslim
Languages: English, Amerindian dialects, Creole, Hindustani, Urdu

Honduras

Area: 43,433 sq mi (112,492 sq km)
Population: 7,755,000
Capital: Tegucigalpa, pop. 1,000,000
Currency: lempira
Religions: Roman Catholic, Protestant
Languages: Spanish, Amerindian dialects

Haiti

Area: 10,714 sq mi (27,750 sq km)
Population: 10,124,000
Capital: Port-au-Prince, pop. 2,643,000
Currency: gourde
Religions: Roman Catholic, Protestant (Baptist, Pentecostal, other)
Languages: French, Creole

Hungary

Area: 35,919 sq mi (93,030 sq km)
Population: 9,972,000
Capital: Budapest, pop. 1,705,000
Currency: forint
Religions: Roman Catholic, Calvinist, Lutheran
Language: Hungarian

You Are There!
The Parthenon, Athens, Greece

Want to know what life looked like more than 2,400 years ago? Then head to the Acropolis overlooking Athens, Greece, where ruins of buildings built in ancient times still stand. Here, you can walk around the grounds of the Parthenon, one of the world's most recognizable buildings. Originally constructed as a temple to the goddess Athena, the Parthenon (which has since served as a church, a fortress, and a place to store ammunition) has literally stood the test of time. The building has been shot at, exploded, set on fire, and rocked by earthquakes—and yet its columns still stand.

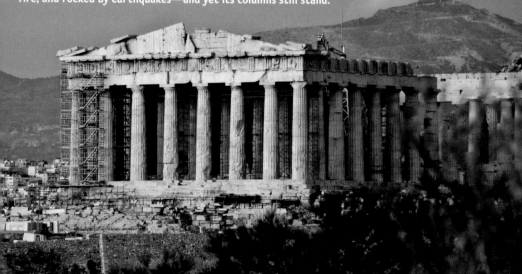

● Asia ● Europe ● North America ● South America

Iceland

Area: 39,769 sq mi
(103,000 sq km)
Population: 319,000
Capital: Reykjavik, pop. 198,000
Currency: Icelandic krona
Religion: Lutheran Church of Iceland
Languages: Icelandic, English, Nordic
languages, German

Indonesia

Area: 742,308 sq mi
(1,922,570 sq km)
Population: 238,181,000
Capital: Jakarta, pop. 9,121,000
Currency: Indonesian rupiah
Religions: Muslim, Protestant, Roman Catholic
Languages: Bahasa Indonesia (modified form of Malay),
English, Dutch, Javanese, local dialects

India

Area: 1,269,221 sq mi (3,287,270 sq km)
Population: 1,241,275,000
Capital: New Delhi, pop. 21,720,000
(part of Delhi metropolitan area)
Currency: Indian rupee
Religions: Hindu, Muslim
Languages: Hindi, 21 other official languages,
Hindustani (popular Hindi/Urdu variant in the north)

Iran

Area: 636,296 sq mi
(1,648,000 sq km)
Population: 77,891,000
Capital: Tehran, pop. 7,190,000
Currency: Iranian rial
Religions: Shiite Muslim, Sunni Muslim
Languages: Persian, Turkic, Kurdish, Luri,
Baluchi, Arabic

You Are There!

Masai Mara National Reserve Kenya, Africa

Just about a four-hour drive from the Kenyan capital of Nairobi, this vast stretch of savanna might as well be a world away from the hustle-and-bustle of city life. Take a safari through the 600 square miles (1,554 sq km) of grasslands. Look closely and you may spot a leopard or even the endangered black rhino. And over there by the acacia tree? It's a pride of lions lazing around in the sun. Here, hippos bathe alongside Nile crocodiles in the Mara River, while African elephants cool off by its banks.

Near the Reserve, the people of the semi-nomadic Maasai live in huts roofed with grass. Known for their elegant beads and colorful dress, the Maasai often travel with their herds of cattle.

COLOR KEY ● Africa ● Australia, New Zealand, and Oceania

Iraq

Area: 168,754 sq mi
(437,072 sq km)
Population: 32,665,000
Capital: Baghdad, pop. 5,751,000
Currency: Iraqi dinar
Religions: Shiite Muslim, Sunni Muslim
Languages: Arabic, Kurdish, Assyrian, Armenian

Japan

Area: 145,902 sq mi (377,887 sq km)
Population: 128,100,000
Capital: Tokyo, pop. 36,507,000
Currency: yen
Religions: Shinto, Buddhist
Language: Japanese

Ireland

Area: 27,133 sq mi
(70,273 sq km)
Population: 4,485,000
Capital: Dublin, pop. 1,084,000
Currency: euro
Religions: Roman Catholic, Church of Ireland
Languages: Irish (Gaelic), English

Jordan

Area: 34,495 sq mi
(89,342 sq km)
Population: 6,632,000
Capital: Amman, pop. 1,088,000
Currency: Jordanian dinar
Religions: Sunni Muslim, Christian
Languages: Arabic, English

Israel

Area: 8,550 sq mi (22,145 sq km)
Population: 7,856,000
Capital: Jerusalem, pop. 768,000
Currency: new Israeli sheqel
Religions: Jewish, Muslim
Languages: Hebrew, Arabic, English

Kazakhstan

Area: 1,049,155 sq mi
(2,717,300 sq km)
Population: 16,553,000
Capital: Astana, pop. 650,000
Currency: tenge
Religions: Muslim, Russian Orthodox
Languages: Kazakh (Qazaq), Russian

Italy

Area: 116,345 sq mi
(301,333 sq km)
Population: 60,769,000
Capital: Rome, pop. 3,357,000
Currency: euro
Religions: Roman Catholic, Protestant, Jewish, Muslim
Languages: Italian, German, French, Slovene

Kenya

Area: 224,081 sq mi (580,367 sq km)
Population: 41,610,000
Capital: Nairobi, pop. 3,375,000
Currency: Kenyan shilling
Religions: Protestant, Roman Catholic, Muslim, indigenous beliefs
Languages: English, Kiswahili, many indigenous languages

Jamaica

Area: 4,244 sq mi
(10,991 sq km)
Population: 2,709,000
Capital: Kingston, pop. 580,000
Currency: Jamaican dollar
Religions: Protestant (Church of God, Seventh-day Adventist, Pentecostal, Baptist, Anglican, other)
Languages: English, English patois

Kiribati

Area: 313 sq mi (811 sq km)
Population: 103,000
Capital: Tarawa, pop. 43,000
Currency: Australian dollar
Religions: Roman Catholic, Protestant (Congregational)
Languages: I-Kiribati, English

Kosovo

Area: 4,203 sq mi (10,887 sq km)
Population: 2,284,000
Capital: Prishtina, pop. 600,000
Currency: euro
Religions: Muslim, Serbian Orthodox, Roman Catholic
Languages: Albanian, Serbian, Bosnian, Turkish, Roma

Kuwait

Area: 6,880 sq mi
(17,818 sq km)
Population: 2,818,000
Capital: Kuwait City,
pop. 2,230,000
Currency: Kuwaiti dinar
Religions: Sunni Muslim, Shiite Muslim
Languages: Arabic, English

Kyrgyzstan

Area: 77,182 sq mi
(199,900 sq km)
Population: 5,600,000
Capital: Bishkek, pop. 854,000
Currency: som
Religions: Muslim, Russian Orthodox
Languages: Kyrgyz, Uzbek, Russian

5 cool things about KYRGYZSTAN

1. Kyrgyzstan is pronounced KIR-gi-stan.

2. Mountains cover close to 75 percent of Kyrgyzstan.

3. The national drink of Kyrgyzstan is fermented milk from a horse, also known as kumyz.

4. Despite its altitude, Kyrgyzstan's Lake Ysyk-Köl, one of Earth's largest mountain lakes, never freezes over.

5. Osh, a city in Kyrgyzstan's Fergana Valley, is believed to be 3,000 years old.

Laos

Area: 91,429 sq mi
(236,800 sq km)
Population: 6,259,000
Capital: Vientiane, pop. 799,000
Currency: kip
Religions: Buddhist, animist
Languages: Lao, French, English, various ethnic languages

Latvia

Area: 24,938 sq mi
(64,589 sq km)
Population: 2,217,000
Capital: Riga, pop. 711,000
Currency: Latvian lat
Religions: Lutheran, Roman Catholic, Russian Orthodox
Languages: Latvian, Russian, Lithuanian

Lebanon

Area: 4,036 sq mi (10,452 sq km)
Population: 4,264,000
Capital: Beirut, pop. 1,909,000
Currency: Lebanese pound
Religions: Muslim, Christian
Languages: Arabic, French, English, Armenian

Lesotho

Area: 11,720 sq mi (30,355 sq km)
Population: 2,194,000
Capital: Maseru, pop. 220,000
Currencies: loti; South African rand
Religions: Christian, indigenous beliefs
Languages: Sesotho, English, Zulu, Xhosa

Liberia

Area: 43,000 sq mi
(111,370 sq km)
Population: 4,133,000
Capital: Monrovia,
pop. 882,000
Currency: Liberian dollar
Religions: Christian, indigenous beliefs, Muslim
Languages: English, some 20 ethnic languages

COLOR KEY ● Africa ● Australia, New Zealand, and Oceania

Libya

Area: 679,362 sq mi
(1,759,540 sq km)
Population: 6,423,000
Capital: Tripoli, pop. 1,095,000
Currency: Libyan dinar
Religion: Sunni Muslim
Languages: Arabic, Italian, English

Liechtenstein

Area: 62 sq mi (160 sq km)
Population: 36,000
Capital: Vaduz, pop. 5,000
Currency: Swiss franc
Religions: Roman Catholic, Protestant
Languages: German, Alemannic dialect

LIECHTENSTEIN is doubly landlocked, or COMPLETELY SURROUNDED by other LANDLOCKED COUNTRIES.

Lithuania

Area: 25,212 sq mi
(65,300 sq km)
Population: 3,211,000
Capital: Vilnius, pop. 546,000
Currency: litas
Religions: Roman Catholic, Russian Orthodox
Languages: Lithuanian, Russian, Polish

Luxembourg

Area: 998 sq mi (2,586 sq km)
Population: 517,000
Capital: Luxembourg, pop. 90,000
Currency: euro
Religions: Roman Catholic, Protestant, Jewish, Muslim
Languages: Luxembourgish, German, French

Macedonia

Area: 9,928 sq mi
(25,713 sq km)
Population: 2,059,000
Capital: Skopje, pop. 480,000
Currency: Macedonian denar
Religions: Macedonian Orthodox, Muslim
Languages: Macedonian, Albanian, Turkish

Madagascar

Area: 226,658 sq mi
(587,041 sq km)
Population: 21,315,000
Capital: Antananarivo,
pop. 1,816,000
Currency: Madagascar ariary
Religions: indigenous beliefs, Christian, Muslim
Languages: English, French, Malagasy

Malawi

Area: 45,747 sq mi
(118,484 sq km)
Population: 15,879,000
Capital: Lilongwe, pop. 821,000
Currency: Malawian kwacha
Religions: Christian, Muslim
Languages: Chichewa, Chinyanja, Chiyao, Chitumbuka

Malaysia

Area: 127,355 sq mi (329,847 sq km)
Population: 28,885,000
Capital: Kuala Lumpur,
pop. 1,494,000
Currency: ringgit
Religions: Muslim, Buddhist, Christian, Hindu
Languages: Bahasa Malaysia, English, Chinese, Tamil, Telugu, Malayalam, Panjabi, Thai, indigenous languages

Maldives

Area: 115 sq mi (298 sq km)
Population: 325,000
Capital: Male, pop. 120,000
Currency: rufiyaa
Religion: Sunni Muslim
Languages: Maldivian Dhivehi, English

Mali

Area: 478,841 sq mi (1,240,192 sq km)
Population: 15,394,000
Capital: Bamako, pop. 1,628,000
Currency: Communauté Financière Africaine franc
Religions: Muslim, indigenous beliefs
Languages: Bambara, French, numerous African languages

Marshall Islands

Area: 70 sq mi (181 sq km)
Population: 55,000
Capital: Majuro, pop. 30,000
Currency: U.S. dollar
Religions: Protestant, Assembly of God, Roman Catholic
Language: Marshallese

Malta

Area: 122 sq mi (316 sq km)
Population: 412,000
Capital: Valletta, pop. 199,000
Currency: euro
Religion: Roman Catholic
Languages: Maltese, English

Mauritania

Area: 397,955 sq mi (1,030,700 sq km)
Population: 3,542,000
Capital: Nouakchott, pop. 709,000
Currency: ouguiya
Religion: Muslim
Languages: Arabic, Pulaar, Soninke, French, Hassaniya, Wolof

You Are There! Chichén Itzá, Mexico

Think pyramids are only found in Egypt? Think again! You can find another ancient pyramid in Mexico, the 1,100-year-old Temple Kukulcan. The standout symbol of the ancient Mayan city of Chichén Itzá, this nine-level, 79-foot (24 m)-tall pyramid is also known as *El Castillo* (the castle). It's believed that the pyramid was built as a tribute to the sacred quetzal bird. In fact, if you stand in front of the pyramid and clap, the resulting echo sounds a lot like the call of the now-endangered bird.

COLOR KEY ● Africa ● Australia, New Zealand, and Oceania

Mauritius

Area: 788 sq mi (2,040 sq km)
Population: 1,286,000
Capital: Port Louis, pop. 149,000
Currency: Mauritian rupee
Religions: Hindu, Roman Catholic, Muslim, other Christian
Languages: Creole, Bhojpuri, French

Mexico

Area: 758,449 sq mi (1,964,375 sq km)
Population: 114,793,000
Capital: Mexico City, pop. 19,319,000
Currency: Mexican peso
Religions: Roman Catholic, Protestant
Languages: Spanish, Mayan, Nahuatl, other indigenous languages

Micronesia

Area: 271 sq mi (702 sq km)
Population: 102,000
Capital: Palikir, pop. 7,000
Currency: U.S. dollar
Religions: Roman Catholic, Protestant
Languages: English, Trukese, Pohnpeian, Yapese, other indigenous languages

Moldova

Area: 13,050 sq mi (33,800 sq km)
Population: 4,109,000
Capital: Chisinau, pop. 650,000
Currency: Moldovan leu
Religion: Eastern Orthodox
Languages: Moldovan, Russian, Gagauz

Monaco

Area: 0.8 sq mi (2.0 sq km)
Population: 36,000
Capital: Monaco, pop. 33,000
Currency: euro
Religion: Roman Catholic
Languages: French, English, Italian, Monegasque

Mongolia

Area: 603,909 sq mi (1,564,116 sq km)
Population: 2,814,000
Capital: Ulaanbaatar, pop. 949,000
Currency: togrog/tugrik
Religions: Buddhist Lamaist, Shamanist, Christian
Languages: Khalkha Mongol, Turkic, Russian

Montenegro

Area: 5,333 sq mi (13,812 sq km)
Population: 637,000
Capital: Podgorica, pop. 144,000
Currency: euro
Religions: Orthodox, Muslim, Roman Catholic
Languages: Serbian (Ijekavian dialect), Bosnian, Albanian, Croatian

Morocco

Area: 172,414 sq mi (446,550 sq km)
Population: 32,273,000
Capital: Rabat, pop. 1,770,000
Currency: Moroccan dirham
Religion: Muslim
Languages: Arabic, Berber dialects, French

Mozambique

Area: 308,642 sq mi (799,380 sq km)
Population: 23,050,000
Capital: Maputo, pop. 1,589,000
Currency: metical
Religions: Roman Catholic, Muslim, Zionist Christian
Languages: Emakhuwa, Xichangana, Portuguese, Elomwe, Cisena, Echuwabo, other local languages

Myanmar (Burma)

Area: 261,218 sq mi (676,552 sq km)
Population: 54,000,000
Capitals: Nay Pyi Taw, pop. 992,000; Yangon (Rangoon), pop. 4,088,000
Currency: kyat
Religions: Buddhist, Christian, Muslim
Languages: Burmese, minority ethnic languages

Namibia

Area: 318,261 sq mi
(824,292 sq km)
Population: 2,324,000
Capital: Windhoek, pop. 342,000
Currencies: Namibian dollar;
South African rand
Religions: Lutheran, other Christian, indigenous beliefs
Languages: Afrikaans, German, English

Nicaragua

Area: 50,193 sq mi
(130,000 sq km)
Population: 5,870,000
Capital: Managua, pop. 934,000
Currency: gold cordoba
Religions: Roman Catholic, Evangelical
Language: Spanish

Nauru

Area: 8 sq mi (21 sq km)
Population: 10,000
Capital: Yaren, pop. 10,000
Currency: Australian dollar
Religions: Protestant, Roman Catholic
Languages: Nauruan, English

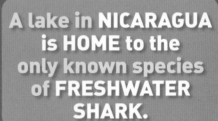

A lake in **NICARAGUA** is **HOME to the** only known species of **FRESHWATER SHARK.**

Nepal

Area: 56,827 sq mi
(147,181 sq km)
Population: 30,486,000
Capital: Kathmandu, pop. 990,000
Currency: Nepalese rupee
Religions: Hindu, Buddhist, Muslim, Kirant
Languages: Nepali, Maithali, Bhojpuri, Tharu, Tamang, Newar, Magar

Niger

Area: 489,191 sq mi (1,267,000 sq km)
Population: 16,096,000
Capital: Niamey, pop. 1,004,000
Currency: Communauté
Financière Africaine franc
Religions: Muslim, other (includes indigenous beliefs and Christian)
Languages: French, Hausa, Djerma

Netherlands

Area: 16,034 sq mi
(41,528 sq km)
Population: 16,694,000
Capital: Amsterdam, pop. 1,044,000
Currency: euro
Religions: Roman Catholic, Dutch Reformed, Calvinist, Muslim
Languages: Dutch, Frisian

Nigeria

Area: 356,669 sq mi
(923,768 sq km)
Population: 162,265,000
Capital: Abuja, pop. 1,857,000
Currency: naira
Religions: Muslim, Christian, indigenous beliefs
Languages: English, Hausa, Yoruba, Igbo (Ibo), Fulani

New Zealand

Area: 104,454 sq mi
(270,534 sq km)
Population: 4,417,000
Capital: Wellington, pop. 391,000
Currency: New Zealand dollar
Religions: Anglican, Roman Catholic, Presbyterian, other Christian
Languages: English, Maori

North Korea

Area: 46,540 sq mi
(120,538 sq km)
Population: 24,457,000
Capital: Pyongyang,
pop. 2,828,000
Currency: North Korean won
Religions: Buddhist, Confucianist, some Christian and syncretic Chondogyo
Language: Korean

COLOR KEY   ● Africa   ● Australia, New Zealand, and Oceania

Norway

Area: 125,004 sq mi
(323,758 sq km)
Population: 4,952,000
Capital: Oslo, pop. 875,000
Currency: Norwegian krone
Religion: Church of Norway (Lutheran)
Languages: Bokmal Norwegian, Nynorsk
Norwegian, Sami

Pakistan

Area: 307,374 sq mi
(796,095 sq km)
Population: 176,940,000
Capital: Islamabad, pop. 832,000
Currency: Pakistani rupee
Religions: Sunni Muslim, Shiite Muslim
Languages: Punjabi, Sindhi, Siraiki, Pashto, Urdu,
Baluchi, Hindko, English

Oman

Area: 119,500 sq mi
(309,500 sq km)
Population: 2,997,000
Capital: Muscat, pop. 634,000
Currency: Omani rial
Religions: Ibadhi Muslim, Sunni Muslim,
Shiite Muslim, Hindu
Languages: Arabic, English, Baluchi, Urdu, Indian dialects

Palau

Area: 189 sq mi (489 sq km)
Population: 21,000
Capital: Melekeok, 1,000
Currency: U.S. dollar
Religions: Roman Catholic, Protestant, Modekngei,
Seventh-day Adventist
Languages: Palauan, Filipino, English, Chinese

You Are There!

Mount Everest South Base Camp, Nepal

It's near freezing and dipping lower here at Mount Everest South Base Camp in Nepal. At an elevation of 18,000 feet (5,486 m), the base camp is higher than the highest peaks in Europe. Just getting to Base Camp is an epic adventure. While some people choose to take a helicopter, others opt for tours guided by Sherpas—natives of Nepal and expert climbers—all the way up to Base Camp (and back).

Because it's so physically tough to tackle Everest, only a small number of people make it to the top each year. That's why it's important to spend a few days at Base Camp gearing up for the trip. Here you begin to adjust to the thin air that only gets thinner as you make your way to the top of Everest—29,035 feet (8,850 m).

 Asia ● Europe ● North America ● South America

Panama

Area: 29,157 sq mi (75,517 sq km)
Population: 3,571,000
Capital: Panama City, pop. 1,346,000
Currencies: balboa; U.S. dollar
Religions: Roman Catholic, Protestant
Languages: Spanish, English

Peru

Area: 496,224 sq mi (1,285,216 sq km)
Population: 29,400,000
Capital: Lima, pop. 8,769,000
Currency: nuevo sol
Religion: Roman Catholic
Languages: Spanish, Quechua, Aymara, minor Amazonian languages

Papua New Guinea

Area: 178,703 sq mi (462,840 sq km)
Population: 6,888,000
Capital: Port Moresby, pop. 314,000
Currency: kina
Religions: indigenous beliefs, Roman Catholic, Lutheran, other Protestant
Languages: Melanesian Pidgin, 820 indigenous languages

Philippines

Area: 115,831 sq mi (300,000 sq km)
Population: 95,739,000
Capital: Manila, pop. 11,449,000
Currency: Philippine peso
Religions: Roman Catholic, Muslim, other Christian
Languages: Filipino (based on Tagalog), English

5 cool things about PAPUA NEW GUINEA

1. Parts of Papua New Guinea are so mountainous and forested that they weren't explored by outsiders until the 1930s.

2. Papua New Guinea is located on the eastern half of New Guinea, the second largest island in the world.

3. The world's largest butterfly can be found in the forests of Papua New Guinea.

4. Scientists recently discovered 30 new species of animals in a crater on Papua New Guinea.

5. Papua New Guinea is home to one of the biggest gold mines on the planet.

Poland

Area: 120,728 sq mi (312,685 sq km)
Population: 38,222,000
Capital: Warsaw, pop. 1,710,000
Currency: zloty
Religion: Roman Catholic
Language: Polish

Portugal

Area: 35,655 sq mi (92,345 sq km)
Population: 10,653,000
Capital: Lisbon, pop. 2,808,000
Currency: euro
Religion: Roman Catholic
Languages: Portuguese, Mirandese

Paraguay

Area: 157,048 sq mi (406,752 sq km)
Population: 6,451,000
Capital: Asunción, pop. 1,977,000
Currency: guarani
Religions: Roman Catholic, Protestant
Languages: Spanish, Guarani

Qatar

Area: 4,448 sq mi (11,521 sq km)
Population: 1,732,000
Capital: Doha, pop. 427,000
Currency: Qatari rial
Religions: Muslim, Christian
Languages: Arabic; English commonly a second language

Romania

Area: 92,043 sq mi
(238,391 sq km)
Population: 21,408,000
Capital: Bucharest, pop. 1,933,000
Currency: new leu
Religions: Eastern Orthodox, Protestant,
Roman Catholic
Languages: Romanian, Hungarian

São Tomé and Príncipe

Area: 386 sq mi (1,001 sq km)
Population: 180,000
Capital: São Tomé, pop. 60,000
Currency: dobra
Religions: Roman Catholic, Evangelical
Language: Portuguese

Russia

Area: 6,592,850 sq mi
(17,075,400 sq km)
Population: 142,847,000
Capital: Moscow, pop. 10,523,000
Currency: ruble
Religions: Russian Orthodox, Muslim
Languages: Russian, many minority languages
Note: Russia is in both Europe and Asia, but its capital is in Europe, so it is classified here as a European country.

Saudi Arabia

Area: 756,985 sq mi
(1,960,582 sq km)
Population: 27,897,000
Capital: Riyadh, pop. 4,725,000
Currency: Saudi riyal
Religion: Muslim
Language: Arabic

Rwanda

Area: 10,169 sq mi
(26,338 sq km)
Population: 10,943,000
Capital: Kigali, pop. 909,000
Currency: Rwandan franc
Religions: Roman Catholic, Protestant,
Adventist, Muslim
Languages: Kinyarwanda, French, English, Kiswahili

Senegal

Area: 75,955 sq mi
(196,722 sq km)
Population: 12,768,000
Capital: Dakar, pop. 2,777,000
Currency: Communauté
Financière Africaine franc
Religions: Muslim, Christian (mostly Roman Catholic)
Languages: French, Wolof, Pulaar, Jola, Mandinka

Samoa

Area: 1,093 sq mi (2,831 sq km)
Population: 191,000
Capital: Apia, pop. 36,000
Currency: tala
Religions: Congregationalist, Roman Catholic,
Methodist, Church of Jesus Christ of Latter-day Saints,
Assembly of God, Seventh-day Adventist
Languages: Samoan (Polynesian), English

Serbia

Area: 29,913 sq mi (77,474 sq km)
Population: 7,257,000
Capital: Belgrade, pop. 1,115,000
Currency: Serbian dinar
Religions: Serbian Orthodox, Roman Catholic, Muslim
Languages: Serbian, Hungarian

San Marino

Area: 24 sq mi (61 sq km)
Population: 32,000
Capital: San Marino, pop. 4,000
Currency: euro
Religion: Roman Catholic
Language: Italian

Seychelles

Area: 176 sq mi (455 sq km)
Population: 88,000
Capital: Victoria, pop. 26,000
Currency: Seychelles rupee
Religions: Roman Catholic, Anglican, other Christian
Languages: Creole, English

Sierra Leone

Area: 27,699 sq mi (71,740 sq km)
Population: 5,364,000
Capital: Freetown, pop. 875,000
Currency: leone
Religions: Muslim, indigenous beliefs, Christian
Languages: English, Mende, Temne, Krio

Slovakia

Area: 18,932 sq mi
(49,035 sq km)
Population: 5,440,000
Capital: Bratislava, pop. 428,000
Currency: euro
Religions: Roman Catholic, Protestant, Greek Catholic
Languages: Slovak, Hungarian

Singapore

Area: 255 sq mi (660 sq km)
Population: 5,167,000
Capital: Singapore, pop. 4,737,000
Currency: Singapore dollar
Religions: Buddhist, Muslim, Taoist, Roman Catholic, Hindu, other Christian
Languages: Mandarin, English, Malay, Hokkien, Cantonese, Teochew, Tamil

Slovenia

Area: 7,827 sq mi
(20,273 sq km)
Population: 2,052,000
Capital: Ljubljana, pop. 260,000
Currency: euro
Religion: Roman Catholic, Muslim, Orthodox
Languages: Slovene, Croatian, Serbian

You Are There!
Cape Town, South Africa

Cape Town, South Africa, was the first place Dutch explorers colonized on Africa's southern tip. And people have been coming ever since! In fact, Cape Town is one of the top tourist destinations in Africa. What's the draw? Hop a cableway up Table Mountain or hit a world-class beach, try skydiving or grab a sea kayak. Simply name your adventure and you're bound to be able to do it in Cape Town!

COLOR KEY ● Africa ● Australia, New Zealand, and Oceania

Solomon Islands

Area: 10,954 sq mi
(28,370 sq km)
Population: 545,000
Capital: Honiara, pop. 72,000
Currency: Solomon Islands dollar
Religions: Church of Melanesia, Roman Catholic,
South Seas Evangelical, other Christian
Languages: Melanesian pidgin, 120 indigenous languages

Somalia

Area: 246,201 sq mi
(637,657 sq km)
Population: 9,926,000
Capital: Mogadishu, pop. 1,353,000
Currency: Somali shilling
Religion: Sunni Muslim
Languages: Somali, Arabic, Italian, English

South Africa

Area: 470,693 sq mi (1,219,090 sq km)
Population: 50,460,000
Capitals: Pretoria (Tshwane),
pop. 1,404,000; Bloemfontein,
pop. 436,000; Cape Town, pop. 3,353,000
Currency: rand
Religions: Zion Christian, Pentecostal, Catholic,
Methodist, Dutch Reformed, Anglican, other Christian
Languages: IsiZulu, IsiXhosa, Afrikaans, Sepedi, English

South Korea

Area: 38,321 sq mi
(99,250 sq km)
Population: 48,989,000
Capital: Seoul, pop. 9,778,000
Currency: South Korean won
Religions: Christian, Buddhist
Languages: Korean, English

South Sudan

Area: 248,777 (644,329 sq km)
Population: 8,260,000
Capital: Juba, pop. 250,000
Currency: South Sudan pound
Religions: animist, Christian
Languages: English, Arabic, regional languages (Dinke,
Nuer, Bari, Zande, Shilluk)

Spain

Area: 195,363 sq mi (505,988 sq km)
Population: 47,262,000
Capital: Madrid, pop. 5,762,000
Currency: euro
Religion: Roman Catholic
Languages: Castilian Spanish, Catalan, Galician, Basque

Sri Lanka

Area: 25,299 sq mi
(65,525 sq km)
Population: 20,858,000
Capital: Colombo, pop. 681,000;
Sri Jayewardenepura Kotte, pop. 120,000
Currency: Sri Lankan rupee
Religions: Buddhist, Muslim, Hindu, Christian
Languages: Sinhala, Tamil

St. Kitts and Nevis

Area: 104 sq mi (269 sq km)
Population: 50,000
Capital: Basseterre, pop. 13,000
Currency: East Caribbean dollar
Religions: Anglican, other Protestant, Roman Catholic
Language: English

St. Lucia

Area: 238 sq mi (616 sq km)
Population: 176,000
Capital: Castries, pop. 15,000
Currency: East Caribbean
dollar
Religions: Roman Catholic, Seventh-day Adventist,
Pentecostal
Languages: English, French patois

St. Vincent and the Grenadines

Area: 150 sq mi (389 sq km)
Population: 109,000
Capital: Kingstown, pop. 28,000
Currency: East Caribbean dollar
Religions: Anglican, Methodist, Roman Catholic
Languages: English, French patois

Sudan

Area: 718,722 sq mi (1,861,484 sq km)
Population: 36,787,000
Capital: Khartoum, pop. 5,021,000
Currency: Sudanese pound
Religions: Sunni Muslim, indigenous beliefs, Christian
Languages: Arabic, Nubian, Ta Bedawie, many diverse dialects of Nilotic, Nilo-Hamitic, Sudanic languages

Suriname

Area: 63,037 sq mi (163,265 sq km)
Population: 529,000
Capital: Paramaribo, pop. 259,000
Currency: Suriname dollar
Religions: Hindu, Protestant (predominantly Moravian), Roman Catholic, Muslim, indigenous beliefs
Languages: Dutch, English, Sranang Tongo, Hindustani, Javanese

Swaziland

Area: 6,704 sq mi (17,363 sq km)
Population: 1,203,000
Capitals: Mbabane, pop. 74,000; Lobamba, pop. 4,557
Currency: lilangeni
Religions: Zionist, Roman Catholic, Muslim
Languages: English, siSwati

Sweden

Area: 173,732 sq mi (449,964 sq km)
Population: 9,447,000
Capital: Stockholm, pop. 1,279,000
Currency: Swedish krona
Religion: Lutheran
Languages: Swedish, Sami, Finnish

Switzerland

Area: 15,940 sq mi (41,284 sq km)
Population: 7,868,000
Capital: Bern, pop. 346,000
Currency: Swiss franc
Religions: Roman Catholic, Protestant, Muslim
Languages: German, French, Italian, Romansh

Syria

Area: 71,498 sq mi (185,180 sq km)
Population: 22,518,000
Capital: Damascus, pop. 2,527,000
Currency: Syrian pound
Religions: Sunni, other Muslim (includes Alawite, Druze), Christian
Languages: Arabic, Kurdish, Armenian, Aramaic, Circassian

Tajikistan

Area: 55,251 sq mi (143,100 sq km)
Population: 7,535,000
Capital: Dushanbe, pop. 704,000
Currency: somoni
Religions: Sunni Muslim, Shiite Muslim
Languages: Tajik, Russian

Tanzania

Area: 364,900 sq mi (945,087 sq km)
Population: 46,218,000
Capitals: Dar es Salaam, pop. 2,930,000; Dodoma, pop. 200,000
Currency: Tanzanian shilling
Religions: Muslim, indigenous beliefs, Christian
Languages: Kiswahili, Kiunguja, English, Arabic, local languages

Thailand

Area: 198,115 sq mi (513,115 sq km)
Population: 69,519,000
Capital: Bangkok, pop. 6,902,000
Currency: baht
Religions: Buddhist, Muslim
Languages: Thai, English, ethnic dialects

Timor-Leste (East Timor)

Area: 5,640 sq mi (14,609 sq km)
Population: 1,186,000
Capital: Dili, pop. 166,000
Currency: U.S. dollar
Religion: Roman Catholic
Languages: Tetum, Portuguese, Indonesian, English, indigenous languages

COLOR KEY   ● Africa   ● Australia, New Zealand, and Oceania

Togo

Area: 21,925 sq mi (56,785 sq km)
Population: 5,847,000
Capital: Lomé, pop. 1,593,000
Currency: Communauté Financière Africaine franc
Religions: indigenous beliefs, Christian, Muslim
Languages: French, Ewe, Mina, Kabye, Dagomba

Trinidad and Tobago

Area: 1,980 sq mi (5,128 sq km)
Population: 1,325,000
Capital: Port of Spain, pop. 57,000
Currency: Trinidad and Tobago dollar
Religions: Roman Catholic, Hindu, Anglican, Baptist
Languages: English, Caribbean Hindustani, French, Spanish, Chinese

Tonga

Area: 289 sq mi (748 sq km)
Population: 104,000
Capital: Nuku'alofa, pop. 24,000
Currency: pa'anga
Religion: Christian
Languages: Tongan, English

Tunisia

Area: 63,170 sq mi (163,610 sq km)
Population: 10,676,000
Capital: Tunis, pop. 759,000
Currency: Tunisian dinar
Religion: Muslim
Languages: Arabic, French

 Phang Nga Bay, Thailand

Welcome to Thailand's Phang Nga Bay! This shallow bay in the Andaman Sea surrounds 42 small islands, including the popular "James Bond Island"—once a setting featured in the famous spy film series. And it's no wonder this bay served as a movie backdrop: After one glimpse of its turquoise water and towering limestone cliffs, you'll likely agree that you're as close to paradise as you can get. In 2004, the nearby island of Phuket was hit hard by a tsunami that devastated most of southern Thailand. But today, the island is back up and running—and welcoming more than five million visitors a year. Many of those visitors flock to Phang Nga Bay to kayak, snorkel, and spot wildlife like spinner dolphins and the blue-ringed octopus.

 Asia   ● Europe   ● North America   ● South America

Turkey

Area: 300,948 sq mi
(779,452 sq km)
Population: 73,950,000
Capital: Ankara, pop. 3,846,000
Currency: new Turkish lira
Religion: Muslim (mostly Sunni)
Languages: Turkish, Kurdish, Dimli (Zaza), Azeri, Kabardian, Gagauz

Turkmenistan

Area: 188,456 sq mi
(488,100 sq km)
Population: 5,105,000
Capital: Ashgabat, pop. 637,000
Currency: Turkmen manat
Religions: Muslim, Eastern Orthodox
Languages: Turkmen, Russian, Uzbek

Tuvalu

Area: 10 sq mi (26 sq km)
Population: 11,000
Capital: Funafuti, pop. 5,000
Currencies: Australian dollar; Tuvaluan dollar
Religion: Church of Tuvalu (Congregationalist)
Languages: Tuvaluan, English, Samoan, Kiribati

Uganda

Area: 93,104 sq mi
(241,139 sq km)
Population: 34,543,000
Capital: Kampala, pop. 1,535,000
Currency: Ugandan shilling
Religions: Protestant, Roman Catholic, Muslim
Languages: English, Ganda, other local languages, Kiswahili, Arabic

Ukraine

Area: 233,090 sq mi
(603,700 sq km)
Population: 45,730,000
Capital: Kiev, pop. 2,779,000
Currency: hryvnia
Religions: Ukrainian Orthodox, Orthodox, Ukrainian Greek Catholic
Languages: Ukrainian, Russian

United Arab Emirates

Area: 30,000 sq mi
(77,700 sq km)
Population: 7,891,000
Capital: Abu Dhabi, pop. 666,000
Currency: Emirati dirham
Religion: Muslim
Languages: Arabic, Persian, English, Hindi, Urdu

5 cool things about UNITED ARAB EMIRATES

1. The U.A.E. is made up of seven emirates: Abu Dhabi, Dubai, Ajman, Fujairah, Ras al Khaimah, Umm al Qaiwain, and Sharjah.

2. There's a mall in Dubai that's bigger than 50 soccer fields and contains more than 1,000 shops.

3. Ferrari World theme park in Abu Dhabi is home to the world's fastest roller coaster, the 150 mile an hour (241 kph) Formula Rossa.

4. There is no mail delivery to street addresses in Abu Dhabi. All mail goes to P.O. boxes at a post office.

5. The Burj Khalifa tower in Dubai is the world's tallest building and man-made structure.

United Kingdom

Area: 93,788 sq mi
(242,910 sq km)
Population: 62,588,000
Capital: London, pop. 8,615,000
Currency: British pound
Religions: Anglican, Roman Catholic, Presbyterian, Methodist
Languages: English, Welsh, Scottish form of Gaelic

United States

Area: 3,794,083 sq mi
(9,826,630 sq km)
Population: 311,695,000
Capital: Washington, D.C., pop. 601,723
Currency: U.S. dollar
Religions: Protestant, Roman Catholic
Languages: English, Spanish

COLOR KEY ● Africa ● Australia, New Zealand, and Oceania

Uruguay

Area: 68,037 sq mi
(176,215 sq km)
Population: 3,369,000
Capital: Montevideo, pop. 1,633,000
Currency: Uruguayan peso
Religion: Roman Catholic
Language: Spanish

Venezuela

Area: 352,144 sq mi
(912,050 sq km)
Population: 29,278,000
Capital: Caracas, pop. 3,051,000
Currency: bolivar
Religion: Roman Catholic
Languages: Spanish, numerous indigenous dialects

Uzbekistan

Area: 172,742 sq mi
(447,400 sq km)
Population: 28,463,000
Capital: Tashkent,
pop. 2,201,000
Currency: Uzbekistani sum
Religions: Muslim (mostly Sunni), Eastern Orthodox
Languages: Uzbek, Russian, Tajik

Vietnam

Area: 127,844 sq mi
(331,114 sq km)
Population: 87,850,000
Capital: Hanoi, pop. 2,668,000
Currency: dong
Religions: Buddhist, Roman Catholic
Languages: Vietnamese, English, French, Chinese, Khmer

Vanuatu

Area: 4,707 sq mi (12,190 sq km)
Population: 252,000
Capital: Port Vila, pop. 44,000
Currency: vatu
Religions: Presbyterian, Anglican, Roman Catholic, other Christian, indigenous beliefs
Languages: more than 100 local languages, pidgin (known as Bislama or Bichelama)

Yemen

Area: 207,286 sq mi
(536,869 sq km)
Population: 23,833,000
Capital: Sanaa, pop. 2,229,000
Currency: Yemeni rial
Religions: Muslim, including Shaf'i (Sunni) and Zaydi (Shiite)
Language: Arabic

Vatican City

Area: 0.2 sq mi (0.4 sq km)
Population: 798
Capital: Vatican City, pop. 798
Currency: euro
Religion: Roman Catholic
Languages: Italian, Latin, French

Zambia

Area: 290,586 sq mi
(752,614 sq km)
Population: 13,475,000
Capital: Lusaka, pop. 1,413,000
Currency: Zambian kwacha
Religions: Christian, Muslim, Hindu
Languages: English, Bemba, Kaonda, Lozi, Lunda, Luvale, Nyanja, Tonga, about 70 other indigenous languages

COOL CLICK

Want to see National Geographic photographs from around the world? Go online.
travel.nationalgeographic.com/travel/travel-photos

Zimbabwe

Area: 150,872 sq mi
(390,757 sq km)
Population: 12,084,000
Capital: Harare, pop. 1,606,000
Currency: Zimbabwean dollar
Religions: Syncretic (part Christian, part indigenous beliefs), Christian, indigenous beliefs
Languages: English, Shona, Sindebele, tribal dialects

● Asia ● Europe ● North America ● South America

THE POLITICAL UNITED STATES

9:00AM PACIFIC TIME

10:00AM MOUNTAIN TIME

Cape Flattery

Seattle
Olympia • Tacoma
WASHINGTON
Yakima
Spokane
Lewiston
Great Falls
Missouri
Helena
MONTANA
Billings
Minot
Grand Forks
NORTH DAKOTA
Bismarck
Fa

Portland
Salem
Eugene
OREGON
Columbia
Butte
Boise
Idaho Falls
Cody
Yellowstone L.
Aberdeen
SOUTH DAKOTA
Pierre

Medford
Klamath Falls
Snake
Pocatello
WYOMING
Casper
Rapid City
Sioux Fa

Eureka
Redding
Great Salt Lake
Ogden
Salt Lake City
Provo
Cheyenne
Laramie
Fort Collins
NEBRASKA
Grand Island
Platte
Linc
Misso

Reno
Carson City
Lake Tahoe
Great Basin
NEVADA
UTAH
Grand Junction
Denver • Boulder
COLORADO
N. Platte
S. Platte

Sacramento
Oakland
San Francisco • San Jose
Salinas
Fresno
SIERRA NEVADA
CALIFORNIA
Mojave
Lake Powell
Colorado
Colorado Springs
Pueblo
KANSAS
Dodge City
Wic
Arkansas

Bakersfield
Point Conception
Desert
Las Vegas
St. George
Lake Mead
Grand Canyon
Flagstaff
Santa Fe
Albuquerque
OKLA
Amarillo
Oklahor
C

Los Angeles
Long Beach
Riverside
Salton Sea
Phoenix • Mesa
Yuma
ARIZONA
NEW MEXICO
Lawton

San Diego
Tucson
Las Cruces
El Paso
Roswell
Wichita Falls
Lubbock
Midland
Odessa
Abilene
Fort Worth
Da
Wac
TEX

7:00AM HAWAI'I-ALEUTIAN TIME

North Slope
Brooks Range
Alaska Range
Juneau
Anchorage
ALASKA
Alaska Peninsula
ALEUTIAN ISLANDS

0   400 miles
0   400 kilometers

8:00AM ALASKA TIME

Kaua'i
Ni'ihau
O'ahu
Honolulu
Moloka'i
Lana'i
Maui
Kaho'olawe
Hilo • Hawai'i
HAWAI'I

0   150 mi
0   150 km

San Antonio
Au
Cor
Chr
Laredo
Browns
Rio Grande

7:00AM HAWAI'I-ALEUTIAN TIME

Like a giant quilt, the United States is made up of 50 states. Each is unique, but together they make a national fabric held together by a constitution and a federal government. State boundaries, outlined in dotted lines on the map, set apart internal political units within the country. The national capital—Washington, D.C.—is marked by a star in a double circle. The capital of each state is marked by a star in a single circle.

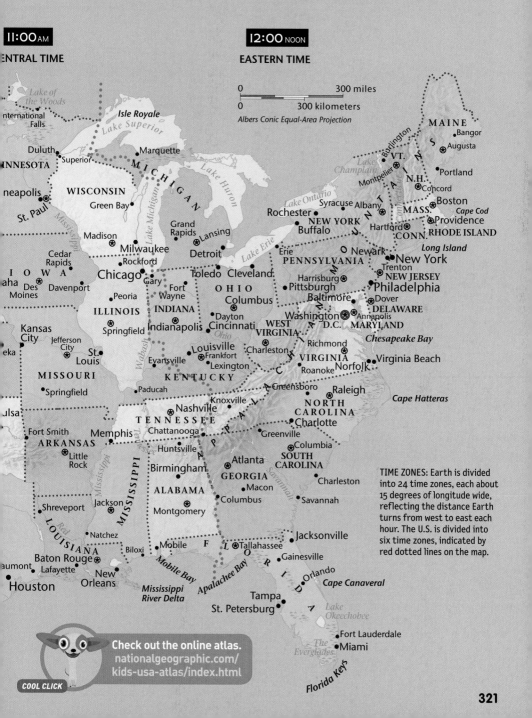

11:00 AM
CENTRAL TIME

12:00 NOON
EASTERN TIME

0   300 miles
0   300 kilometers
Albers Conic Equal-Area Projection

TIME ZONES: Earth is divided into 24 time zones, each about 15 degrees of longitude wide, reflecting the distance Earth turns from west to east each hour. The U.S. is divided into six time zones, indicated by red dotted lines on the map.

Check out the online atlas.
nationalgeographic.com/
kids-usa-atlas/index.html

COOL CLICK

321

THE PHYSICAL UNITED STATES

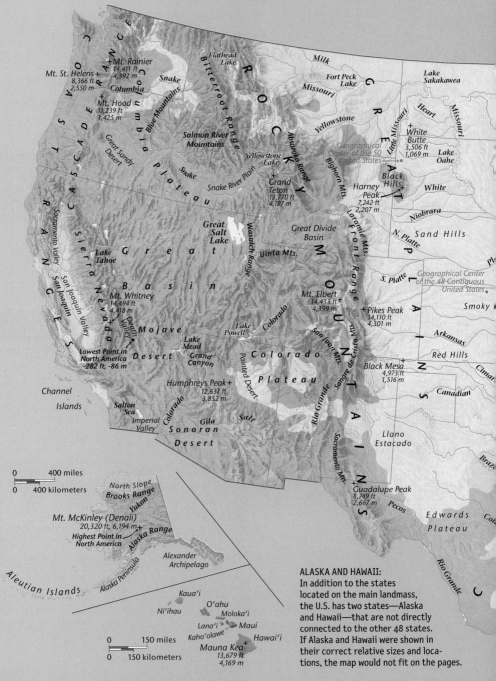

Mt. Rainier
14,411 ft
4,392 m

Mt. St. Helens
8,366 ft
2,550 m

Mt. Hood
11,239 ft
3,425 m

Columbia

Snake

Flathead Lake

Bitterroot Range

Blue Mountains

Salmon River Mountains

Great Sandy Desert

Snake

Snake River Plain

Columbia Plateau

CASCADE RANGE

COAST RANGE

Milk

Fort Peck Lake

Missouri

Yellowstone

Yellowstone Lake

Absaroka Range

Grand Teton
13,770 ft
4,197 m

Bighorn Mts.

Geographical Center of the 50 United States

Little Missouri

Missouri

Heart

White Butte
3,506 ft
1,069 m

Lake Sakakawea

Lake Oahe

Black Hills

Harney Peak
7,242 ft
2,207 m

White

Niobrara

N. Platte

Sand Hills

ROCKY

GREAT

Sacramento Valley

San Joaquin

San Joaquin Valley

Sierra Nevada

Lake Tahoe

Great Salt Lake

Wasatch Range

Uinta Mts.

Great Divide Basin

Laramie Mts.

Front Range

Geographical Center of the 48 Contiguous United States

S. Platte

Smoky

Great Basin

Mt. Whitney
14,494 ft
4,418 m

Death Valley

Mojave Desert

Lake Mead

Lake Powell

Colorado

Mt. Elbert
14,433 ft
4,399 m

Pikes Peak
14,110 ft
4,301 m

Arkansas

Red Hills

Lowest Point in North America
-282 ft, -86 m

Grand Canyon

Colorado Plateau

Colorado

San Juan Mts.

Black Mesa
4,973 ft
1,516 m

Sangre de Cristo Mts.

Cimar.

Canadian

Channel Islands

Salton Sea

Imperial Valley

Colorado

Gila

Salt

Humphreys Peak
12,637 ft
3,852 m

Painted Desert

Sonoran Desert

Rio Grande

Llano Estacado

MOUNTAINS

Pl.

Braz.

0 400 miles
0 400 kilometers

North Slope

Brooks Range

Yukon

Mt. McKinley (Denali)
20,320 ft, 6,194 m
Highest Point in North America

Alaska Range

Alaska Peninsula

Aleutian Islands

Alexander Archipelago

Sacramento Mts.

Guadalupe Peak
8,749 ft
2,667 m

Pecos

Edwards Plateau

Rio Grande

Cot.

Kaua'i

Ni'ihau

O'ahu

Moloka'i

Lana'i

Kaho'olawe

Maui

Hawai'i

Mauna Kea
13,679 ft
4,169 m

0 150 miles
0 150 kilometers

ALASKA AND HAWAII:
In addition to the states located on the main landmass, the U.S. has two states—Alaska and Hawaii—that are not directly connected to the other 48 states. If Alaska and Hawaii were shown in their correct relative sizes and locations, the map would not fit on the pages.

Stretching from the Atlantic Ocean in the east to the Pacific Ocean in the west, the United States is the third largest country (by area) in the world. Its physical diversity ranges from mountains to fertile plains and dry deserts. Shading on the map indicates changes in elevation, while colors show different vegetation patterns.

| 0 | | | | 400 miles |
| 0 | | | | 400 kilometers |

Albers Conic Equal-Area Projection

Lake of the Woods

Isle Royale

Eagle Mt. 2,301 ft 701 m

Lake Superior

Source of the Mississippi (Lake Itasca)

Upper Peninsula

Lake Champlain

+Mt. Washington 6,288 ft 1,917 m

Minnesota

Mississippi

Wisconsin

Lake Michigan

Lower Peninsula

Lake Huron

Lake Ontario

←Niagara Falls

Adirondack Mts.

Green Mts.

Connecticut

Catskill Mts.

Hudson

Cape Cod

Cedar

Lake Winnebago

Lake St. Clair

Lake Erie

Allegheny

Appalachian Plateau

Delaware

Long Island

CENTRAL

Des Moines

Illinois

Wabash

Ohio

Allegheny Mts.

Susquehanna

Potomac

Delaware Bay

LOWLAND

Missouri

Lake of the Ozarks

Ohio

Kentucky Lake

Lake Barkley

Cumberland Plateau

Cumberland Plateau

James

Roanoke

Chesapeake Bay

Harry S. Truman Res.

Ozark Plateau

Tennessee

APPALACHIAN MOUNTAINS

+Mt. Mitchell 6,684 ft, 2,037 m

Cape Fear

Great Pee Dee

Cape Hatteras

Magazine Mt. 2,753 ft 839 m+

Arkansas

Mississippi

Cape Fear

Ouachita Mts.

Black Belt

Chattahoochee

Savannah

COASTAL PLAIN

Red

Ouachita

Altamaha

Trinity

Sabine

Red

Alabama

Okefenokee Swamp

Cape Canaveral

COASTAL PLAIN

Lake Pontchartrain

Mississippi River Delta

Lake Okeechobee

The Everglades

Florida Keys

NATURAL VEGETATION

- NEEDLELEAF FOREST
- BROADLEAF FOREST
- MIXED FOREST
- GRASSLAND
- TROPICAL VEGETATION
- DESERT
- TUNDRA

To see more great maps, go online. maps.national geographic.com/maps

COOL CLICK

THE STATES

From sea to shining sea, the United States of America is a nation of diversity. In the more than 235 years since its creation, the nation has grown to become home to a wide range of peoples, industries, and cultures. The following pages present a general overview of all 50 states in the U.S.

The country is generally divided into five large regions: the Northeast, the Southeast, the Midwest, the Southwest, and the West. Though loosely defined, these zones tend to share important similarities, including climate, history, and geography. The color key below provides a guide to which states are in each region.

Flags of each state and highlights of demography and industry are also included. These details offer a brief overview of each state.

In addition, each state's official flower and bird are identified.

Color Key by Region

Alabama

Area: 52,419 sq mi (135,765 sq km)
Population: 4,779,736
Capital: Montgomery, pop. 205,764
Largest city: Birmingham, pop. 212,237
Industry: Retail and wholesale trade, services, government, finance, insurance, real estate, transportation, construction, communication
State flower/bird: Camellia/northern flicker

Alaska

Area: 663,267 sq mi (1,717,862 sq km)
Population: 710,231
Capital: Juneau, pop. 31,275
Largest city: Anchorage, pop. 291,826
Industry: Petroleum products, government, services, trade
State flower/bird: Forget-me-not/willow ptarmigan

Arizona

Area: 113,998 sq mi (295,256 sq km)
Population: 6,392,017
Capital: Phoenix, pop. 1,445,632
Largest city: Phoenix, pop. 1,445,632
Industry: Real estate, manufactured goods, retail, state and local government, transportation and public utilities, wholesale trade, health services, tourism
State flower/bird: Saguaro/cactus wren

Arkansas

Area: 53,179 sq mi (137,732 sq km)
Population: 2,915,918
Capital: Little Rock, pop. 193,524
Largest city: Little Rock, pop. 193,524
Industry: Services, food processing, paper products, transportation, metal products, machinery, electronics
State flower/bird: Apple blossom/mockingbird

California

Area: 163,696 sq mi (423,972 sq km)
Population: 37,253,956
Capital: Sacramento, pop. 466,488
Largest city: Los Angeles, pop. 3,792,621
Industry: Electronic components and equipment, computers and computer software, tourism, food processing, entertainment, clothing
State flower/bird: Golden poppy/California quail

DEATH VALLEY, CALIFORNIA, is the HOTTEST PLACE in NORTH AMERICA.

Colorado

Area: 104,094 sq mi (269,602 sq km)
Population: 5,029,196
Capital: Denver, pop. 600,158
Largest city: Denver, pop. 600,158
Industry: Real estate, government, durable goods, communications, health and other services, nondurable goods, transportation
State flower/bird: Columbine/lark bunting

COLOR KEY ● Northeast ● Southeast

Connecticut

Area: 5,543 sq mi (14,357 sq km)
Population: 3,574,097
Capital: Hartford, pop. 124,775
Largest city: Bridgeport, pop. 144,229
Industry: Transportation equipment, metal products, machinery, electrical equipment, printing and publishing, scientific instruments, insurance
State flower/bird: Mountain laurel/robin

Delaware

Area: 2,489 sq mi (6,447 sq km)
Population: 897,934
Capital: Dover, pop. 36,047
Largest city: Wilmington, pop. 70,851
Industry: Food processing, chemicals, rubber and plastic products, scientific instruments, printing and publishing, financial services
State flower/bird: Peach blossom/blue hen chicken

Florida

Area: 65,755 sq mi (170,304 sq km)
Population: 18,801,310
Capital: Tallahassee, pop. 181,376
Largest city: Jacksonville, pop. 821,784
Industry: Tourism, health services, business services, communications, banking, electronic equipment, insurance
State flower/bird: Orange blossom/mockingbird

Georgia

Area: 59,425 sq mi (153,910 sq km)
Population: 9,687,653
Capital: Atlanta, pop. 420,003
Largest city: Atlanta, pop. 420,003
Industry: Textiles and clothing, transportation equipment, food processing, paper products, chemicals, electrical equipment, tourism
State flower/bird: Cherokee rose/brown thrasher

ROME, GEORGIA, is home to the country's only NATURAL FOREST within a city.

Hawaii

Area: 10,931 sq mi (28,311 sq km)
Population: 1,360,301
Capital: Honolulu, pop. 337,256
Largest city: Honolulu, pop. 337,256
Industry: Tourism, trade, finance, food processing, petroleum refining, stone, clay, glass products
State flower/bird: Hibiscus/Hawaiian goose (nene)

Idaho

Area: 83,570 sq mi (216,447 sq km)
Population: 1,567,582
Capital: Boise, pop. 205,671
Largest city: Boise, pop. 205,671
Industry: Electronics and computer equipment, tourism, food processing, forest products, mining
State flower/bird: Syringa (Lewis's mock orange)/mountain bluebird

Illinois

Area: 57,914 sq mi (149,998 sq km)
Population: 12,830,632
Capital: Springfield, pop. 116,250
Largest city: Chicago, pop. 2,695,598
Industry: Industrial machinery, electronic equipment, food processing, chemicals, metals, printing and publishing, rubber and plastics, motor vehicles
State flower/bird: Violet/cardinal

Indiana

Area: 36,418 sq mi (94,322 sq km)
Population: 6,483,802
Capital: Indianapolis, pop. 820,445
Largest city: Indianapolis, pop. 820,445
Industry: Transportation equipment, steel, pharmaceutical and chemical products, machinery, petroleum, coal
State flower/bird: Peony/cardinal

Iowa

Area: 56,272 sq mi (145,743 sq km)
Population: 3,046,355
Capital: Des Moines, pop. 203,433
Largest city: Des Moines, pop. 203,433
Industry: Real estate, health services, industrial machinery, food processing, construction
State flower/bird: Wild rose/American goldfinch

Kansas

Area: 82,277 sq mi (213,097 sq km)
Population: 2,853,118
Capital: Topeka, pop. 127,473
Largest city: Wichita, pop. 382,368
Industry: Aircraft manufacturing, transportation equipment, construction, food processing, printing and publishing, health care
State flower/bird: Sunflower/western meadowlark

Kentucky

Area: 40,409 sq mi (104,659 sq km)
Population: 4,339,367
Capital: Frankfort, pop. 25,527
Largest city: Louisville, pop. 597,337
Industry: Manufacturing, services, government, finance, insurance, real estate, retail trade, transportation, wholesale trade, construction, mining
State flower/bird: Goldenrod/cardinal

Louisiana

Area: 51,840 sq mi (134,265 sq km)
Population: 4,533,372
Capital: Baton Rouge, pop. 229,493
Largest city: New Orleans, pop. 343,829
Industry: Chemicals, petroleum products, food processing, health services, tourism, oil and natural gas extraction, paper products
State flower/bird: Magnolia/brown pelican

5 cool things about LOUISIANA

1. Louisiana is home to the country's tallest state capitol building, at 450 feet (137 m) and 34 stories high.

2. There are nearly two million wild alligators living in Louisiana.

3. The 24-mile-long (55 km) Lake Pontchartrain causeway is one of the longest over-water bridges in the world.

4. Each spring, more than a million people party in New Orleans, Louisiana, during Mardi Gras, the celebration before the start of the Christian season of Lent.

5. Southern Louisiana's Atchafalaya Basin is the country's biggest wetland.

Maine

Area: 35,385 sq mi (91,646 sq km)
Population: 1,328,361
Capital: Augusta, pop. 19,136
Largest city: Portland, pop. 66,194
Industry: Health services, tourism, forest products, leather products, electrical equipment, food processing
State flower/bird: White pine cone and tassel/chickadee

Maryland

Area: 12,407 sq mi (32,133 sq km)
Population: 5,773,552
Capital: Annapolis, pop. 38,394
Largest city: Baltimore, pop. 620,961
Industry: Real estate, federal government, health services, business services, engineering services
State flower/bird: Black-eyed Susan/northern (Baltimore) oriole

Massachusetts

Area: 10,555 sq mi (27,336 sq km)
Population: 6,547,629
Capital: Boston, pop. 617,594
Largest city: Boston, pop. 617,594
Industry: Electrical equipment, machinery, metal products, scientific instruments, printing and publishing, tourism
State flower/bird: Mayflower/chickadee

Michigan

Area: 96,716 sq mi (250,495 sq km)
Population: 9,883,640
Capital: Lansing, pop. 114,297
Largest city: Detroit, pop. 713,777
Industry: Motor vehicles and parts, machinery, metal products, office furniture, tourism, chemicals
State flower/bird: Apple blossom/robin

Minnesota

Area: 86,939 sq mi (225,172 sq km)
Population: 5,303,925
Capital: St. Paul, pop. 285,068
Largest city: Minneapolis, pop. 382,578
Industry: Real estate, banking and insurance, industrial machinery, printing and publishing, food processing, scientific equipment
State flower/bird: Showy lady's slipper/common loon

COLOR KEY ● Northeast ● Southeast

COOL CLICK

Check out great state facts online. www.state.me.us This is for Maine. For each state insert the two-letter state abbreviation (see p. 331) where "me" is now.

Nevada

Area: 110,561 sq mi (286,352 sq km)
Population: 2,700,551
Capital: Carson City, pop. 55,274
Largest city: Las Vegas, pop. 583,756
Industry: Tourism and gaming, mining, printing and publishing, food processing, electrical equipment
State flower/bird: Sagebrush/mountain bluebird

Mississippi

Area: 48,430 sq mi (125,434 sq km)
Population: 2,967,297
Capital: Jackson, pop. 173,514
Largest city: Jackson, pop. 173,514
Industry: Petroleum products, health services, electronic equipment, transportation, banking, forest products, communications
State flower/bird: Magnolia/mockingbird

New Hampshire

Area: 9,350 sq mi (24,216 sq km)
Population: 1,316,470
Capital: Concord, pop. 42,695
Largest city: Manchester, pop. 109,565
Industry: Machinery, electronics, metal products
State flower/bird: Purple lilac/purple finch

Missouri

Area: 69,704 sq mi (180,534 sq km)
Population: 5,988,927
Capital: Jefferson City, pop. 43,079
Largest city: Kansas City, pop. 459,787
Industry: Transportation equipment, food processing, chemicals, electrical equipment, metal products
State flower/bird: Hawthorn/eastern bluebird

New Jersey

Area: 8,721 sq mi (22,588 sq km)
Population: 8,791,894
Capital: Trenton, pop. 84,913
Largest city: Newark, pop. 277,140
Industry: Machinery, electronics, metal products, chemicals
State flower/bird: Violet/American goldfinch

Montana

Area: 147,042 sq mi (380,840 sq km)
Population: 989,415
Capital: Helena, pop. 29,939
Largest city: Billings, pop. 105,845
Industry: Forest products, food processing, mining, construction, tourism
State flower/bird: Bitterroot/western meadowlark

New Mexico

Area: 121,590 sq mi (314,917 sq km)
Population: 2,059,179
Capital: Santa Fe, pop. 67,947
Largest city: Albuquerque, pop. 545,852
Industry: Electronic equipment, state and local government, real estate, business services, federal government, oil and gas extraction, health services
State flower/bird: Yucca/roadrunner

Nebraska

Area: 77,354 sq mi (200,346 sq km)
Population: 1,826,341
Capital: Lincoln, pop. 258,379
Largest city: Omaha, pop. 408,958
Industry: Food processing, machinery, electrical equipment, printing and publishing
State flower/bird: Goldenrod/western meadowlark

New York

Area: 54,556 sq mi (141,300 sq km)
Population: 19,378,102
Capital: Albany, pop. 97,856
Largest city: New York City, pop. 8,175,133
Industry: Printing and publishing, machinery, computer products, finance, tourism
State flower/bird: Rose/eastern bluebird

● Midwest ● Southwest ● West

North Carolina

Area: 53,819 sq mi (139,390 sq km)
Population: 9,535,483
Capital: Raleigh, pop. 403,892
Largest city: Charlotte, pop. 731,424
Industry: Real estate, health services, chemicals, tobacco products, finance, textiles
State flower/bird: Flowering dogwood/cardinal

North Dakota

Area: 70,700 sq mi (183,113 sq km)
Population: 672,591
Capital: Bismarck, pop. 61,272
Largest city: Fargo, pop. 105,549
Industry: Services, government, finance, construction, transportation, oil and gas
State flower/bird: Wild prairie rose/western meadowlark

8,962 people made SNOW ANGELS at the same time on the grounds of the NORTH DAKOTA STATE CAPITOL.

Ohio

Area: 44,825 sq mi (116,097 sq km)
Population: 11,536,504
Capital: Columbus, pop. 787,033
Largest city: Columbus, pop. 787,033
Industry: Transportation equipment, metal products, machinery, food processing, electrical equipment
State flower/bird: Scarlet carnation/cardinal

Oklahoma

Area: 69,898 sq mi (181,036 sq km)
Population: 3,751,351
Capital: Oklahoma City, pop. 579,999
Largest city: Oklahoma City, pop. 579,999
Industry: Manufacturing, services, government, finance, insurance, real estate
State flower/bird: Mistletoe/scissor-tailed flycatcher

Oregon

Area: 98,381 sq mi (254,806 sq km)
Population: 3,831,074
Capital: Salem, pop. 154,637
Largest city: Portland, pop. 583,776
Industry: Real estate, retail and wholesale trade, electronic equipment, health services, construction, forest products, business services
State flower/bird: Oregon grape/western meadowlark

Pennsylvania

Area: 46,055 sq mi (119,283 sq km)
Population: 12,702,379
Capital: Harrisburg, pop. 49,528
Largest city: Philadelphia, pop. 1,526,006
Industry: Machinery, printing and publishing, forest products, metal products
State flower/bird: Mountain laurel/ruffed grouse

Rhode Island

Area: 1,545 sq mi (4,002 sq km)
Population: 1,052,567
Capital: Providence, pop. 178,042
Largest city: Providence, pop. 178,042
Industry: Health services, business services, silver and jewelry products, metal products
State flower/bird: Violet/Rhode Island red

South Carolina

Area: 32,020 sq mi (82,932 sq km)
Population: 4,625,364
Capital: Columbia, pop. 129,272
Largest city: Columbia, pop. 129,272
Industry: Service industries, tourism, chemicals, textiles, machinery, forest products
State flower/bird: Yellow jessamine/Carolina wren

South Dakota

Area: 77,117 sq mi (199,732 sq km)
Population: 814,180
Capital: Pierre, pop. 13,646
Largest city: Sioux Falls, pop. 153,888
Industry: Finance, services, manufacturing, government, retail trade, transportation and utilities, wholesale trade, construction, mining
State flower/bird: Pasqueflower/ring-necked pheasant

COLOR KEY ● Northeast ● Southeast

Tennessee

Area: 42,143 sq mi (109,151 sq km)
Population: 6,346,105
Capital: Nashville, pop. 601,222
Largest city: Memphis, pop. 646,889
Industry: Service industries, chemicals, transportation equipment, processed foods, machinery
State flower/bird: Iris/mockingbird

Texas

Area: 268,581 sq mi (695,624 sq km)
Population: 25,145,561
Capital: Austin, pop. 790,390
Largest city: Houston, pop. 2,099,451
Industry: Chemicals, machinery, electronics and computers, food products, petroleum and natural gas, transportation equipment
State flower/bird: Bluebonnet/mockingbird

Utah

Area: 84,899 sq mi (219,888 sq km)
Population: 2,763,885
Capital: Salt Lake City, pop. 186,440
Largest city: Salt Lake City, pop. 186,440
Industry: Government, manufacturing, real estate, construction, health services, business services, banking
State flower/bird: Sego lily/California gull

Vermont

Area: 9,614 sq mi (24,901 sq km)
Population: 625,741
Capital: Montpelier, pop. 7,855
Largest city: Burlington, pop. 42,417
Industry: Health services, tourism, finance, real estate, computer components, electrical parts, printing and publishing, machine tools
State flower/bird: Red clover/hermit thrush

Virginia

Area: 42,774 sq mi (110,785 sq km)
Population: 8,001,024
Capital: Richmond, pop. 204,214
Largest city: Virginia Beach, pop. 437,994
Industry: Food processing, communication and electronic equipment, transportation equipment, printing, shipbuilding, textiles
State flower/bird: Flowering dogwood/cardinal

Washington

Area: 71,300 sq mi (184,666 sq km)
Population: 6,724,540
Capital: Olympia, pop. 46,478
Largest city: Seattle, pop. 608,660
Industry: Aerospace, tourism, food processing, forest products, paper products, industrial machinery, printing and publishing, metals, computer software
State flower/bird: Coast rhododendron/Amer. goldfinch

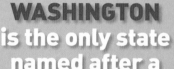

WASHINGTON is the only state named after a U.S. PRESIDENT.

West Virginia

Area: 24,230 sq mi (62,755 sq km)
Population: 1,852,994
Capital: Charleston, pop. 51,400
Largest city: Charleston, pop. 51,400
Industry: Tourism, coal mining, chemicals, metal manufacturing, forest products, stone, clay, oil, glass products
State flower/bird: Rhododendron/cardinal

Wisconsin

Area: 65,498 sq mi (169,639 sq km)
Population: 5,686,986
Capital: Madison, pop. 233,209
Largest city: Milwaukee, pop. 594,833
Industry: Industrial machinery, paper products, food processing, metal products, electronic equipment, transportation
State flower/bird: Wood violet/robin

Wyoming

Area: 97,814 sq mi (253,337 sq km)
Population: 563,626
Capital: Cheyenne, pop. 59,466
Largest city: Cheyenne, pop. 59,466
Industry: Oil and natural gas, mining, generation of electricity, chemicals, tourism
State flower/bird: Indian paintbrush/western meadowlark

THE TERRITORIES

The United States has 14 territories—political divisions that are not states. Three of these are in the Caribbean Sea, and the other eleven are in the Pacific Ocean.

St. John, U.S. Virgin Islands

U.S. CARIBBEAN TERRITORIES

Puerto Rico

Area: 3,508 sq mi (9,086 sq km)
Population: 3,989,133
Capital: San Juan, pop. 2,730,000
Languages: Spanish, English

Note: Population figures for territories do not reflect the 2010 census.

U.S. Virgin Islands

Area: 149 sq mi (386 sq km)
Population: 109,666
Capital: Charlotte Amalie, pop. 54,000
Languages: English, Spanish or Spanish Creole, French or French Creole

U.S. PACIFIC TERRITORIES

American Samoa

Area: 77 sq mi (199 sq km)
Population: 67,242
Capital: Pago Pago, pop. 60,000
Language: Samoan

Guam

Area: 217 sq mi (561 sq km)
Population: 183,286
Capital: Hagåtña (Agana), pop. 153,000
Languages: English, Chamorro, Philippine languages

Northern Mariana Islands

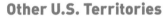

Area: 184 sq mi (477 sq km)
Population: 46,050
Capital: Saipan (Capital Hill), pop. 1,500
Languages: Philippine languages, Chinese, Chamorro, English

Other U.S. Territories

Baker Island, Howland Island, Jarvis Island, Johnston Atoll, Kingman Reef, Midway Islands, Palmyra Atoll, Wake Island, Navassa Island (in the Caribbean)

THE U.S. CAPITAL

District of Columbia

Area: 68 sq mi (177 sq km)
Population: 601,723

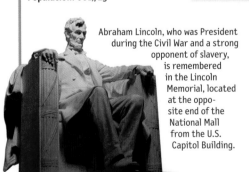

Abraham Lincoln, who was President during the Civil War and a strong opponent of slavery, is remembered in the Lincoln Memorial, located at the opposite end of the National Mall from the U.S. Capitol Building.

The Library of Congress is one of the world's oldest and largest libraries. Established in 1800 by an act of Congress, the library's current collection includes more than 33 million books and other print materials!

COLOR KEY ● Territories ● Northeast

Bet you didn't know

There is a place called **ROACH, Missouri.**

EIGHT United States Presidents **were BORN IN VIRGINIA.**

BALD EAGLES live in **EVERY U.S. STATE** EXCEPT Hawaii.

NO ROADS lead to **Juneau,** the capital of Alaska.

A CORNFLAKE shaped like the state of Illinois **SOLD FOR $1,350.**

Two-Letter Postal Abbreviations

AK	Alaska
AL	Alabama
AR	Arkansas
AS	American Samoa
AZ	Arizona
CA	California
CO	Colorado
CT	Connecticut
DC	District of Columbia
DE	Delaware
FL	Florida
GA	Georgia
GU	Guam
HI	Hawaii
IA	Iowa
ID	Idaho
IL	Illinois
IN	Indiana
KS	Kansas
KY	Kentucky
LA	Louisiana
MA	Massachusetts
MD	Maryland
ME	Maine
MI	Michigan
MN	Minnesota
MO	Missouri
MP	Northern Mariana Islands
MS	Mississippi
MT	Montana
NC	North Carolina
ND	North Dakota
NE	Nebraska
NH	New Hampshire
NJ	New Jersey
NM	New Mexico
NV	Nevada
NY	New York
OH	Ohio
OK	Oklahoma
OR	Oregon
PA	Pennsylvania
PR	Puerto Rico
RI	Rhode Island
SC	South Carolina
SD	South Dakota
TN	Tennessee
TX	Texas
UT	Utah
VA	Virginia
VI	U.S. Virgin Islands
VT	Vermont
WA	Washington
WI	Wisconsin
WV	West Virginia
WY	Wyoming

URBAN GIANT

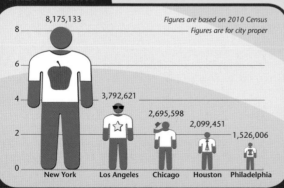

Figures are based on 2010 Census
Figures are for city proper

New York: 8,175,133
Los Angeles: 3,792,621
Chicago: 2,695,598
Houston: 2,099,451
Philadelphia: 1,526,006

With more than twice the population of the next-largest city, New York—known as the Big Apple—is the largest city in the U.S.

Go on Vacati🛰️n

Want to get away? Consider these unique destinations for your next vacation.

GRAND CANYON
SKYWALK

Grand Canyon Skywalk

GRAND CANYON WEST, ARIZONA

You hover above the Grand Canyon and gaze down at its jagged bottom 4,000 feet (1,219 m) below. It may feel like you're flying, but you're actually standing on the Grand Canyon Skywalk—a see-through platform that extends 70 feet (21 m) beyond the rim of the canyon and gives you a bird's-eye view. The only thing that's keeping you from free-falling is five layers of thick glass.

Don't worry about plummeting, though. The structure is built to withstand strong winds and earthquakes, and can hold about 71 million pounds (32 million kg)—or the weight of almost 71 Boeing 747 airplanes. As you make your way around the horseshoe-shaped walkway, gaze down at the winding Colorado River and scan the sky for bald eagles and red-tailed hawks. One word of advice: Leave your fear of heights at home.

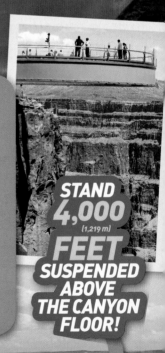

STAND 4,000 [1,219 m] FEET SUSPENDED ABOVE THE CANYON FLOOR!

POLAR BEAR ADVENTURE

THE TUNDRA BUGGY

Tundra Buggy Lodge
CHURCHILL, CANADA

SMILE FOR THE CAMERA!

You grip your camera and look through the viewfinder. A wild polar bear stares back at you, its nose almost touching the lens. Whoa! Sounds impossible? Not if you roam across northern Canada in the Tundra Buggy—an off-road vehicle that looks like a supersize bus. From a deck on the buggy that's safely out of a polar bear's reach, you can watch the bears stroll by. Keep a lookout for Dancer, a polar bear known for leaning against the buggy and then shuffling backward on two legs like he's getting his groove on.

Icy winds too cold? At Polar Bear Point—an area that's home to nearly a thousand bears—the Tundra Buggy hooks up to a lodge. Once inside, grab a cup of hot cocoa and gaze out at the bears on the tundra. You definitely won't see these sights at the zoo!

TAKE A WALK ON THE WILD SIDE

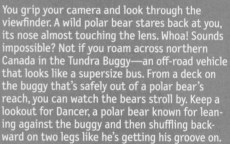

BREAKFAST VISITOR

The Giraffe Manor
KENYA, AFRICA

This hotel is home to nine Rothschild's giraffes that roam free on the property—and they're definitely not shy. Some of the giraffes may stick their heads into your second-story bedroom window or eat food right off the breakfast table! When they want a snack, the giraffes have been known to pluck flowers from the manor's vases. Patrick and Helen, the two youngest giraffes, are often seen playfully running across the lawn after warthogs, the hotel's pet dog, and sometimes even the guests. But no one thinks they're a pain in the neck!

GET UP CLOSE!

WACKY HOTELS

These three weird-but-cool places are so wacky, they'll make a huge splash on anyone's vacation. Hold your breath and dive in!

CHECK OUT THESE FUN WATER-THEMED PLACES TO STAY ON VACATION.

② MAGIC MOUNTAIN LODGE

WHERE: Puerto Fuy, Chile

WHY IT'S COOL: This 66-foot-tall hotel (20-m) looks like a volcano. But instead of lava, a waterfall erupts out of the top and continuously cascades down the sides. Inspired by nearby Mocho Choshuenco volcano and Huilo-Huilo Falls, the lodge draws its waterfall from a local river.

① BURJ AL ARAB

WHERE: Dubai, United Arab Emirates

WHY IT'S COOL: No beach? No problem! The builders behind the Burj Al Arab made their own island so that this sail-shaped hotel appears to be cruising 919 feet (280 m) into the Arabian Gulf. A simulated submarine ride takes you to a seafood restaurant with a giant aquarium.

INSIDE

③ CAPSULE HOTEL

WHERE: The Hague, Netherlands

WHY IT'S COOL: You *could* call these orange saucers UFOs—Unusual Floating Objects! These floating hotel rooms were once rescue capsules for workers on offshore oil rigs. Docked in a canal, the basic capsule comes with a seat, a toilet, and a hammock made from old fishing nets. A "superdeluxe" version livens things up with a DVD player, disco ball, and karaoke machine!

The ORIGINAL 7 WONDERS of the WORLD

More than 2,000 years ago, many travelers wrote about sights they had seen on their journeys. Over time, seven of those places made history as the "wonders of the ancient world." There are seven because the Greeks, who made the list, believed the number seven to be magical.

THE PYRAMIDS OF GIZA, EGYPT
BUILT: ABOUT 2600 B.C.
MASSIVE TOMBS OF EGYPTIAN PHARAOHS, THE PYRAMIDS ARE THE ONLY ANCIENT WONDERS STILL STANDING TODAY.

HANGING GARDENS OF BABYLON, IRAQ
BUILT: DATE UNKNOWN
LEGEND HAS IT THAT THIS GARDEN PARADISE WAS PLANTED ON AN ARTIFICIAL MOUNTAIN, BUT MANY EXPERTS SAY IT NEVER REALLY EXISTED.

TEMPLE OF ARTEMIS AT EPHESUS, TURKEY
BUILT: SIXTH CENTURY B.C.
THIS TOWERING TEMPLE WAS BUILT TO HONOR ARTEMIS, THE GREEK GODDESS OF THE HUNT.

STATUE OF ZEUS, GREECE
BUILT: FIFTH CENTURY B.C.
THIS 40-FOOT (12-M) STATUE DEPICTED THE KING OF THE GREEK GODS.

MAUSOLEUM AT HALICARNASSUS, TURKEY
BUILT: FOURTH CENTURY B.C.
THIS ELABORATE TOMB WAS BUILT FOR KING MAUSOLUS.

COLOSSUS OF RHODES, RHODES (AN ISLAND IN THE AEGEAN SEA)
BUILT: FOURTH CENTURY B.C.
A 110-FOOT (34-M) STATUE HONORING THE GREEK SUN GOD HELIOS.

LIGHTHOUSE OF ALEXANDRIA, EGYPT
BUILT: THIRD CENTURY B.C.
THE WORLD'S FIRST LIGHTHOUSE, IT USED MIRRORS TO REFLECT SUNLIGHT FOR MILES OUT TO SEA.

The NEW 7 WONDERS of the WORLD

Why name new wonders of the world? Most of the original ancient wonders no longer exist. To be eligible for the new list, the wonders had to be man-made before the year 2000 and in preservation. They were selected in 2007 through a poll of more than 100 million voters!

TAJ MAHAL, INDIA
COMPLETED: 1648
THIS LAVISH TOMB WAS BUILT AS A FINAL RESTING PLACE FOR THE BELOVED WIFE OF EMPEROR SHAH JAHAN.

PETRA, SOUTHWEST JORDAN
COMPLETED: ABOUT 200 B.C.
SOME 30,000 PEOPLE ONCE LIVED IN THIS ROCK CITY CARVED INTO CLIFF WALLS.

MACHU PICCHU, PERU
COMPLETED: ABOUT 1450
OFTEN CALLED THE "LOST CITY IN THE CLOUDS," MACHU PICCHU IS PERCHED 7,972 FEET (2,430 M) HIGH IN THE ANDES.

THE COLOSSEUM, ITALY
COMPLETED: A.D. 80
WILD ANIMALS—AND HUMANS—FOUGHT EACH OTHER TO THE DEATH BEFORE 50,000 SPECTATORS IN THIS ARENA.

CHRIST THE REDEEMER STATUE, BRAZIL
COMPLETED: 1931
TOWERING ATOP CORCOVADO MOUNTAIN, THIS STATUE IS TALLER THAN A 12-STORY BUILDING AND WEIGHS ABOUT 2.5 MILLION POUNDS (1.1 MILLION KG).

CHICHÉN ITZÁ, MEXICO
COMPLETED: TENTH CENTURY
ONCE THE CAPITAL CITY OF THE ANCIENT MAYA EMPIRE, CHICHÉN ITZÁ IS HOME TO THE FAMOUS PYRAMID OF KUKULCÁN.

GREAT WALL OF CHINA, CHINA
COMPLETED: 1644
THE LONGEST MAN-MADE STRUCTURE EVER BUILT, IT WINDS OVER AN ESTIMATED 4,500 MILES (7,000 KM).

335

Finding Your Way Around

Every map has a story to tell, but first you have to know how to read one. Maps represent information by using a language of symbols. Knowing how to read these symbols provides access to a wide range of information. Look at the scale and compass rose or arrow to understand distance and direction (see box below).

To find out what each symbol on a map means, you must use the key. It's your secret decoder—identifying information by each symbol on the map.

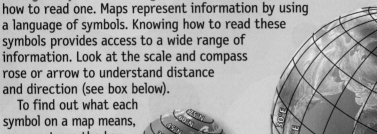

90°N (North Po

Latitude

Longitude

LATITUDE AND LONGITUDE

Latitude and longitude lines (above) help us determine locations on Earth. Every place on Earth has a special address called absolute location. Imaginary lines called lines of latitude run west to east, parallel to the Equator. These lines measure distance in degrees north or south from the Equator (0° latitude) to the North Pole (90°N) or to the South Pole (90°S). One degree of latitude is approximately 70 miles (113 km).

Lines of longitude run north to south, meeting at the poles. These lines measure distance in degrees east or west from 0° longitude (prime meridian) to 180° longitude. The prime meridian runs through Greenwich, England.

SCALE AND DIRECTION

The scale on a map can be shown as a fraction, as words, or as a line or bar. It relates distance on the map to distance in the real world. Sometimes the scale identifies the type of map projection. Maps may include an arrow or compass rose to indicate north on the map.

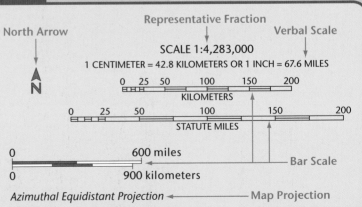

North Arrow

Representative Fraction

Verbal Scale

SCALE 1:4,283,000
1 CENTIMETER = 42.8 KILOMETERS OR 1 INCH = 67.6 MILES

0 25 50   100   150   200
KILOMETERS

0   25   50   100   150   200
STATUTE MILES

Bar Scale

0   600 miles
0   900 kilometers

Azimuthal Equidistant Projection ◄──── Map Projection

SYMBOLS

There are three main types of map symbols: points, lines, and areas. Points, which can be either dots or small icons, represent locations of things, such as schools, cities, or landmarks. Lines are used to show boundaries, roads, or rivers and can vary in color or thickness. Area symbols use patterns or color to show regions, such as a sandy area or a neighborhood.

POINT
A point symbol, a black dot, indicates a city, such as Omdurman.

LINE
Sudan's country boundary appears as a line symbol: a dotted line with a colored edge.

AREA
Sandy places, such as parts of the Sahara Desert, are shown by a tan, speckled area.

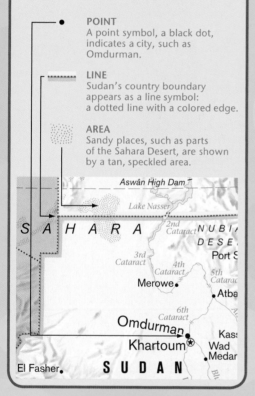

What's an ATLAS?

An atlas, or collection of maps, is usually chock-full of information, charts, and illustrations. You can look up specific places or just browse. Atlases are full of photographs, statistics, quick facts, and—most of all—lots of detailed maps and charts.

MAKING A PROJECTION. Globes present a model of Earth as it is—a sphere—but they are bulky and can be difficult to use and store. Flat maps are much more convenient but certain problems can result from transferring Earth's curved surface to a flat piece of paper, a process called projection. Imagine a globe that has been cut in half like this one has. If a light is shined into it, the lines of latitude and longitude and the shapes of the continent will cast shadows that can be "projected" onto a piece of paper, as shown here. Depending on how the paper is positioned, the shadows will be distorted in different ways.

ABSOLUTE LOCATION. Suppose you are using latitude and longitude to play a game of global scavenger hunt. The clue says the prize is hidden at absolute location 30°S, 60°W. You know that the first number is south of the Equator, and the second is west of the prime meridian. On the map at left, find the line of latitude labeled 30°S. Now find the line of longitude labeled 60°W. Trace these lines with your fingers until they meet. Identify this spot. The prize must be located in central Argentina (see arrow, right).

GAME ANSWERS

Splash Down, pages 164–165

We Gave It a Swirl, page 168

1. pink flamingo, 2. chameleon, 3. koala, 4. cow, 5. fish.

April Showers, page 169

Signs of the Times, page 175

Signs #5 and #8 are fake.

What in the World? page 176

Top row: pineapples, leis, coconut.
Middle row: Hawaiian shirt, a toy hula dancer, sea turtle.
Bottom row: volcano, surfboard, ukulele.

Animal Jam, page 177

The Bargain Hunt, page 180

Stump Your Parents, page 182

1. A, 2. C, 3. B, 4. B, 5. D, 6. A, 7. C, 8. B, 9. D.

Just for Kicks, page 183

Your World 2013 (8–17)
p. 11 "Simon Says" by Stephen Ornes; all other articles in section by Sarah Wassner Flynn

Amazing Animals (18–79)
pp. 20–21 "What Is Taxonomy?" & "Vertebrates/Invertebrates" by Susan K. Donnelly; pp. 22-23 "Giraffe Hangs with Goat" & "Dog Loves Owl" by Kitson Jazynka; p. 23 "Raccoon Adopts Cat" by C.M. Tomlin; p. 24 "Critter Creations" by Kitson Jazynka; p. 25 "Animal Myths Busted" by C.M. Tomlin; p. 26 "Mystery of the Disappearing Frogs" by Fiona Sundquist; p. 27 "Do Animals Have Feelings?" by Aline Alexander Newman; pp. 28–29 "The Fox Next Door" by Karen De Seve; pp. 30–31 "6 Tips Every Polar Bear Should Know" by David George Gordon; p. 32 "Meerkat City" by Graeme Stemp-Morlock; p. 33 "Wild Dogs of Africa" by Crispin Boyer; pp. 34–35 "Supershark Awards" by Ruth A. Musgrave; pp. 36–37 "Dolphins in Disguise" by Crispin Boyer; p. 37 "Problem Solved!" by Aline Alexander Newman; p. 38 "Under the Ice" by Norbert Wu; p. 39 "Incredible Powers of the Octopus" by Mark Norman; pp. 40–41 "Secret Life of Sea Turtles" by Ruth Musgrave; p. 44 "Do Fish Sleep?" by Dr. Seymour Katz; p p. 42 "5 Cool Things About Harp Seals" by Sharon Thompson; p. 43–44 "Panda Shake-up" & "Rock-a-bye Monkey" by Ruth A. Musgrave; p. 45 "Will the Red Panda Survive?" by Fiona Sunquist; p. 45 "Saving the Blue Iguana" by Jennifer Weeks; 46–47 "Bear" and "Wombat" by Scott Elder; p. 47 "Dog" by Kitson Jazynka; pp. 48–49 "Wild Cat Family Reunion" by Fiona Sunquist; p. 50 "Leopards: Nature's Supercats" by Crispin Boyer; pp. 52–53 "Think Like a Tiger" by Aline Alexander Newman; pp. 54–55 "Cheetahs: Built for Speed" &"The Mystery of the Black Panther" by Fiona Sunquist; p. 56 "5 Cool Things About Butterflies" by Erin Whitmer; pp. 58–59 "Bizarre Insects" by Sarah Wassner Flynn; pp. 60–61 "Silly Pet Tricks" by Margaret J. Krauss; p. 62 "Why Do Dogs and Cats Need Tails?" by Dr. Seymour Katz; p. 63 "The Smart Way to Find a Lost Pet" by Heather E. Schwartz; pp. 64–65 "Lifestyles of the Rich and Furry" by Sarah Wassner Flynn; pp. 66–67 "28 Cool Things About Pets"; p. 68 "What Killed the Dinosaurs?" nationalgeographic.com; pp. 68–71 "Prehistoric Timeline" & "Who Ate What?" by Susan K. Donnelly; p. 70 "What Color were Dinosaurs?" by Sarah Wassner Flynn; p. 72 "Dino Classification" by Susan K. Donnelly;

Awesome Adventure (80–99)
pp. 80–81 "Dare to Explore!" by Sarah Wassner Flynn; pp. 80–85 "5 Cool Dudes Who Changed the World" by Michael N. Smith; p. 86 "Mystery in the Desert" by Kristin Baird Rattini; p. 87 "Fearless Fliers" by Sarah Wassner Flynn; pp. 88–89 "Crystal Cave" by Jennifer Cutraro; pp. 90–91 "The Seal Who Loved Me" by Paul Nicklen; p. 92 "Will My Toy Car..." by Brady Barr as told to Maggie Zackowitz; p. 93 "How to Survive..." by Michael N. Smith; pp. 94–95 "No Limits" by Sarah Wassner Flynn; p. 97 "How to Take Great Photos" Excerpted from The National Geographic Kids Photo Field Guide by Neil Johnson

Culture Connection (100–125)
p. 110 "Kwanzaa" & "Chinese Dragon Boat Festival" by Sarah Wassner Flynn; p. 111 "What's Your Chinese Horoscope?" by Geoff Williams; p. 108 "Myths Busted" by Jamie Kiffel-Alcheh; p. 108 "Pop History" by Jamie McCoy; pp. 110-111 "Let Them Eat Cake" by Sean McCollum; p. 116 "Money Around the World" by Kristin Baird Rattini; pp. 118–1119 "World Religions" by Mark Bockenhauer; pp. 120–122 "Mythology" & "The Olympics" by Susan K. Donnelly;

Super Science (126–161)
p. 129 "The Three Domains of Life" by Susan K. Donnelly; p. 130 "Your Amazing Body" by Susan K. Donnelly; p. 131 "Myths Busted" by Sarah Wassner Flynn; p. 132 "Your Amazing Eyes" by Douglas E. Richards; p. 133 "What Your Favorite Color..." by Sarah Wassner Flynn; p. 134 "Your Amazing Brain" by Douglas E. Richards; p. 136 "Get Fit!" by Susan K. Donnelly/Sarah Wassner Flynn; pp. 138–139 "...Big Bang" by David A. Aguilar; p. 142 "Dwarf Planets" by Sarah Wassner Flynn; pp. 145–147 "Solar and Lunar Eclipses" & "Constellations" by Sarah Wassner Flynn; pp. 149-153: "Rock Stars," "It's a Rocky World," & "Birthstones" by Steve Tomecek; pp. 154-155 "Cool Inventions" by Cathy Lu; p. 156 "Space Robots" by Douglas E. Richards; p. 157 "5 Ways You Use Satellites" by Sean Price; pp. 158–159 "Space Vacation" by Douglas E. Richards

Wonders of Nature (184–205)
pp. 186–187 "World Climate" & "Climate Change" by Mark Bockenhauer; pp. 188–189 "Freaky Weather" by Douglas E. Richards; p. 190 "Hurricane" by Renee Skelton; p. 191–192 "Tornado!" "Triple Disaster," & "Wildfire!" by Sarah Wassner Flynn; pp. 194–196 "Biomes" & "How Does Your Garden Grow?" by Susan K. Donnelly; p. 197 "Grow an Indoor Herb Garden" by Jill Yaworski; p. 198 "World Water" by Mark Bockenhauer; pp. 200–201 "Oceans" by Mark Bockenhauer; pp. 202–203 "Coral Reefs" by Crispin Boyer

Going Green (206–225)
pp. 208–209 "Trapped by Trash!" by Scott Elder; pp. 210–211 "Global Warming," by Sarah Wassner FLynn; pp. 212–213 "Pollution," "Declining Biodiversity," & "Habitat Destruction" by David George Gordon; pp. 214–215 "World Energy & Minerals" by Mark Bockenhauer; 216 "Ocean Alert" by Enric Sala; pp. 220–221 "Green Cool Inventions" by Cathy Lu; pp. 222–223 "Green Houses" by Sarah Wassner Flynn

History Happens (226–257)
pp. 228–229 "Discovering Tut's Treasures" by Sean Price; p. 229 "Animal Mummies" by Sarah Wassner Flynn; pp. 230–231 "The Lost City of Pompeii" by Kristin Baird Rattini; p. 233 "5 Cool Things About Ancient Greece" by Sarah Wassner Flynn; pp. 234–237 "Guardians of the Tomb" "The Greatest Heists of All Time" &"Curse of the Hope Diamond" by Kristin Baird Rattini pp. 238–239 "Solving the Ancient Mystery of Stonehenge by Kristin Baird Rattini and Sarah Wassner Flynn; pp. 240–241 "War!" by Susan K. Donnelly/Sarah Wassner Flynn; p. 241 "Gettysburg" by Sarah Wassner Flynn; pp. 242, 244–245 by Susan K. Donnelly; p. 243 "George Washington's Real Look" by Cathy Lu; p. 251 "The Indian Experience" by Martha B. Sharma; pp. 252–253 "Civil Rights" by Susan K. Donnelly/Sarah Wassner Flynn; pp. 254–255"Women Fighting for Equality" by Sarah Wassner Flynn

Geography Rocks (258–337)
pp. 260–265 by Mark Bockenhauer; pp. 266–293 by Mark Bockenhauer and Susan K. Donnelly; pp. 297-317 "You Are There!" by Sarah Wassner Flynn; pp. 332-333 "Go on Vacation" by Amanda Sandlin; p. 334 "Wonders of the World" by Elisabeth Deffner; pp. 335 "Wacky Hotels" by Kristin Baird Rattini

All "Homework Help" by Vicki Ariyasu

ABBREVIATIONS:

AL: Alamy
CB: Corbis
DA: David Aguilar
GI: Getty Images
IS: iStockphoto.com
JI: Jupiter Images
MP: Minden Pictures
MW: Martin Walz
MVLA: Mount Vernon Ladies' Association
NGS: NationalGeographicStock.com
NPL: naturepl.com
PR: Photo Researchers, Inc.
SP: SeaPics.com
SS: Shutterstock
SU: SuperStock
WHHA: White House Historical Association

All Maps
By NGS unless otherwise noted.

All Illustrations & Charts
By Stuart Armstrong unless otherwise noted.

Zipper Artwork
By Nathan Jurevicius.

Front cover/Spine
Frog, Tim Flach/Stone/GI; surfer, EpicStockMedia/SS; tiger, Ron Kimball/Kimball Stock; penguin, Tom Brakefield/Corbis; panda, Brandon Beccarelli/NGYS

Back Cover
Koala, Craig Dingle/IS; earth, Alex Staroseltsev/SS; cake, Ocean/CO; Eiffel Tower, vichie81/SS; bicyclist, Brooke Whatnall/SS; butterfly, David Maska/SS; coyote, John Pitcher/IS; dolphin, Kristian Sekulic/IS

Inside Front Cover
Giraffe, Roy Toft/NGS; T. Rex, CB

Front Matter (2–7)
2–3, Alaska Stock Images/NGS; 5 (UP), SS; 5 (UP CTR), ChinaFotoPress/GI; 5 (LO CTR), WILDLIFE GmbH/AL; 5 (LO), Red Bull Content Pool - Images; 6 (UP), Martine Perret/UNMIT/UN Photo; 6 (UP CTR), NASA/JPL Caltech; 6 (LO CTR), Terra/CB; 6 (LO), Gary Bell/OceanwideImages.com; 7 (UP), Ian Nichols/NGS; 7 (CTR), Adrian Pope/GI; 7 (LO), Donald M. Jones/MP

Your World 2013 (8–17)
8–9, ChinaFotoPress/GI; 10 (UP LE), Alexander Cherednichenko/IS; 10 (UP RT), Simon Grosset/AL; 10 (LE CTR), jorisvo/SS; 10 (RT CTR), Maria Stenzel/NGS; 10 (LO LE), Maxim Tupikov/SS; 10 (LO CTR), Igor Plotnikov/SS; 10 (LO RT), AfriPics.com/AL; 10 (UP LE), Rui Manuel Teles Gomes/SS; 11 (UP), Buena Vista/Zuma Press; 11 (CTR), Twentieth Century Fox Film/Zuma Press; 11 (LO), Courtesy of Georgia Institute of Technology; 12 (LE), AP Images/Green Renaissance/WWF; 12 (RT), AP Images/Green Renaissance/WWF; 13 (UP), Shattil & Rozinski/NPL/MP; 13 (UP CTR), Shattil & Rozinski/SU; 13 (LO CTR LE), Brent Stephenson/NPL; 13 (LO LE), NHPA/

Photoshot; 13 (UP CTR RT), John M. Burnley/PR; 13 (LO CTR RT), Mark Bowler/AL; 13 (LO RT), David Haring/Photolibrary RM/GI; 14 (UP), DA; 14 (CTR), Marvel Enterprises/Zuma Press; 14 (LO LE), Illumination Entertainment/Zuma Press; 14 (LO RT), KRT/Newscom; 15 (UP LE), Royal Geographical Society/NGS; 15 (UP RT), HO/Reuters/CB; 15 (UP BACK), David Poole/Robert Harding World Imagery/CB; 15 (LO), AP Images/Bebeto Matthews; 16 (UP LE), Michael Nichols/NGS; 16 (UP RT), DanielW/SS; 16 (UP CTR RT), Bettmann/CB; 16 (LO CTR LE), Johan Swanepoel/SS; 16 (LO CTR RT), Nancy Bauer/SS; 16 (LO LE), AP Images/Scanpix/Kenneth Paulsson; 16 (LO RT), Artem Povarov/IS; 16 (UP CTR LE), Le Do/SS; 17 (UP), Martha Holmes/NPL/MP; 17 (LO LE), Chris Hunt/ZUMA Press/CB; 17 (LO RT), Steven G. Smith/CB;

Amazing Animals (18–79)
18–19, WILDLIFE GmbH/AL; 20 (LO), Eric Isselée/SS; 20 (UP), Craig Dingle/IS; 21 (UP LE), FloridaStock/SS; 21 (RT CTR), Karen Massier/IS; 21 (UP RT), cbpix/SS; 21 (LE CTR), mashe/SS; 21 (LO), Eric Isselée/SS; 22, Noah Goodrich/Caters News Agency; 23 (UP), Andrea Klostermann; 23 (LO), South West News Service; 24 (LO), Ross Parry; 24 (UP LE), Brian Terry/The Oklahoman; 24 (UP RT), Coutesy of Oklahoma City Zoo; 25 (UP), Dean MacAdam; 25 (CTR), Dean MacAdam; 25 (LO), Dean MacAdam; 26 (UP), George Grall/NGS; 26 (LO), Chris Collins Studio; 27, Michael K. Nichols/NGS; 28 (UP), Sergey Gorshkov/MP; 28 (LO), John Hawkins/MP; 29 (UP RT), Wendy Shattil/Photolibrary/GI; 29 (UP LE), Elliot Neep/MP; 29 (LO), Peter Bisset/Photolibrary/GI; 30 (UP), Norbert Rosing/NGS; 30 (CTR), Alaska Stock LLC/AL; 30 (LO), David Pike/NPL; 31 (UP LE), Paul Nicklen/NGS; 31 (UP RT), Art Wolfe/The Image Bank/GI; 31 (LO Back), David Hiser/Stone/GI; 32 (UP RT), Paul Souders/GI; 32 (UP LE), EcoPrint/SS; 32 (LO LE), Age Fotostock/SU; 32 (LO RT), Beverly Joubert/NGS; 33 (UP), Andy Rouse/Stone/GI; 33 (LO), Albert Froneman; 34 (UP), David Doubilet/NGS; 34 (LO LE), Norbert Wu/MP; 34 (LO RT), Mark Conlin/SP; 35 (UP), Mark Strickland/SP; 35 (CTR), David Doubilet/NGS; 35 (LO RT), Ronald C. Modra/Sports Imagery/GI; 36–37 (UP), Doug Perrine/NPL; 36 (A), SP; 36 (B), WWF, Kathleen Sullivan; 36 (C), Brandon Cole; 37 (A), Hiroya Minakuchi/MP; 37 (LO RT), Julian Finn/Museum Victoria; 38 (LO), Paul Souders/GI; 38 (UP), © 2005 Norbert Wu/www.norbertwu.com; 38 (CTR), © 2007 NGHT, Inc.; 39 (UP), John C. Lewis/SP; 39 (LE CTR), Gary Bell/OceanwideImages.com; 39 (RT CTR), Gary Bell/OceanwideImages.com; 39 (LO LE), Jeff Rotman/SP; 39 (LO RT), Doug Perrine/SP; 40 (LE), National Geographic Remote Imaging/Crittercam; 40 (RT), Lisa Steiner/SP; 40–41 (Background), Dave Fleetham/Pacific Stock/PhotoLibrary; 41 (LO), NOAA Permit # 1591; 42 (UP), Lisa & Mike Husar/

Team Husar; 42 (LO), Keren Su/GI; 43 (UP), Katherine Feng/MP; 43 (CTR), Katherine Feng/MP; 43 (UP back), Gerry Ellis/MP; 44 (UP back), Djuna Ivereigh; 44 (UP), Djuna Ivereigh; 44 (LO), Djuna Ivereigh; 45 (UP), Fritz Polking; Frank Lane Picture Agency/CB; 45 (LO), Michael D. Kern/NPL; 46 (UP), Heinz Plenge; 46 (LO LE), Craig Borrow/Newspix/Rex USA; 46 (LO RT), Newspix/Rex/Rex USA; 47 (LO), Newspix/Rex/Rex USA; 47 (UP), Institute of Meteorology and Water Management; 47 (CTR), AP Images/Maciej Czoska; 48 (LO), DLILLC/CB; 48 (CTR LE), Randy Green/GI; 48 (CTR RT), Lynn M. Stone/NPL; 48 (UP), Peter Blackwell/NPL; 49 (A), Dr. Gertrud Neumann-Denzau/NPL; 49 (C), Henk Bentlage/SS; 49 (D), Anup Shah/NPL; 49 (E), Lynda Richardson/CB; 49 (F), Vladimir Sazonov/SS; 49 (H), Joel Sartore/NGS; 49 (I), Philip Perry/CB; 49 (G), Fritz Polking; Frank Lane Picture Agency/CB; 49 (B), Art Wolfe; 50 (UP), Francois Savigny/NPL; 50 (RT CTR), Beverly Joubert/NGS; 50 (LO LE), Beverly Joubert/NGS; 50 (LO RT), Mark Thiessen/NGS; 51, Chris Johns/NGS; 52 (LE), T.J. Rich/NPL; 52 (RT), Konrad Wothe/MP; 52–53 (BACK), Pixtal Images/Photolibrary/GI; 53 (LO), E.A. Kuttapan/MP; 54 (CTR), Andy Rouse/NHPA/Photoshot; 54 (LO LE), Stephen Belcher/MP; 54 (LO RT), Suzi Eszterhas/MP; 55 (LO), Rodney Griffiths; 55 (UP), Erwin & Peggy Bauer; 56 (UP LE), Brian Kenney; 56 (UP RT), Art Wolfe/Stone/GI; 56 (LO), Ingo Arndt/MP; 57, Cisca Castelijns/MP; 58 (UP CTR LE), Ingo Arndt/NPL; 58 (UP CTR RT), Dr. James L. Castner/Visuals Unlimited, Inc.; 58 (LO CTR), Alex Hyde/NPL; 58 (LE LE), NHPA/SU; 58 (LO RT), Chris Mattison/FLPA/MP; 58 (UP), Cosmin Manci/SS; 59 (UP LE), Photolibrary.com; 59 (UP RT), PREMAPHOTOS/NPL; 59 (LE CTR), Alex Hyde/NPL; 59 (RT CTR), Kazuo Unno/Nature Production/MP; 59 (LO), NH/SS; 60 (UP LE), Karine Aigner/NGS; 60 (UP CTR), Karine Aigner/NGS; 60 (UP RT), Karine Aigner/NGS; 60 (LO), Courtesy of Henry Lizardlover; 61 (UP), Karine AIgner/NGS; 61 (UP RT), Heather Brook; 61 (LE LE), Burnell Yow!; 62 (LO RT), Demark/SS; 62 (RT CTR), Ellustrations/IS; 62 (UP LE), Damien Richard/SS; 62 (LO LE), DLILLC/CB; 62 (UP RT), haveseen/SS; 63, Tom Cocotos; 64 (LO LE), Ruth Regina/Wiggles; 64–49, age fotostock/SU; 64–49, SU; 64 (LO CTR), Ruth Regina/Wiggles; 64 (UP CTR), Tim Flach/GI; 65 (LE), Michael Grecco/UpperCut Images/GI; 65 (RT), Ted Soqui/Sygma/CB; 65 (UP CTR), PhotoDisc/Punchstock; 65 (LO), Mark Thiessen/NGS Staff; 66 (UP LE), Martin Harvey/Kimball Stock; 66 (UP RT), NaturePL/SU; 66 (CTR), age fotostock/SU; 66 (LO LE), Stephen Dalton/MP; 66 (LO RT), Klein-Hurbert/Kimball Stock; 67 (UP LE), Brian Bevan/ARDEA; 67 (UP CTR), age fotostock/SU; 67 (UP RT), Ron Kimball/Kimball Stock; 67 (RT CTR), avatra images/AL; 67 (LE CTR), Mark Conlin/SP; 67 (LO), Jean Michel Labat/ARDEA; 68 (UP), Chris

Butler/Science Photo Library/PR; 68 (CTR), Publiphoto/PR; 68 (LO), Pixeldust Studios/NGS; 69 (B), Laurie O'Keefe/PR; 69 (C), Chris Butler/PR; 69 (D), Publiphoto/PR; 69 (A), Publiphoto/PR; 69 (E), image courtesy of Project Exploration; 70–71 (CTR), Pixeldust Studios/NGS; 70 (LE), NGS; 71 (UP), Ira Block; 71 (UP RT), Ira Block; 72 (UP), Paul B. Moore/SS; 72 (LO), Andrea Meyer/SS; 73, Franco Tempesta; 74, Franco Tempesta; 75, Franco Tempesta; 76, Franco Tempesta; 77 (UP), AP Images/Jeffrey Martz; 77 (LO LE), Rodrigo Vega; 77 (LO RT), HO/AFP/GI; 78, Barry Mansell/NPL/MP; 79, Gelpi/SS

Awesome Adventure (80–99)

80–81, Red Bull Content Pool - Images; 82 (UP LE), CB2/ZOB/WENN.com/News com; 82–83 (CTR), Mikey Schaefer/NGS; 83 (UP LE), Bates Littlehales/NGS; 83 (UP RT), Natalie B. Fobes/NGS; 84 (UP), Tom Richmond; 84 (CTR), Tom Richmond; 84 (LO), Tom Richmond; 84 (B), MW; 84, MW; 85 (UP), Tom Richmond; 85 (LO), Tom Richmond; 85 (C), MW; 85 (A), MW; 85 (B), MW; 86 (UP), Yoshino Tomi Photo Studio/Photolibrary; 86 (LO LE), JTB Photo/PhotoLibrary; 86 (Background), Robert Clark/Institue; 87 (B), Bettmann/CB; 87 (C), Bettmann/CB; 87 (A), CB; 87 (UP), Skyscan/CB; 88–89, Carsten Peter/SPELEORESEARCH & FILMS/NGS; 90 (UP LE), Paul Nicklen/NGS; 90–91, Paul Nicklen/NGS; 91 (UP RT), Paul nicklen/NGS; 92, Martin Harvey, www.wildimagesonline .co.za; 93 (LO), Barbara Kinney; 93 (UP), Renee Lynn/GI; 94 (UP), Berbar Halim/SIPA/Newscom; 94 (LO LE), James Cheadle; 94 (LO RT), Thomas Lohnes/AFP/GI/News com; 95 (UP LE), imago sportfotodienst/Newscom; 95 (UP RT), Jeff Hall; 95 (LO), Barry Bland/AL; 96 (UP LE), aftica7/NG KIDS My Shot; 96 (UP), loveusike/NG KIDS My Shot; 96 (LE CTR), juniorasparagus/NG KIDS My Shot; 96 (RT CTR), Matt/NG KIDS My Shot; 96 (LO LE), the_future_batman/NG KIDS My Shot; 96 (LO RT), Alexander/NG KIDS My Shot; 96 (UP LE), Willowpix/IS; 97 (CTR), Martin Vrlik/IS; 97 (RT), Berenika Lychak/IS; 98, Grady Reese/IS

Culture Connection (100–125)

100–101, Martine Perret/UNMIT/UN Photo; 102 (LO LE), Comstock; 102 (LO RT), Comstock;102 (UP LE), Christophe Testi/SS; 102 (UP RT), Elinag/SS; 104 (UP), Lonny Shavelson/ZUMAPRESS.com; 104 (LO), So Hing-Keung/CB; 105, Scott Matthews; 106 (UP LE), Tom Nick Cocotos; 106 (UP RT), Tom Nick Cocotos; 106 (LO), Ron Nickel/Design Pic/CB; 107, Brand X/SU; 108–108 (UP), Debbie Goard/Rex USA; 108 (LO LE), Debbie Goard/Rex USA; 108–109 (BOARDER), Goss Images/AL; 109 (UP RT), Debbie Goard/Rex USA; 109 (LO), Debbie Goard/Rex/Rex USA; 110, Mark Thiessen, NGS Staff; 111 (UP), Mark Thiessen, NGS Staff; 111 (LO), Mark Thiessen, NGS Staff; 112, Lonely Planet Images; 113 (UP), JTB Photo/Photolibrary; 113 (CTR), AP Photo/

Charles City Press/Mark Wicks; 113 (LO LE), AP Photo/The Alpena News/Amy Lisenbe; 113 (LO RT), AP Photo/Al Grillo; 114 (UP LE), Stock Connection/SU; 114 (UP RT), Exactostock/SU; 114 (CTR), Top Photo Corporation/CB; 114 (LO LE), James Urbach/SU; 114 (LO CTR LE), David Knopf/AL; 114 (LO CTR), David Doty; 114 (LO CTR RT), Esa Hiltula CC/AL; 114 (LO RT), Don Klein/Purestock/SU; 115, Mark Thiessen, NGS Staff; 116, Ocean/CB; 117, IS; 118 (UP), Randy Olson; 118 (LO LE), Martin Gray/NGS; 118 (LO RT), Sam Panthaky/AFP/GI; 119 (LO LE), Reza/NGS; 119 (LO RT), Richard Nowitz/NGS; 119 (UP), Winfield Parks/NGS; 120 (UP LE), John Hazard; 120 (UP RT), Jose Ignacio Soto/SS; 120 (LO), Photosani/SS; 121 (LE), Corey Ford/Dreamstime.com; 121 (RT), IS; 123 (UP), G.K. Hart/Vikki Hart/GI; 123 (LO LE), Andy Crawford/GI; 123 (LO RT), Gary S. Chapman/GI; 124 (UP), Neftali/SS; 124 (CTR), Ajay Bhaskar/IS; 124 (LO), Sunil Menon/IS

Super Science (126–161)

126–127, NASA/JPL-Caltech; 128, DA; 129 (E), Marie C. Fields/SS; 129 (D), Fedor A. Sidorov/SS; 129 (F), sgame/SS; 129 (A), Sebastian Kaulitzki/SS; 129 (B), Steve Gschmeissner/PR; 129 (C), Volker Steger/Christian Bardele/PR; 129 (G), Benjamin Jessop IS; 130 (UP LE), Sebastian Kaulitzki /SS; 130 (UP RT), David Aguilar; 130 (LO), David Arky/CB; 131 (UP), Jacek Chabraszewski/IS; 131 (LO), Photographer/SS; 132 (UP), Dennis Cooper/CB; 132 (LO), Linda Nye; 134, Robert J. Demarest; 135 (BACK), Hiroya Minakuchi/MP; 135, Photo Pool/Anwar Hussein Collection/WENN/News com; 135, Hiroya Minakuchi/MP; 135, age fotostock/SU; 135, Michael & Patricia Fogden/MP; 135, Courtesy of Royal Caribbean International; 135, AP Images; 135, Photodisc/SU; 135, GI; 135, C. Huetter/Peter Arnold, Inc.; 135, Rod Williams/NPL; 136, Jani Bryson/IS; 137, Dan Westegren/NGS Staff; 137 (LE CTR), Jean-Michel Serin/ASNL; 137 (LO RT), Dania Maxwell;137 (LO RT), Dylan Lagheim; 138–139 (Background), Take 27 Ltd/PR; 139 (A), DA; 139 (B), DA; 139 (C), DA; 139 (D), DA; 139 (E), DA; 140–141, DA; 142, DA; 142 (LE), DA; 143, DA; 144 (A), Giovanni Benintende/SS; 144 (C), peresanz/SS; 144 (B), Tony & Daphne Hallas/PR; 144 (Background), Gabe Palmer/CB; 145, DA; 145 (UP LE), DA; 145 (CTR), DA; 145 (UP RT), DA; 146, DA; 146–147 (Background), AlaskaStock/AL; 147, DA; 149 (UP), Ralph Lee Hopkins/NGS; 149 (UP CTR LE), Visuals Unlimited/GI; 149 (UP CTR RT), Visuals Unlimited/GI; 149 (LO CTR LE), Doug Martin/PR; 149 (LO CTR RT), DEA/C. Dani/GI; 149 (LO LE), Michael Baranski/SS; 149 (LO RT), Terry Davis/SS; 150 (UP LE), Panoramic Stock Images/NGS; 150 (CTR), Ted Clutter/PR; 150 (UP RT), Charles D. Winters/PR; 150 (LO LE), Jim Lopes/SS; 150 (LO RT), Jim Richardson/NGS; 151 (UP LE), Scenics & Science/AL; 151 (UP RT), Mark A. Shneider/PR; 151 (UP CTR LE), Visuals Unlimited/CB; 151 (UP CTR RT), Carsten

Peter/NGS; 151 (LO CTR), Dirk Wiersma/PR; 151 (LO LE), Arturo Limon/SS; 151 (LO RT), Goran Bogicevic/SS; 152 (LE), JewelryStock/AL; 152 (A), Manamana/SS; 152 (B), Jens Mayer/SS; 152 (G), PjrStudio/AL; 152 (H), E.R. Degginer/PR; 153 (C), Alexander Maksimov/SS; 153 (D), Biophoto Assoc./PR; 153 (E), DEA/C. Bevilaqua/GI; 153 (F), DAE/A. Rizzi/GI; 153 (I), DAE/C. Bevilaqua/GI; 153 (J), DEA/GI; 153 (K), Suponev Vladimir/SS; 153 (L), Mark A. Shneider/PR; 153 (UP LE), Palani Mohan/GI; 153 (UP RT), Amritaphotos/AL; 154 (UP), Matthias Schmiedbauer; 154 (LO LE), Courtesy of Van der Led; 154 (LO RT), Mark Thiessen, NGS Staff; 155 (UP), Jog A Dog; 155 (LO), Virgin Galactic; 156 (UP), NASA/iGOAL; 156 (CTR), NASA/iGOAL; 156 (LO LE), NASA/iGOAL; 156 (LO RT), NASA/iGoal; 157, courtesy of Lockheed Martin; 157 (RT), Johnee Bee; 158–159 (UP), Mondolithic Studios, Inc; 158 (LO), Mondolithic Studios, Inc; 158–159 (Background), Don Farrall/GI; 159 (LO LE), NASA; 159 (LO RT), Pat Rawlings; 160 (LO), Chris Gorgio/SS; 160 (UP), Rob Marmion/SS; 161, pixhook/IS

Fun and Games (162–183)

162–163, Terra/CB; 164–165, James Yamasaki; 166 (UP LE), Gary Fields; 166 (UP RT), Gary Fields; 166 (LO LE), Gary Fields; 166 (LO RT), Gary Fields; 167 (UP), David Aubrey/CB; 167 (LE CTR), Stockbyte/SS; 167 (RT CTR), Larry Lilac/AL; 167 (LO LE), GK Hart/Vikki Hart/GI; 167 (LO RT), Jim Cornfield/CB; 168 (UP LE), B.S.P.I./CB; 168 (UP RT), Image99/JI; 168 (CTR), gillmar/SS; 168 (LO LE), Erik Sampers/JI; 168 (LO RT), Comstock/JI; 169, Clayton Hanmer; 170, Tom Brakefield/CB; 171 (UP LE), Sumio Harada/MP; 171 (UP RT), Ivonne Wierink/SS; 171 (LE CTR), Royalty-FreeCB; 171 (RT CTR), Digital Vision/Punchstock; 171 (LO LE), Stephen Dalton/MP; 171 (LO RT), Gabe Palmer/AL; 172–173, Strika Entertainment; 174, Marty Baumann LLC; 175 (3), Slim Aarpms/Hulton Archive/GI; 175 (1), Charles Gullung/GI; 175 (4), Thinkstock Images/JI; 175 (5), Joseph Sohm/Visions of America/CB; 175 (6), Celeste Janosko/Lonely Planet; 175 (7), Jack Sullivan/AL; 175 (2), Michael T. Sedam/CB; 175 (8), Doug Lansky/Lonely Planet; 175 (9), © Dale O'Dell 2008; 176 (UP LE), Eising FoodPhotography/StockFood; 176 (UP CTR), Craig Auness/CB; 176 (UP RT), BananaStock/JI; 176 (LE CTR), BananaStock/JI; 176 (CTR), PhotoObjects.net/JI; 176 (RT CTR), Stephen Frink Collection/AL; 176 (LO LE), James L. Amos/NGS; 176 (LO CTR), Douglas Peebles/eStock Photo; 176 (LO RT), Siede Preis/GI; 177, Mondolithic Studios, Inc.; 178 (UP), Hiroya Minakuchi/MP; 178 (LO LE), Laurel/AL; 178 (CTR), Sonny Poole/Wink/Jupiterimages/GI; 178 (LO RT), Paul A. Souders/CB; 179 (UP LE), Gary Fields; 179 (UP RT), Chris Ware; 179 (LO LE), Clayton Hanmer; 179 (LO RT), Clayton Hanmer; 180, James Yamasaki; 181, Marty Bauman LLC; 182 (UP RT), Jana Brusch/Zuma Red West Photos/Newscom; 182 (LE CTR), Rebecca

Hale, NGS Staff; 182 (RT CTR), Stocktrek/ CB; 182 (LO LE), cbpix/SS; 182 (LO RT), Gerry Ellis/Digital Vision; 182 (UP LE), Andesign101/SS; 183, Craig Thompson

Wonders of Nature (184–205)
184–185, Gary Bell/OceanwideImages.com; 186, Klimapark; 187 (LE), Artem Efimov/ SS; 187 (CTR), Weiss and Overpeck, The University of Arizona; 187 (RT), Weiss and Overpeck, The University of Arizona; 188 (LO RT), Spectrum Photofile.com; 188 (UP), Thomas Allen/GI; 188 (LO LE), Chris Ne-whall/USGS; 189 (UP), U.S. Navy photo; 189 (CTR), Cathy & Gordon ILLG; 189 (LO LE), Sygma/CB; 189 (LO RT), AP Images; 190, NOAA; 191 (BACK), Carsten Peter/NGS; 191 (RT), Eric Nguyen/Jim Reed Photography/ GI/PR; 192 (UP), The Asahi Shimbun/GI; 192 (LO), AP Images/Air Photo Service; 193 (UP), AP Images; 193 (LO LE), Mark Thies-sen/NGS; 193 (LO RT), Rebecca Hale/NGS; 194 (UP), AVTG/IS; 194 (LO), Brad Wynnyk/ SS; 195 (A), Rich Carey/SS; 195 (B), Rich-ard Walters/IS; 195 (C), Karen Graham/ IS; 195 (D), Michio Hoshino/MP/NGS; 196, PR; 197, Mark Thiessen, NGS Staff; 198, Jarvis Gray/SS; 199, Stuart Armstrong; 199 (LO LE), Octavio Aburto/NGS; 199 (LO RT), Zafer Kizilkaya/NGS; 200–201, Jason Edwards/NGS; 202 (UP), Image 100/SU; 202 (LO), GI; 202–189 (Background), John A. Anderson/IS; 203 (UP), Paul Souders/ CB; 203 (LO), Rebecca Hale, NGS Staff; 205, AVAVA/SS

Going Green (206–225)
206–207, Ian Nichols/NGS; 208 (UP), Wildlife in Crisis; 208 (BACK), Wildlife in Crisis; 209 (UP), Marie De Stefanis/ The Marine Mammal Center; 209 (CTR RT), Wildlife in Crisis; 209 (LO), Wildlife in Crisis; 209 (LE CTR), Sue Pemberton/The Marine Mammal Center; 210 (LO), Erlend Kvalsvik/IS; 210 (UP), Paul Souders/CB; 211 (UP LE), Michael DeYoung/CB; 211 (UP RT), Catalin Petolea/SS; 211 (CTR), NASA/ JPL; 212 (LE), Stéphane Bidouze/SS; 212 (Background), Mujka Design Inc./IS; 213 (UP), 33karen33/IS; 213, Nick Garbutt/ NPL; 215 (LE CTR), Walter Rawlings/CB; 215 (RT CTR), Sarah Leen; 215 (CTR), Richard Nowitz/NGS; 215 (UP), Marc Moritsch/ NGS; 215, WENN/Newscom; 216 (UP RT), Index Stock Imagery/Photolibrary; 216 (Background), Brian Skerry; 217 (A), Su-sann Parker/Photolibrary/GI; 217 (b), Mark Thiessen, NGS Staff; 217 (c), A.N.T. Photo Library/NHPA/Photoshot; 217 (D), Pat Morris/ARDEA; 217 (E), Wilfried Krecich-wost/Photographer's Choice/GI; 217 (F), age fotostock/SU; 217 (G), Exactostock/ SU; 217 (H), Ron Chapple Photography/ SuperFusion/SU; 217 (I), Kevin Schafer/ NHPA/Collection/Photoshot; 217 (BACK), Design Pics/SU; 218 (UP), Rebecca Hale, NGS Staff; 218 (LO), FogStock LLC/Index Stock; 218, Digital Vision/Punchstock;

218, Royalty-Free/CB; 218, Photodisc Green/GI; 218, Royalty-Free/CB; 218, Burke/Triolo/Brand X Pictures/JI; 218, Burke/Triolo/Brand X Pictures/ JI; 218, Rubberball Productions/GI; 218, Thinkstock/JI; 219 (UP), Rebecca Hale, NGS Staff; 220 (UP LE), Courtesy of Seymourpowell; 220 (UP RT), Courtesy of Seymourpowell; 220 (LO), Rex/Rex USA; 221 (UP), Kevin Hand; 221 (LO), Kaleidoscope; 222 (UP LE), N55/Wysing Arts Centre; 222 (UP RT), N55/Wysing Arts Centre; 222 (LO), Giga Plex Inc.; 223 (UP), WENN/Newscom; 223 (CTR), courtesy Lower Mill Estate; 223 (LO), VIEW Pictures Ltd/AL; 224, Albo003/SS

History Happens (226–257)
226–227, Adrian Pope/GI; 228 (UP), Araldo De Luca/White Star; 228 (LO LE), Araldo De Luca/White Star; 228 (LO CTR LE), Araldo De Luca/White Star; 228 (LO CTR RT), Araldo De Luca/White Star; 228 (LO RT), Araldo De Luca/White Star; 229 (UP), Richard Barnes/NGS; 229 (LO), Art by Elisabeth Daynes; 230–231 (UP), Mondolithic Studios; 231 (UP RT), Seamas Culligan/Zuma/CB; 231 (LO), Roger Ressmeyer/CB; 232, Kirill Vorobyev/SS; 233 (LO), Photoservice Electa/SU; 233 (UP), James L. Stanfield/NGS; 234, Wang da Gang; 235 (UP LE), O. Louis Mazzatenta/ NGS; 235 (LO LE), Wang da Gang; 235 (UP RT), O. LOUIS MAZZATENTA/NGS; 235 (RT CTR), O. Louis Mazzatenta; 235 (LO RT), O. Louis Mazzatenta/NGS; 236 (UP), Chip Wass; 236 (CTR), Chip Wass; 236 (LO), Chip Wass; 237 (UP RT), Index Stock Imagery/ Jupiterimages/GI; 237 (CTR), Chip Clark/ NMNH/Smithsonian Institution; 237 (LO), SU, Inc./SU; 238–239, Glenn Beanland/ Lonely Planet; 238 (LO), Alan Sorrell Stonehenge drawing/English Heritage Photo Library; 240–241, AP Images/Adam Butler; 241, ©1993 Mot Künstler, Inc.; 242 (UP), Scott Rothstein/SS; 243 (UP LE), mack2happy/SS; 243 (BACK), Courtesy of the Mount Vernon Ladies' Association; 243 (UP), Courtesy of Partnership for Research in Spatial Modeling (PRISM), Arizona State University; 243 (LE CTR), MVLA; 243 (RT CTR), Courtesy of the Mount Vernon Ladies' Association; 243 (LO LE), Courtesy of the MVLA; 243 (LO RT), Courtesy of the MVLA; 244 (UP), Aleksan-darNakic/IS; 244 (LO), Stephen Coburn/ SS; 245 (LO), Gary Blakely/SS; 245 (UP), S. Borisov/SS; 246–250 (B), WHHA; 250 (LO RT), The White House; 250 (LO), The White House; 251, Tom Till/SU; 252 (LO), Bettmann/CB; 252 (UP), Bettmann/CB; 253 (UP), AP Photo/Gene Herrick; 253 (LE CTR), Central Press/GI; 253 (RT CTR), Topham/ The Image Works; 253 (LO), Central Press/ GI; 254, History/AL; 255 (UP LE), Women's Suffrage, 1920The Granger Collection, New York/The Granger Collection/Art Resource, NY; 255 (UP RT), The Bloomer

Costume. Lithograph, 1851, by Nathaniel Currier; The Granger Collection, NY/The Granger Collection/Art Resource, NY; 255, Frontpage/SS; 256, Alessia Pierdomenico/ Reuters/CB; 257, bluehill/SS

Geography Rocks (258–337)
258–259, Donald M. Jones/MP; 265 (CTR CTR), Maria Stenzel/NGS; 265 (LO CTR), Bill Hatcher/NGS; 265 (UP), Carsten Peter/ NGS; 265 (RT CTR), Gordon Wiltsie/NGS; 265 (LO LE), James P. Blair/NGS; 265 (CTR LE), Thomas J. Abercrombie/NGS; 265 (LO RT), Bill Curtsinger/NGS; 266 (UP), George F. Mobley/NGS; 266 (LO), THEGIFT777/IS; 267, VicZA/IS; 270–271 (UP), Neil Lucas/ NPL; 271 (UP), Sue Flood/NPL; 274, ssguy/ SS; 275 (LO), David Edwards/NGS; 275 (UP), Thomas Marent/MP; 278 (UP), Frans Lanting; 278 (LO), Thomas Marent/MP; 279, JamersonG/IS; 282 (LO), Peter Wey/ SS; 282 (UP), Paul Thompson/Danita Delimont.com; 283, Joe Beynon/GI; 286 (UP), Robert Fried/AL; 286 (LO), Henry Georgi/GI; 287, Justin Jager/National Geographic Your Shot; 290, Tier und Naturfotografie/V; 291 (UP), John & Lisa Merrill/DanitaDelimont.com; 291 (LO), Glowimages/GI; 297, Cindy Miller Hopkins/ Danita Delimont.com; 300, absolutely_ frenchy/IS; 303, dovate/IS; 304, catalo-nia/SS; 308, Steve Elmore/GI; 311, Robert Preston/AL; 314, Mark Van Overmeire/ SS; 317, Frank Lukasseck/CB; 330 (LO LE), PhotoDisc; 330 (LO RT), Albert H. Teich/ SS; 330 (UP), Panoramic Images/GI; 332, John Burcham/NGS; 332 (INSET), Craig Ruttle/Bloomberg via GI; 333 (UP), Thomas Sbampato/Photolibrary/GI; 333 (UP CTR), Jörn Friederich/Photolibrary/GI; 333 (LO CTR), Steve Mann; 333 (LO), Design Pics Inc. - RM Content/AL; 334, The Jumeirah Group; 334 (LO LE), The Jumeirah Group; 334 (LO RT), © Denis Oudendijk Refunc. NL; 334 (UP), Hulio Hulio; 335 (A), David Sutherland/GI; 335 (B), Ferdinand Knab/ GI; 335 (C), Ferdinand Knab/GI; 335 (D), Ferdinand Knab/GI; 335 (E), Wilhelm van Ehrenberg/GI; 335 (F), Ferdinand Knab/GI; 335 (G), DEA Picture Library/GI; 335 (H), Holger Mette/SS; 335 (I), Holger Mette/ SS; 335 (J), Jarno Gonzalez Zarraonandia/ SS; 335 (K), David Iliff/SS; 335 (L), Ostill/SS; 335 (M), Hannamariah/SS; 335 (n), Jarno Gonzalez Zarraonandia/SS

345

346

348